Treatment Planning for Person-Centered Care: Shared Decision Making for Whole Health

Treatment Planning for Person-Centered Care: Shared Decision Making for Whole Health

Second Edition

NEAL ADAMS, MD, MPH

Deputy Director, California Institute for Mental Health

DIANE M. GRIEDER, MEd

President, Alipar, Inc., Suffolk, VA

Amsterdam • Boston • Heidelberg • London • New York • Oxford
Paris • San Diego • San Francisco • Singapore • Sydney • Tokyo
Academic Press is an imprint of Elsevier

Academic Press is an imprint of Elsevier
32 Jamestown Road, London NW1 7BY, UK
225 Wyman Street, Waltham, MA 02451, USA
525 B Street, Suite 1800, San Diego, CA 92101-4495, USA

Second edition

Notice
No responsibility is assumed by the publisher for any injury and/or damage to persons or
property as a matter of products liability, negligence or otherwise, or from any use or
operation of any methods, products, instructions or ideas contained in the material herein.
Because of rapid advances in the medical sciences, in particular, independent verification
of diagnoses and drug dosages should be made

British Library Cataloguing-in-Publication Data
A catalogue record for this book is available from the British Library

Library of Congress Cataloging-in-Publication Data
A catalog record for this book is available from the Library of Congress

ISBN: 978-0-12-394448-1

For information on all Academic Press publications
visit our website at www.store.elsevier.com

Typeset by TNQ Books and Journals

Printed and bound in United States of America

14 15 16 17 18   10 9 8 7 6 5 4 3 2 1

  Working together
to grow libraries in
developing countries

www.elsevier.com • www.bookaid.org

CONTENTS

See: www.booksite.elsevier.com/9780123944481 for
additional content for this title, including 1e chapters for reference.

ACKNOWLEDGMENTS

The impulse to write a second edition of this book came from a wide range of experiences, learning, teaching and observing over the past eight years since the publication of the first edition. It has been enormously gratifying to see the response of the behavioral health community—from policy makers to educators to providers to service users and their families, among many others—and the endorsement for what has come to be referred to by some as "*the* book" on person-centered care and recovery practice in our field.

That said, in the same eight-year period our field has undergone enormous changes and advances. We came to feel that so much has changed, that the book was becoming somewhat outdated and less relevant and useful. Thus, the impetus for a revised and updated second edition that builds on the core of the first volume, and at the same time brings forward new insights, ideas, strategies and examples to promote person-centered planning and care as health care systems and practices continue to evolve and change.

In completing this second edition, we owe many thanks to our colleagues who were willing to read, offer comments and support, and even edit portions of the book as it evolved—and a special thanks to Janis Tondora PhD from Yale who has grown to be a friend and colleague in this journey.

But most of all, we want to acknowledge the many individuals providing, as well as receiving, services from the behavioral health services system. Over the past eight years in our efforts to "spread the word" we have met many exceptional people who have truly been a source of inspiration to us. They have both encouraged us to forge on as well taught us how to listen, to have hope, and to be more convinced than ever of the power and importance of person-centered care.

Finally, we wish to thank our editor, Nikki Levy, for her tireless encouragement, and our close friends and family for their enduring support and forbearance.

FOREWORD

Since writing the first edition of this book eight years ago, many things have changed substantially, if not dramatically, in the mental health and addictions treatment field related to recovery and treatment planning that warrant a second edition. These include but are by no means limited to:

1. new information and perspectives derived from consultations with provider organizations, hospitals and entire state systems
2. sharing the international dialog and experience in providing person-centered care/medicine
3. the growing evidence base supporting shared decision making as part of providing person-centered care and planning
4. health care reform in USA, which has brought a new focus to person-centered care and integrated health care
5. a shift to person-centered health care homes as a way to organize and deliver health care services
6. advances in primary care and mental health integration

The intent of writing a second edition is to address all of these changes and provide a more current and therefore useful and relevant book. Our hope is that this update can better help practitioners move from a values-based approach to care to successfully addressing the complexities of policy, financing and system redesign/reform that challenge the implementation of person-centered care principles in daily practice.

It is increasingly clear that simply focusing on redesign and refinancing of the service delivery system will not in and of itself produce person-centered care. Regardless of how the pieces of the system are organized, care *must* be driven by shared decision making and an effective partnership between persons receiving services and all types of providers. Shared decision making is the essence of person-centered care and is a key strategy for assuring that people's values and preferences are consistently reflected in the actual care plan and services provided.

Recovery is a term that came from the addictions treatment community, was adapted by mental health practitioners and now is being used to look at wellness outcomes for people living with a wide range of chronic and often co-occurring health problems—including chronic medical conditions, mental health disorders and addictions. Ultimately, recovery is about the hope and empowerment that are essential to living beyond the challenges of illness and enjoying a meaningful life in the community. We continue to believe that a focus on person-centered planning is an effective strategy for helping to promote recovery and wellness.

In the first edition, we built on the metaphor of recovery as a journey and each of the sections introduced another phase of the trip. This has been retained although the subtitle of the book *The Road to Mental Health and Addictions Recovery* has changed. The original Section I was entitled *Planning the Trip* and included three chapters that provided background on the history of person-centered thinking and examined how then recent changes in mental health care policy made the case for person-centered approaches to care. In the past eight years, that information has become generally well known and accepted, and did not seem to fit well with this new edition. Those chapters are still available on the Internet for the interested reader and can be accessed at http://booksite.elsevier.com/9780123944481/. For the second edition, we have written a new Chapter 1 entitled *The Landscape* to replace the original three and try to address recent changes in health care delivery systems and policy that describe the health care environment as well as impact and advance person-centered practice.

The following six chapters, now numbered 2 through 7, are revisions of the original Chapters 4 through 9; they continue to offer practical and updated guidance on how to provide person-centered approaches to planning and care in routine practice with a focus on the elements or components of the assessment and planning process. In an effort to make sure that this part of the second edition remains a useful "how-to" book, we have maintained the division of each chapter into three sections. The first section is *Stating the Case* and is a look at the status quo as well as emerging trends in both theory and practice and lays out the background and issues related to assuring that care is person-centered. The second section, *Creating the Solution*, examines the essentials of a person-centered approach to preparing and implementing individual plans and provides practical guidance on how to actually implement person-centered planning and care. The third section, *Making it Happen*, largely provides commentary on the four case examples in the appendices that are included to illustrate the issues and solutions identified in each chapter and how a person-centered plan can be developed based upon shared understanding/decision making and a whole health approach to recovery.

As all travelers know, a map is an indispensable tool to help guide any journey—especially in traversing an uncertain landscape. Thinking about individual planning for recovery as a trip to be mapped helps us to better explore and understand the process. Ultimately, creating a plan is about helping an individual to envision his or her own journey (creating a map that directs their trip) to health and wellness. Practitioners' ability to be helpful and stay on track is greatly enhanced by also knowing the terrain, having the course laid out and the destination identified.

Bon voyage!

Neal Adams, MD, MPH
Diane Grieder, MEd

Our book, *Treatment Planning for Person-Centered Care: The Road to Mental Health and Addiction Recovery*, was first published in 2005. Since then we have traveled the country—and even some places around the world—providing training, consulting and technical assistance to direct care staff, supervisors and administrators about how to promote systems transformation, recovery practice and more person-centered approaches to delivering services and supports. These colleagues have come from a variety of behavioral health care settings including private/public, outpatient/inpatient, association groups, learning collaboratives and even entire state systems of care.

It seems that regardless of the country, state or setting, there are significant barriers to transforming systems, truly adopting person-centered principles and changing practices. Almost everyone is struggling with how best to implement strengths-based shared decision making, person-centered planning and meet recipient expectations while also satisfying regulatory and payer requirements. Despite progress, old medical-model deficit-based approaches are seen as required for meeting payer and regulatory requirements and addressing perceived audit threats.

It has also become abundantly clear that training alone cannot change practice. Not only do direct care staff need opportunities for experiential as well as didactic learning, practice change must be built into supervisory practice to assure clinical competence as well as the organization's overall performance and quality goals. The need to address a variety of systems-level organizational and administrative workflow/care process barriers to implementing new practices is even more critical than training.

Perhaps the greatest stumbling block we encounter is the lack of training and/or experience of most care staff in a critical phase of person-centered recovery-oriented work: achieving shared understanding and establishing common ground. Clinically this is often referred to as formulation. Moving beyond assessment and data gathering to promoting engagement and achieving understanding must be the foundation of a healing partnership and a successful recovery-oriented plan.

The journey is now taking us all into uncharted territory with health care reform, etc. As a field we have been on a journey to rethink our work, our purpose, and this transformation of the behavioral health system. On the one hand, there has been a huge uptake on person-centeredness in the medical and behavioral health care fields, this can be found in new books/journal articles, conferences/institutes, and even in the research arena, e.g., PCORI (Person-Centered Outcomes Research Institute). On the other hand, recipients of services still seem to play a marginal role directing their care and clinicians struggle with how to implement more person-centred approaches. The tension between the traditional "medical model" and the rehabilitation practice of specialty mental health is now increasingly challenged by the call for integration with primary care as well as substance abuse services. We realize the guidance on Person-Centred Planning (PCP) needs to be "upgraded" for the first decade of the millennium: how to actually *apply* the basic principles.

The treatment/recovery planning process and the product or plan should be the heart and soul of a recovery-oriented partnership between individuals and providers. Using both participants' expertise (the provider's knowledge, skills and abilities, and the person's knowledge of his/her own self) to develop the goals on the plan, the action steps needed to achieve those goals, and the services and supports to attain the objectives and goals, is all about shared decision making.

However, one of the serious challenges facing the behavioral health field is how to help consumers find their voice so they can actively participate. This book builds upon *Treatment Planning for Person-Centered Care: The Road to Mental Health and Addiction Recovery*, which included concrete information on recovery values, the process of planning and the technical elements to create a plan. This updated version of the book will provide readers with ideas and tools from a shared decision-making perspective and offer practical guidance on how to organize and conduct the recovery plan meeting, prepare and engage individuals in the treatment planning process, help with goal setting, actually use the plan in daily practice, as well as how to evaluate and improve the results.

See: www.booksite.elsevier.com/9780123944481 for additional content for this title, including 1e chapters for reference.

Land of Opportunity

Thinking about the pursuit of whole health and recovery inevitably invokes some notion of travel across an often poorly charted landscape. It has been said that "life is a journey…not a destination" and this is true at both an individual and systems level for those seeking help as well as those providing health care services and supports. If we consider person-centered planning as the process of creating a map, it is an apt metaphor by which to organize this book and its several sections and chapters.

A journey is about traversing the landscape, and knowing the physical and social terrain is essential before we begin to think about making more detailed and specific plans. Are there challenges we can anticipate? Are there resources along the way? Have others traveled this way before? Are the countrymen welcoming or hostile? Are there shortcuts or detours that need to be considered?

Section I, Chapter 1 offers an overview of the current health care landscape in which providers and those seeking help and services must travel. Knowing the lay of the land and the scenic vistas, as well as the rivers and mountains that we are likely to encounter, is an essential precursor to Section II—"Getting Started."

The Health Care Landscape

Ever charming, ever new,
When will the landscape tire the view?

John Dyer

I. INTRODUCTION

The overall purpose of this book is to advance person-centered care—primarily but not exclusively in mental health and substance abuse service as well as integrated health care delivery systems—by focusing on the role and contribution of treatment planning to the individual's experience of care, the provider's work and outcomes. The pursuit of person-centered care is highly aligned with notions of holism, integration, empowerment, self-management, recovery and wellness.

Done right, treatment planning can play a critical role in helping to assure that care is in fact person-centered. The plan of care is intended to create a detailed roadmap—a personalized, highly individualized health management program—to actively drive appropriate treatment and supports that are oriented towards health and wellness.

Implementing person-centered planning requires knowledge, skills and abilities on the part of providers and the active participation of persons receiving services. However, efforts to improve routine practice do not occur in a vacuum; rather they are influenced—both positively and negatively—by the design and operation of the health care delivery system, financing, and regulation along with social and professional attitudes and values among other factors. Mastery and promotion of person-centered planning occurs in this milieu. Understanding the opportunities and challenges created by these "environmental" factors that shape provider efforts as well as health care consumer experience is an important precursor to a more detailed look at the specifics of person-centered planning.

The health care delivery system in the United States is in the midst of a profound transformational process. This includes not only changes in insurance, finance and organization prompted by the Patient Protection and Affordable Care Act (ACA), but also changes in access to services protected

Treatment Planning for Person-Centered Care
http://dx.doi.org/10.1016/B978-0-12-394448-1.00001-9

by the Mental Health Parity and Addiction Equity Act of 2008, as well as many other initiatives to improve the experience of care, promote better outcomes and lower cost.

Before considering the detailed "nuts and bolts" of person-centered planning in Chapters 2 through 7, this chapter attempts to provide an overview of this changing policy and practice landscape in order to provide a context for learning and practicing person-centered care. We start by considering what is meant by person-centered care and consider a range of related topics including whole health, shared decision making, service delivery models, health care reform and integrated care among others; together they begin to describe the environment and the opportunities it offers to advance person-centered care and recovery-oriented whole health practice.

II. PERSON-CENTERED CARE

The notion of person-centered care is becoming increasingly common in all of health care—we have person-centered medical homes, person-centered care/services, person-centered planning and even the Association for the Development of the Person-Centered Approach (ADPCA) as well as the International College of Person-Centered Medicine and the Person-Centered Outcomes Research Institute (PCORI). With this proliferation of use, there is some concern that the term "person-centered" will soon become a cliché and lose its value and significance. But what does it mean to be person-centered? Hasn't health care always been person-centered? Is person-centeredness a matter of principles, a statement of values, or is it a defined set of practices? Does it mean the same thing in general health care settings as it does in the realm of mental health and substance use treatment systems?

Many interpretations and definitions of person-centeredness abound, but there is no one concise operational description that can be applied across settings. The idea of being person-centered has been called a "fuzzy concept," meaning that everyone recognizes the overall intent of the term but it has a range of connotations and implications or interpretations for different people and different settings. While the core elements of the concept may be clear, it often seems unclear on the periphery and it is difficult to operationalize in measurable elements.

Don Berwick, an internationally respected thought leader in health care policy and quality improvement, defines person-centeredness as "the experience (to the extent the informed individual desires) of transparency, individualization, recognition, respect, dignity, and choice in all matters, without exception, related to one's person, circumstances, and relationships in health care"[1]. Berwick identified three maxims of person- or patient-centered care:

1. The needs of the patient come first.
2. Nothing about me without me.
3. Every patient is the only patient.

Berwick goes on to argue that beyond whatever moral, ethical, economic or political imperative that might accompany the need to be person-centered in health care, "most researchers who have studied it systematically have found that it does often have a positive relationship to classical health status outcomes." Berwick also believes that "a [truly] patient- and family-centered health care system would be radically and uncomfortably different from most today."

In an effort to make clear its importance, Berwick suggests that "we should without equivocation make patient-centeredness a primary quality dimension all its own." This was effectively done when the Institute of Medicine (IOM) included person-centeredness as one of six core aims of a quality health care system in its *Crossing the Quality Chasm* report[2]. The importance of person-centeredness on the mental health and substance abuse arena was emphasized in both the *President's New Freedom Commission* report and the IOM's quality chasm report, which focused on these two clinical arenas[3,4].

There are some who have argued that especially in mental health the need to be more person-centered is the most important of all the aims and rules. The IOM urged that in order to successfully promote person-centered care, all parties involved in health care for mental or substance use conditions should support the decision-making abilities and preferences for treatment and recovery of persons with mental and substance use (M/SU) problems and disorders. Specifically they called for organizations providing M/SU treatment to "have in place policies that implement informed, person-centered participation and decision-making in treatment, illness self-management, and recovery plans as well as involve persons served and their families in the design, administration, and delivery of treatment and recovery services."

In the delivery of mental health and substance use services—also sometimes referred to as "behavioral health"—person-centeredness invokes the need for a comprehensive approach to understanding and responding to each individual and their family in the context of their history, needs, strengths, recovery hopes and dreams, culture and spirituality. Providing person-centered care means that assessments, recovery plans, services and supports, and quality of life outcomes are all tailored to respect the unique preferences, strengths, vulnerabilities (including trauma history) and dignity of each whole person. In addition, person-centeredness lies at the heart of recovery approaches to mental health and substance use services. In the effort to respond to multiple calls for system reform and transformation of this specialty sector—driven in large part by the emerging new paradigm of recovery—the need to be person-centered holds a unique position in the change agenda[4].

For the purposes of this book, person-centered care and planning is first and foremost about always considering the perceptions, needs, "truths," preferences and priorities, as well as experiences, of the individual seeking help. Person-centeredness refers to care that is of the person (of the totality of the person's health, both ill and positive), by the person (with clinicians adopting humanistic and ethical attitudes and extending themselves as full human beings), for the person (assisting the fulfillment of the person's life goals) and with the person (in respectful collaboration with the person who consults)[5]. Many providers of general health care, as well as behavioral health care, resonate with these concepts and feel that they are already person-centered in their daily work. However, being truly person-centered often requires a far more profound shift in attitudes, policies and practices across a broad spectrum of health care services/settings than is often realized or achieved. All too frequently we are limited by blind spots in our ability to recognize the difference between well-intended "usual care" and truly person-centered approaches.

This seems to be especially, but not exclusively by any means, the case in the world of mental health and addictive disorders treatment. While there has been tremendous progress in shifting the care paradigm over the past 20 plus years, there also remains much more to be done if this essential and fundamental shift in providing health care services and its benefits is to be fully realized[6]. Recovery-oriented approaches to mental health and substance abuse treatment are highly correlated with person-centeredness, but consumer frustration with the lack of truly person-centered approaches remains[7]. Treatment planning should be central to the process of providing mental health and substance abuse services. Attention to person-centeredness in working with individuals in the creation of their plan can go a long way towards advancing person-centeredness as routine practice.

III. WHOLE HEALTH

Traditional approaches to health care have not only separated mental health and addictive disorders from general health care, but they have also tended to focus on disease, deficits, symptoms and the illusion of cure more than a holistic understanding of illness as well as health and well-being. Some people believe that in reality we have a "*sick* care" not a "*health* care" system[8] that is inherently reductionist and plagued by fragmentation in both understanding of as well as responding to human needs.

In contrast, person-centered approaches are very much aligned with the World Health Organization's (WHO) definition of health:

> Health is a state of complete physical, mental and social well-being and not merely the absence of disease or infirmity.*

Recently, we have seen the term "whole health" used in an effort to succinctly capture and express this definition, and with it recognize the interdependence of physical and mental well-being[9]. This has become somewhat of a companion concept to person-centeredness as it attempts to acknowledge the importance of holistic approaches to understanding the human experience of illness and the pursuit of health. It is said: "there can be no health without mental health"; the obverse is equally true and relevant[10].

In contrast to traditional and more limited definitions of health, person-centered approaches are focused on understanding the whole person, aligning with their unique and individual definitions of quality of life, health and illness as well as supporting their empowerment and ability to realize their hopes and dreams for a fulfilling life even in the face of illness and disability. Many persons with mental and addictive disorders have asserted: "I am not my diagnosis"[11], in an effort to assure that their personhood is not overshadowed or lost in the face of the inevitable challenges that come with having a behavioral health disorder. Recovery and the idea of living beyond one's illness has become an increasingly popular and applicable term to describe a person-centered vision of health, resilience and wellness.

From this perspective, understanding the strengths and abilities as well as the needs and challenges each individual faces in the context of their personal whole health vision is the essence of being person-centered. When people are challenged by physical illness, mental health problems, addictions

---

*Preamble to the Constitution of the World Health Organization as adopted by the International Health Conference, New York, 19–22 June 1946; signed on 22 July 1946 by the representatives of 61 states (Official Records of the World Health Organization, no. 2, p. 100) and entered into force on 7 April 1948.

or social needs, the role of the health care system should be to help people get the health, behavioral health and social services and supports they specifically need to promote recovery and make those hopes and dreams a reality.

In person-centered care, the focus is not just on physical health, mental health or addictions recovery, but on overall or whole health as well. It includes understanding that wellness, self-responsibility, empowerment and having a meaningful role as part of the community for each individual are all part of health. Each person has their own values, priorities and perspectives that should shape the kinds of help they receive—acknowledging and respecting those is also part of being person-centered. In this way, person-centered care is also culturally competent care[12].

Here is an example of how health, mental health and problems with addiction can be interrelated and how they can confound both help seeking and providing services. Consider a person diagnosed with diabetes, depression and alcoholism that feels ill and distressed but not sure about how best to seek help. One day the person has a hangover, and perceives his drinking as his greatest problem and says "I had better go get some substance abuse help." On another day the person may feel so depressed that he can't get out of bed and determines "I need to go get some mental health help." On yet another day the same individual may be focused on their elevated blood sugar levels and decides "I had better get back to my primary care doctor." But all of these issues are highly intertwined and cannot be reduced to three isolated and independent problems or health care responses; yet all too often that is exactly what happens.

The road to health and wellness, and success in managing these problems, requires a holistic, integrated and individualized approach. In this way the notions of whole health, recovery and person-centeredness come together. Without this integrated approach to understanding the individual and the impact of their multiple concerns and needs, any vision of health and well-being will be difficult to realize. This also makes clear the value and importance of creating "no wrong door" approaches to organizing and providing health care services[13].

Person-centered planning is a strategy to promote and foster whole health that builds on this integrative approach to assessing and understanding each person's needs and can go a long way to help each person articulate and realize his or her unique individual wellness vision. In some instances it is also referred to as "person-*driven*" which carries its own implications[4]. Understanding how physical and behavioral health and social needs interact and impact each individual is critical for success. The road to whole health is best traveled with a personal map; a clear individualized and person-centered plan for the journey to health and recovery can serve as that guide. Planning is not just meeting an administrative or regulatory requirement—rather it is the collaborative creation of a "social contract" between individuals and providers of whole health services that can, in and of itself, be empowering. This requires a change from what has been usual or customary practice—and in some instances that change can be profound.

> It is well accepted as a general principle that self-determination is essential to everyone's mental health and well-being and is often regarded as a basic human right. The need for improvement in the development of individual plans as a key element in system reform speaks to the shortcomings of current practice. Success in creating and implementing individual plans that are experienced by consumers and families as person-centered is essential if we are to succeed in creating the [health], mental health and addictive disorders service delivery system that people want and deserve.[14]

Or in the words of Janis Tondora at Yale's University School of Medicine, Program for Recovery and Community Health, "consumers demand it, public service systems endorse it, medical and professional programs are encouraged to teach it, and researchers investigate it." Yet, people continue to struggle to understand exactly what "it" is and what "it" might look like in practice"[15]. Sheila Clay, CEO at Detroit's Neighborhood Service Organization, has said to providers, "Your job is *not* to tell people what treatment they need, or how to live their lives, but rather to help facilitate people's dreams"[16]. Person-centered planning is a strategy to make high levels of consumer and patient involvement in identifying desired outcomes and "driving" their care the new "treatment as usual." A focus on shared decision making is a strategy for assuring this.

IV. SHARED DECISION MAKING

> Shared Decision Making is an opportunity to make recovery [and whole health] real. By developing and promoting shared decision making in mental healthcare, we can advance consumer-centered care and recovery[17].
>
> **Kathryn Power 10 July 2007**

There is a substantial and growing body of evidence that shared decision making dramatically improves service outcomes[18]. *Shared decision making is the essence of person-centered care and practice* and a treatment/recovery plan can be regarded as a logically organized record of the process and outcomes of shared decision making. Although there is not a strong evidence base for the effectiveness of person-centered planning *per se*, there is overwhelming evidence of the value, impact and effectiveness of shared decision making across all of health care. For example, in a recent study, person-centered planning and collaborative documentation[†] were associated with greater engagement in services and higher rates of treatment adherence[19]. Done right, treatment planning can be considered to be a way to organize and facilitate shared decision making.

Shared decision making is a complex topic in and of itself—and worthy of its own text; a few basic definitions are in order. For our purposes here, decision making is the process of choosing between alternatives, which may include doing nothing. Competent decision makers need to understand and consider the courses of action open to them, the chances of positive and negative effects and the desirability or value of these effects. People are more likely to choose an option they think is likely to achieve valued outcomes and to avoid undesirable outcomes. Shared decision making can be considered to be an interactive and collaborative process between individuals and their health care practitioners about decisions pertinent to the individual's treatment, services and ultimately their personal recovery.

An optimal decision is one that is informed, consistent with personal values and acted upon. Participants are satisfied with the process used to make the decision. For the sake of clarity, "informed" decision making refers to any intervention in communities or health care systems intended to promote informed decisions, while shared decision making is a subset of informed decision making concerning interventions that are carried out between one person served and his/her health care provider(s) in clinical settings. The greater the degree of uncertainty about potential risk and benefits, the more difficult the process of making a decision can be.

The 2011 Commonwealth Fund *Report on Patient Engagement* found that when persons served are actively involved in their health care, including decision making, they have better quality care and a better care experience[20]. Shared decision making is a way of increasing consumer engagement and what is often referred to as "activation." Engaged individuals are also more likely to have more positive views of the health care system as a whole as well as of their individual providers and experience of care. Overall, individuals who are actively engaged in their own care receive higher

---

[†]Collaborative documentation refers to the growing practice of having the person served and the provider jointly create a written entry into the clinical record during a meeting or clinical encounter.

quality care, receive fewer medical errors and have more positive views of the health system.

The treatment planning process, and the written record, should be the heart and soul of a whole health and recovery-oriented partnership between persons seeking services and providers. Collaboratively engaging both participants' expertise (the provider's knowledge, skills and abilities, and the individual's knowledge of his/her own self and experience) to develop a whole health recovery plan is all about shared decision making. Success in this kind of healing partnership must start with a shared understanding of the nature of the problems that incorporates and integrates both the individual's experience and the provider's perspective. This shared understanding and decision making should be reflected in the goals and objectives included in a plan, as well as the action steps, services and supports needed to attain the objectives and goals.

However, helping individuals to "find their voice" and supporting their active participation in planning and decision making can sometimes be a challenge. A 2008 report from the Bazelon Center[21], a national consumer advocacy group, reinforces the same message as the Institute of Medicine[22] (IOM) and the New Freedom Commission reports: service delivery systems are not meeting people's needs—in large part because they are not sufficiently person-centered. There is growing evidence that when people receiving services are directly involved in designing their own care plan, the experience of care and outcomes are improved. But this involvement must be real, genuine and transparent. Active efforts at decision support can help to promote the individual's active and meaningful involvement and can include:

- providing help in defining one's goals and wellness vision
- assuring that information about effective service options are readily accessible
- helping to choose or select among service and treatment options
- promoting active participation in developing treatment plans
- providing ongoing assessment of progress, and review of treatment decisions

Despite this, we find too often that even when health care consumers and other advocates are involved in care planning, they are only allowed a marginal role and are not provided with information and support that could enable them to participate more fully and effectively; this is not acceptable. Providers often believe and assert that the person served has had input into the plan because they met with the clinical staff and signed the plan. From this perspective, it should be no surprise to find that when people receiving services are asked what they think about the notion of being in the driver's seat of articulating their wellness goals and creating their plans, they will sometimes respond, "In the driver's seat? Heck, I'm not even in the car!" It should be clear that this is *not* what is intended by active person-centered participation in the development of one's own care plan.

Establishing common ground and shared understanding between persons served and providers is a virtual pre-condition for effective shared decision making. Shared decision making clearly rests in the paradigm of person-centered medicine…and the concept of finding common ground[23]. This notion of "common ground" has since been taken and expanded upon by Patricia Deegan, a psychologist and psychiatric survivor, who has written eloquently on the topic and created a web-based application, *Common Ground*, to help people with a mental illness become more empowered and take a more active role in their treatment, including developing their recovery plan, making informed decisions about medication use, and so on.

Yet, research indicates that all too often physicians still fail to find common ground with patients[24]. In the primary care system, models of clinical decision making can be represented on a spectrum from a paternalistic approach on one end, to self-direction and informed choice on the other. While the paternalistic approach and unilateral decision making has some merit in the face of a provider's "duty of beneficence," it negates the individual's perspectives, experience and expertise. In comparison, self-direction risks placing near full responsibility for decision making on the person seeking help—almost as if they have been abandoned by the provider. In between these extremes lies the "sweet spot" of shared decision making—a point that balances authority and duty with consumer autonomy empowerment and activation with the value of collaboration. There is a growing body of evidence confirming that problems in effective communication and collaboration between doctors and patients contribute substantially to nonadherence with therapy, advice or other management plans. However, in a shared decision-making approach we find that people who take an active part in making decisions about their care have better health outcomes.

Without common ground and agreement about the nature of the problem that is prompting an individual to seek help, it is difficult for a patient and doctor to agree on a plan that is acceptable, or even rational, to both. It is not essential that the recipient of services and the provider entirely share the same perspective at all times—differences will and do occur. However, the doctor's explanations and recommended treatments must at least be consistent with the person's own experience and point of view and make sense in the person's world. For example, if a young man perceives his hearing the voice of God to be a blessed moment of spiritual grace and enlightenment, but the physician insists the experience is a psychotic symptom that needs to be extinguished, there can be little if any basis for even considering a shared decision about treatment. Even in these circumstances, physicians will all too often persist in prescribing medications and ordering treatment only to be frustrated by the lack of patient follow-through and improvement.

However, organizing the health care delivery system to promote person-centered care and shared decision making is critical for success. Fortunately there are models we can turn to for guidance.

V. WAGNER CARE MODEL

The Wagner care model[25], also known as the chronic care model, was initially proposed as a way of better understanding the role of health care systems and communities in promoting optimal outcomes for persons receiving health care services. Wagner and his colleagues developed the model as part of the Improving Chronic Illness Care Program (a Robert Wood Johnson [RWJ] funded project)[26] over 10 years ago. The model is based on a synthesis of the scientific literature and has been used internationally in quality improvement collaboratives involving over 1000 health care systems to date. The model has been adapted to a number of different settings including mental health as well as public health and prevention.

Wagner suggested that positive outcomes were the result of "productive interactions" between a receptive and capable provider team and an activated hopeful and empowered consumer. Those productive interactions are the essence of person-centered care and encompass establishing common ground, shared decision making and collaboration in achieving desired outcomes. According to the model, the role of the health care delivery system, and to some extent the community as well, is to create and support the conditions needed to promote those positive interactions.

Wagner specifically identified *self-management support* (how we help individuals live with and beyond their conditions), *delivery system design* (who's on the health care team and in what ways do they interact with individuals), *decision support* (what is the most appropriate and efficacious care and how do we make it happen every time) and *clinical information systems* (how do we capture and use critical information for clinical care). These four essential and somewhat interdependent resources or functions within the health care system all help to set the stage and provide the supports needed to promote effective collaborations between providers/teams and activated/ empowered individuals.

The health care system itself exists in a larger community. Resources and policies in the community also influence the kind of care that can be delivered. It is not accidental that self-management support is on the edge between the health system and the community; some programs and services that provide substantial support to individuals exist in the community outside of the health care systems.

The adaptation of the Wagner model for mental health and substance abuse recovery practice is depicted in Figure 1.1. This has proven to be helpful in understanding the importance of service user/provider partnership and collaboration in promoting successful recovery outcomes. These productive interactions are effectively about "making recovery real" as both a process and an outcome. In adapting the model, emphasis was given to end result: recovery/wellness outcomes; in accord, the term "chronic" was dropped due to the potential implication of permanent illness and disability as well as system dependence.

The model has been especially useful in helping clinical practice teams successfully change how they organize and provide services for individuals with complex and/or chronic illness and promote wellness recovery outcomes. The model makes clear that collaborative/shared decision making

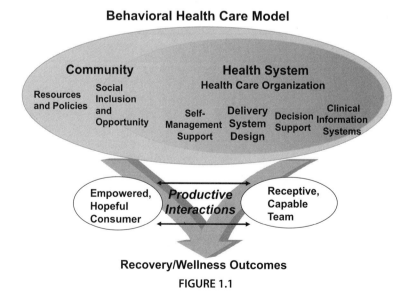

Behavioral Health Care Model

FIGURE 1.1

and "productive interactions" between service recipients and providers is the path to improved health outcomes; both the community and the health services delivery system play an important role in promoting and supporting this partnership. The creation of a person-centered plan is effectively a written record of the outcomes from a process of shared decision making. The structure of the plan, and its inherent hierarchical logic model of goals → barriers → objectives → interventions → desired outcomes help to organize and facilitate the desired positive and collaborative interactions. In other words, treatment planning is far from a mere administrative task or paperwork burden—it is at the core of what we must do to as providers to promote and support wellness and health outcomes among clients and service recipients. And if it's worth doing, it's worth writing down.

According to a Commonwealth Fund supported study in *Health Affairs*, patients in a large care delivery system in Minnesota who were identified as the most "activated"—that is, they participated in treatment decisions and took part in managing their own care—had significantly lower costs than those who were the least activated[27]. However, exactly what occurs in these productive interactions is not entirely clear. Focusing on the process of creating a person-centered plan and utilizing the implicit logical model of the plan to organize those interactions is a way of operationalizing the model. The work required to create a plan can help guide and shape the collaborative process and interactions as identified in the care model. This helps providers and individuals to engage in a collaborative partnership or team that includes the individual as a key member of that team and works to help the individual achieve their desired life goals beyond the illnesses that threaten their hopes and dreams.

A somewhat more precise but still brief description of each model element follows, along with some examples of the kind of steps and activities that might be pursued in each to promote and support productive interactions between service recipients and provider teams to promote personalized care[28].

Health system: Create a culture, organization and mechanisms that promote safe, high-quality care
- Visibly support improvement at all levels of the organization, beginning with the senior leader.
- Promote effective improvement strategies aimed at comprehensive system change.
- Encourage open and systematic handling of errors and quality problems to improve care.

- Provide incentives based on quality of care.
- Develop agreements that facilitate care coordination within and across organizations.

Delivery system design: Assure the delivery of effective, efficient clinical care and self-management support
- Define roles and distribute tasks among team members.
- Use planned interactions to support evidence-based care.
- Provide clinical case management services for individuals with complex needs.
- Ensure regular follow-up by the care team.
- Give care that individuals understand and that fits with their cultural background.

Decision support: Promote care that is consistent with scientific evidence and individual preferences
- Embed evidence-based guidelines into daily clinical practice.
- Share evidence-based guidelines and information with persons served to encourage their participation.
- Use proven provider education methods.

Clinical information systems: Organize person-level and population-based data to facilitate efficient and effective care
- Provide timely reminders for providers and person served.
- Identify relevant subpopulations for proactive care.
- Facilitate individual care planning.
- Share information with persons served and providers to coordinate care.
- Monitor performance of practice team and care system.

Self-management support: Empower and prepare individuals to manage their health and health care
- Emphasize the persons served's central role in managing their health.
- Use effective self-management support strategies that include assessment, goal setting, action planning, problem solving and follow-up (these self-management strategies often translate into interventions on the recovery plan).
- Organize internal and community resources to provide ongoing self-management support to persons served.

The community: Mobilize community resources to meet needs of individuals
- Encourage persons served to participate in effective community programs.

- Form partnerships with community organizations to support and develop interventions that fill gaps in needed services.
- Advocate for policies to improve care.

If we can imagine a circumstance where all the resources we believed necessary to have an optimal system became available, would we really know what to do? What would we prioritize? Where would we spend the first dollars? The last dollars? Another value of the Wagner model is that it helps us to identify strengths within the existing system, and at the same time it highlights opportunities for change and improvement that can work towards optimizing the interrelationships between various functions and possible strategies. But in the end, it distills down to improving the interactions and shared decisions between providers and persons served, promoting shared decisions creating person-centered plans, and ultimately improving outcomes. The opportunity to "get it right" may lie ahead embedded in health care reform.

VI. HEALTH CARE REFORM

Full implementation of the Affordable Care Act and health care reform in United States health care is slated for January 2014. No doubt, efforts at improving implementation and reforms along with policy and system refinements will continue well into the foreseeable future. Health care reform provides both an opportunity and an obligation to advance person-centered care. One of the primary motivations for and objectives of health care reform has been the need to improve care and outcomes and reduce costs. Somewhat of a companion and complimentary effort to improve the performance of the US health care system has been the focus on the Triple Aim put forward by the Institute for Healthcare Improvement and then championed by Don Berwick during his tenure as the Administrator for the Center for Medicare and Medicaid Services (CMS)[29]. The Triple Aim calls for[30]:

Better care
- Improve the overall quality, by making behavioral health care more person-centered, reliable, accessible and safe.

Healthy people/healthy communities
- Improve the behavioral health of the US population by supporting proven interventions to address behavioral, social and environmental determinants of positive behavioral health in addition to delivering higher-quality behavioral health care.

Affordable care
- Increase the value (cost-effectiveness) of behavioral health care for individuals, families, employers and government.

The importance of leveraging person-centered care and shared decision making as part of an overall strategy for reform of health care systems and success in achieving these cannot be understated. Health care reform and the advancement of person-centered medicine are interwoven. An April 2013 report from the Brooking Institute proposes a framework for improving care and slowing health care cost growth[31]. The report states:

> We propose a framework for health care reform that focuses on supporting person-centered care. With continued innovation toward more personalized care, this is the best way to improve care and health while also bending the curve of health care cost growth.... Our report's person-focused reforms aim to support these changes in care—not as an afterthought or as an addition to our health care financing and regulation, but as the core goal.

In fact, the focus on the need to improve the person-centeredness of care is ingrained in the law itself. The United States' Patient Protection and Affordable Care Act (ACA) championed by President Obama has identified and mandated the use of measures of the quality of care, public reporting and performance as part of what is required to improve the health care delivery system[32]. The law repeatedly refers to patient-centeredness, patient satisfaction, patient experience of care, patient engagement and shared decision making in its provisions.

In order to assure that needed mental health and substance abuse are included in health care reform, the ACA identifies these services as one of 10 "essential benefits" to be included in any insurance plan offered through the states' health insurance exchanges/marketplaces. In addition, the ACA also cites and invokes the Paul Wellstone and Pete Domenici Mental Health Parity and Addiction Equity Act of 2008 (MHPEAA). This law requires:

- Equity coverage apply to all financial requirements, including deductibles, copayments, coinsurance, and out-of-pocket expenses, and to all treatment limitations, including frequency of treatment, number of visits, days of coverage or other similar limits.
- Health plans may not apply separate cost sharing requirements or treatment limitations to mental health and substance use disorder benefits.

The ACA calls for increased consumer involvement in decision making, transparency and quality in health care. One overarching provision directs the Secretary of Health and Human Services (HHS) to develop a common framework that establishes the principles and process elements supporting participant direction across the department and all its programs (Section 2402(a)). Other specific Medicaid provisions require a person-centered or participant-directed approach to service delivery. These provisions strengthen and increase access to home- and community-based services while also giving consumers more of a say about their care[33,34].

Health care reform legislation, with its three core components—universal coverage, payment system reform and delivery system redesign—will extend mental health and substance treatment benefits to over 30 million Americans who are currently medically indigent or simply uninsured. Additionally, the focus on payment and delivery system reform will offer vital opportunities to reshape how services are actually provided. We must begin to consider what system reforms in the behavioral health sector are required to build a foundation for more effectively engaging and enabling consumers as true partners in the delivery of person-centered care. Clearly, any effort at health care reform must address the need for both general health care as well as specialty services for mental health and substance treatment to succeed in being more person-centered. The essential issues in mental health and substance abuse treatment services are really no different than in general health care, but the challenges may be greater.

Today's behavioral health care services environment can be described by high rates of disorders, low rates of detection, limited access to treatment and barriers to the provision of appropriate, effective, evidence-based treatments personalized for culturally diverse populations that are responsive to individual consumer needs and wants; and the structural, financing and organizational problems of the delivery system can be directly implicated. Against this backdrop, the structural and administrative barriers and challenges to quality person-centered care that face practitioners, consumers and families are many and include: the enormous complexity and fragmentation of services for individuals with mental illness and substance use and in some instances criminal justice involvement; the cross system needs of children and families, particularly those who are involved in the public welfare or juvenile justice systems; and the delicate balance between issues of public safety and consumer choice. In addition, efforts at providing services are often complicated by stigma, fear and confusion, by poverty and a lack of stable housing, along with the risk of suicide. One tragic outcome is the undertreatment of co-morbid physical illnesses that has led to the premature deaths of individuals with serious mental illnesses; it has been clearly documented that they die 25 years earlier than their age- and sex-matched cohorts[35].

The struggle to transform lives and communities, to find practical solutions to complex problems, and to effectively deliver recovery-focused and person-centered services is confounded by a number of factors that include:

- Public mental health and substance use services operate within unique and distinctly different state systems without uniform standards of care and by all measures are grossly underfunded. A behavioral health care system of the highest quality that delivers personalized care every time requires an adequately and rationally financed system.

- Incentives to service organizations are left to the states, and too often the people who are stigmatized for their behavioral health disorders and who receive care paid for with public dollars are an easy target for funding reductions.

- There is not a standard model for forecasting and costing behavioral health service demand and capacity as well as revenues and expenses based on accepted prevalence data, delivery of evidence-based practices, appropriate staffing levels, salaries and benefits. Moreover, there is not a quality improvement infrastructure that supports the delivery of person-centered care.

- The workforce is underpaid and unprepared to provide services in a new paradigm which is further complicated by shortages in the availability of capable staff. Many lack the ability and experience to find common ground for establishing "a continuous healing relationship" which lies at the heart of person-centered practice.

- Person-centered care depends upon the availability of a full range of research-based services. While considerable resources are being dedicated to the "science to service" agenda, it still falls far short of the need.

- There is little technology infrastructure and it will be virtually impossible to achieve the type of care envisioned by policy experts and hoped for by consumers without significant deployment of electronic health records that are interconnected through Health Information Networks (HINs).

- Services and compensation are siloed and tied to the billable hour when the need is for customized services provided in a wide range of settings coordinated among multiple systems and agencies.

- Provider organizations lack the capacity for outcome measurement and quality improvement activity necessary for success in the reduction of errors, practice based on research and the delivery of personalized care.

- Implementation of practice change is fundamentally a systems management function and organizational processes are the missing link between science and service, but we lack the design and implementation of more effective organizational processes necessary for making and sustaining practice change.

To date, there has been very little health care reform design work focused on the needs of Americans with serious mental health and substance use disorders. A set of funding and structural problems has resulted in a public behavioral health care system that is lacking in essential payment and regulatory supports necessary for success—in many cases to a much greater degree than the general health care system. Few to none of the redesign efforts that have been attempted have resulted in improved care nor moved us toward what Berwick identified as the three maxims of person-centered care.

Whatever health care reform may bring in terms of new financing and new service delivery models, we will be challenged to assure that services are person-centered and promote recovery. If we accept that this is our most critical task or process, then we must organize the efforts needed to achieve success and optimal outcomes for individuals, families and communities. Practical action steps include:

1. Adopting the Mental Health Care Model as the standard for the delivery of personalized services that promote shared decision making, recovery and social inclusion.

2. Explicitly include shared decision making and person-centered care competencies as provider performance measures and a focus of clinical supervision.

3. Routinely monitor key performance indicators of person-centered care and initiate data-driven efforts at quality/process improvement.

4. Include peer providers and self-help resources as part of routine care to explicitly help support and promote person-centered services.

It is essential to remember that health insurance and managed care remain as core components of how health care reform will actually be implemented. For better or worse, this means that we must continue to address the issue of medical necessity to help manage resources and utilization.

VII. MEDICAL NECESSITY

One of the several functions of a treatment plan is the clear demonstration and documentation of the "medical necessity" of services. Medical necessity has been a concept in both public and private insurance programs since the initial introduction of the Medicare and Medicaid programs in the

1960s—if not before. Simply stated, the demonstration of medical necessity requires that there is a legitimate clinical need and that services provided are an appropriate response. While there is often some confusion about how best to document and demonstrate medical necessity, the clearest and most effective approach is through the proper development of a clinically relevant individual plan.

Medical necessity is not only about *what* services are provided but also includes some consideration of *where* services are provided (i.e., at what level of care). For example, motivational counseling for addictive disorders can occur in an outpatient program or in a residential program—the most appropriate and necessary setting is determined by a host of specific issues and needs for a given individual and all are components of medical necessity.

Medical necessity is also about billing and revenue. Today, most organized systems of care have some form of utilization review or quality management function. Increasingly, health care providers are concerned about how scarce resources are applied and want to minimize waste and unnecessary services while at the same time assuring that individuals and families receive indicated and needed services. The plan helps to organize decisions about services and the documentation of medical necessity.

The concept of medical necessity can be divided into five components. Most payers will only pay for services that satisfy these five criteria. Services must be:

- indicated
- appropriate
- efficacious
- effective
- efficient

While these components can be considered individually, they are also very interrelated.

Services are *indicated* when there is a diagnosis. The latest version of the *International Classification of Disease Manual* (ICDM-9/10) or the *Diagnostic and Statistical Manual of Mental Disorders* (DSM-5) is typically the reference used. While psychosocial factors may complicate an individual's needs, there must be a recognized and diagnosable "medical" condition identified in order to demonstrate the need for services and to justify billings. In some settings, eligibility for services is closely tied to the concept of indication and plays a part in determining program enrollment and service availability.

Appropriateness refers to the match between a service and the individual's or family's needs and is closely linked with the idea of efficacy. Often, cultural factors as well as other individual attributes will play a part in determining appropriateness. For example, it is not appropriate to treat an individual at imminent risk of self-harm in an outpatient setting; nor is it appropriate to automatically place an individual in residential treatment when they have an adequate support system and have never before attempted or failed to seek help for their problems. In past years, depth-oriented psychoanalytic psychotherapy was considered to be an appropriate treatment for schizophrenia. Today, while there is an important role for some psychotherapy and counseling for individuals with this disorder, antipsychotic medications and psychosocial rehabilitation are seen as the most appropriate primary intervention.

Efficacy is about the likelihood that a particular intervention or service will be effective, and is tightly linked to the principles of evidence-based practice. Efficacy is often determined in research and controlled settings. While predictive of outcome and helpful in deciding which course of action to pursue, efficacy alone does not guarantee the desired results or outcome. In initiating any service or intervention, the challenge is to identify those activities that are most likely to have a positive impact for that individual and family. At the same time, individual choice and preference must be a factor in determining efficacy, and should be balanced with expert opinion and research data in determining what will most likely work for a given individual. Unacceptable interventions, no matter how powerful the evidence base to support them, will in all likelihood ultimately fail.

Effectiveness refers to determining the actual impact and value of the services and interventions provided. Did they work? Did they have the intended impact? Were there unanticipated negative consequences? Was a partial result obtained? These are all essential questions in the process of reviewing and updating a plan. It is surprising, if not shocking, how often ineffective services are provided on an ongoing basis. How can services be "necessary" if they do not in fact make a difference and support desired change?

Efficiency is closely tied to the concepts of appropriateness, efficacy and effectiveness. It is not efficient to provide inappropriate, inefficacious or ineffective services that are inherently wasteful of resources. For example, it is not efficient to provide services in a costly 24-hour setting when the individual can safely receive indicated treatment in an outpatient setting. Another element of efficiency is related to questions about the intensity, frequency and duration of services. Intensity refers to how much of a service is provided: is case management for 30 minutes or for 90 minutes? Frequency refers to the pattern of service: is counseling provided twice a week or only once every other week? Duration describes the length of the intervention: will residential treatment be for two weeks or for six months? It can be difficult at times to determine the most efficient way to provide services, but understanding common practice and evaluating individual response to services can help. Regardless, it is essential to consider the question of efficiency in determining and demonstrating the medical necessity of services.

Medical necessity can be a useful and helpful concept in developing a plan of action in response to the needs of individuals and families. The concept is sound, useful and central to developing meaningful and effective individual plans. The individual's plan should provide the clearest and most cogent documentation of medical necessity. When asked to demonstrate the medical necessity of a service for prior authorization or billing review, the capable provider should be able to present an organized and coherent plan clearly documenting the five core components.

This is true whether care is provided within a dedicated mental health and substance abuse services delivery system or in the context of integrated primary care/behavioral health setting.

VIII. INTEGRATED CARE

The Institute of Medicine (IOM) defines mental health integration (MHI) as a comprehensive approach to promoting the health of individuals, families and communities based on communication and coordination of evidence-based primary care and mental health services. It emphasizes integration as an example of quality health care delivery design that facilitates communication and coordination based on consumer and family preferences and sound economics. Integration of care should also include mental health and substance abuse integration as well as substance abuse and primary care coordination.

There are multiple advantages to care integration as well as challenges that can be summarized as follows:

Integrating mental health services into a primary care setting offers a promising, viable, and efficient way of ensuring that people have access to needed mental health services. Additionally, mental health care delivered in an integrated setting can help to minimize stigma and discrimination, while increasing opportunities to improve overall health outcomes. Successful integration requires the support of a strengthened primary care delivery system as well as a long-term commitment from policymakers at the federal, state, and private levels[36].

And there are multiple reasons to pursue integration[37]:

- The burden of mental disorders is great. They produce significant economic and social hardships that affect society as a whole.
- Mental and physical health problems are interwoven. Many people suffer from both physical and mental health problems.
- The treatment gap for mental disorders is enormous. Coordinating primary care and mental health helps close this divide.
- Primary care settings for mental health services enhance access. When mental health is integrated into primary care, people can access mental health services closer to their homes.
- Delivering mental health services in primary care settings reduces stigma and discrimination.
- Treating common mental disorders in primary care settings is cost-effective.
- The majority of people with mental disorders treated in collaborative primary care have good outcomes, particularly when linked to a network of services at a specialty care level and in the community.

Integrated care occurs when mental health specialty and general medical care providers work together to address both the physical and mental health and addictive disorder needs of their patients. Integration can work in two directions: either (1) specialty mental health and substance use care is introduced into primary care settings, or (2) primary health care is introduced into specialty behavioral health care settings. By definition, integration must involve linking primary care providers with mental health providers, but the models differ widely in terms of the nature of these linkages and the strategies used to target various aspects of the care process[38].

There has been a tendency to focus on the issues of location/co-location as part of the effort to integrate care. The Affordable Care Act promotes the idea of a person-centered medical home as a place where all essential services are either located or coordinated and fixes a central point of access and responsibility for each person seeking care. Collins et al.[36] propose a continuum of models for achieving care integration which is captured in Figure 1.2.

While some might argue that co-location is necessary for care coordination and integration, this is not necessarily true. According to the Canadian Collaborative Mental Health Initiative (CCMHI)[39], "there are almost as

COLLABORATION CONTINUUM
FIGURE 1.2

many ways of 'doing' collaborative mental health care as there are people writing about it"; there are a wide range of strategies to achieve care collaboration and understanding this is made even more complicated because most models are implemented as hybrids. Some believe that the ideal is "one team, one plan" however that might be achieved.

What is clear is that a person–centered plan can and should figure prominently in any effort at care integration. Like an orchestra, the plan creates a score that assures the various components of a symphony come together as beautiful music rather than cacophony. Collins et al. make this point clearly[36]:

> *Behavioral health care may be coordinated with primary care, but the actual delivery of services may occur in different settings. As such, treatment (or the delivery of services) can be co-located (where behavioral health and primary care are provided in the same location) or integrated,* **which means that behavioral health and medical services are provided in one treatment plan.** *Integrated treatment plans can occur in co-location and/or in separate treatment locations aided by Web-based health information technology. Generally speaking, co-located care includes the elements of coordinated care, and integrated care includes the elements of both coordinated care and co-located care.*

Not only does the idea of a medical home provide new models of how best to provide care, we must also consider that there are important new members of the health care team to consider and include in the process.

IX. WORKFORCE CHANGES

The past 25 years have seen a revolution in our understanding of the impact of mental health and substance use disorders on people's lives. Research within the United States and around the world began to challenge the old notion that people with these conditions could not succeed in regaining their full capacity and status in life following the onset of their disorders[40]. Instead, the vision of recovery articulated by consumers became common wisdom and mainstream thinking. The vision was based on these realizations:

- People could and did recover even from severe mental illness; and
- Recovery should build on a person's strengths[41].

As part of this shift, there has been increasing recognition of the value of "lived experience" and the unique ability of persons who themselves have experienced a mental health or substance abuse problem to help others. This has led to the evolution of persons in recovery as members of the treatment team with a distinct and valuable perspective and set of skills. In the words of Katherine Power, former Director of the Center for Mental Health Services at SAMHSA:

> *The peer-to-peer model is an exceptional example of the innovative ways in which we can help the system overcome its own barriers. Peer-support programs are not just empowerment programs. They are an expression and an example of the way the system is going to have to fundamentally change to foster healing relationships, and create an environment conducive for recovery.*

This has been part of the emergence of the certified peer specialist (CPS) as a trained and competent peer provider (although different terminology may be used, such as peer navigators, recovery coaches, etc.). A peer specialist has a unique ability to help a person reclaim control over his/her life and is now recognized as a vital member of the behavioral health workforce.

The CPS accomplishes this work by providing assistance in the development and application of personalized coping skills, by teaching and modeling self-help group process and networking skills, by assisting in the development of skills for empowerment and successful community living and by providing individual and systems advocacy within the mental health services and community health systems[42]. Peers can often connect with those in need of help in ways that a professional provider can't— there are issues of trust, recognition and empathy that all play a role. In addition, the CPS can be of tremendous assistance in helping to motivate individuals, helping them to articulate their goals and supporting them in the process of working with the other members of the team to create a person-centered plan.

For example, at Clarks Summit State Hospital in Pennsylvania, peers have assumed very specific roles and responsibilities that include:
- Peer mentoring and advocacy.
- Counseling with individuals to address a myriad of issues such as
  - medications/family relationships/peer relationships/substance use issues/spirituality/dealing with stigma/recognizing and
  - identifying stressors/developing management techniques.
- Sharing a recovery journey with others—providing a positive role model.
- Group facilitation with an occupational therapist and psychologist.

- Assessment of patient satisfaction questionnaire to be utilized by the advocacy group.
- Facilitation of the recovery center; which includes drop-in, community support program and consumer/family satisfaction teams.
- Supporting and assisting individuals to protect their rights in the mental health system and other related service systems.
- Completing peer assessments.
- Being an active member of the recovery team—visiting consumers and providing mentoring services within the community setting.

At Austin State Hospital in Austin, Texas, the certified peer specialists are full members of the multidisciplinary treatment team that meet with the person served to help develop the recovery plan. They also prepare the person for the treatment planning meeting by getting together with the individual prior to the team meeting and conducting a recovery inventory with the person (see example in Chapter 4). The purpose of the meeting can also be to determine what *kind* of support the person needs during a treatment team meeting. Are they having trouble defining what they want to say or request at the meeting? Are they afraid of speaking in front of a group? Do they need help in deciding what will be possible? Can they write a list of what they want to say? In some of these sessions, actually rehearsing with some people on how to present themselves can be a successful intervention for some people[43].

There is also growing evidence about the effectiveness of helping individuals to remain in the community and stay out of hospitals. One of the major benefits to the mental health service delivery system is the potential cost savings that are likely to result to the system from peer provided services[44]. Anecdotal reports from Optum Behavioral Health, a managed behavioral health care company, include:

- Enrollees in the Wisconsin PeerLink program had a 71% reduction in average number of acute inpatient days per month.
- Enrollees in the Tennessee PeerLink program showed a 90% drop in the average number of acute inpatient days per month.
- Optum Texas has seen a 70% reduction in hospital days associated with the work of peers.
- Optum Pierce County, Washington, observed a 79.2% reduction in hospital admissions year over year in a cohort of 125 individuals following the introduction of peer services resulting in a saving of over $550,000.
- The New York Association of Psychosocial Rehabilitation Services.

This is not intended to be an extensive list but rather a few examples of the financial benefits attributed to peer support services.

Peer support services are part of the array of services necessary for a culturally competent, recovery-based mental health and substance abuse system. Peer support services should be equal in value to more traditional clinical services. At the same time there is a risk that peer support is used as a cost-saving substitute for clinical services. As means of insuring quality care, peer services should include a certification process and should be available to all in need, regardless of the financing mechanism[45].

In the public sector, where services are largely funded by Medicaid, peer support services must be coordinated within the context of a comprehensive, individualized plan of care that includes specific individualized goals. In addition, Medicaid requires a person-centered planning process to help promote participant ownership of the plan of care. Such methods actively engage and empower the participant, and individuals selected by the participant, in leading and directing the design of the service plan and, thereby, ensure that the plan reflects the needs and preferences of the participant in achieving the specific, individualized goals that have measurable results and are specified in the service plan[46]. Peers can play a vital role in this process.

Peers have also helped to make clear the importance of better recognition of the prevalence of trauma among persons with mental health and substance abuse disorders. As a result people seeking help are especially vulnerable in ways that had not previously been understood or appreciated. This has led to an increased focus on trauma-informed care.

X. TRAUMA-INFORMED CARE

The prevalence of trauma in our society is shockingly high. The Substance Abuse and Mental Health Services Administration (SAMHSA) has defined trauma as the results from an event, series of events or set of circumstances that is experienced by an individual as physically and emotionally harmful or threatening and that has lasting adverse effects on the individual's physical, social, emotional or spiritual well-being[47]. Individuals with histories of violence, abuse and neglect from childhood onward make up the majority of clients served by public mental health and substance abuse service systems[48]. Some statistics about the occurrence of trauma include:

- Ninety-eight percent of public mental health clients with severe mental illness, including schizophrenia and bipolar disorder, have been exposed to childhood physical and/or sexual abuse. Most have multiple experiences of trauma.

- Seventy-five percent of women and men in substance abuse treatment report abuse and trauma histories.
- In Massachusetts, 82% of all children and adolescents in continuing care inpatient and intensive residential treatment have trauma histories.
- Teenagers with alcohol and drug problems are six to 12 times more likely to have a history of being physically abused and 18 to 21 times more likely to have been sexually abused compared with teenagers without alcohol and drug problems.

Often people seeking mental health services, especially in the public sector, have suffered multiple traumatic events and not just a single traumatic event such as natural disasters, accidents, terrorist acts or crimes occurring in adulthood such as rape and domestic violence[49]. Rather, the traumatic experiences of adults, adolescents and children with the most serious mental health problems are interpersonal in nature, intentional, prolonged and repeated, occur in childhood and adolescence, and may extend over years of a person's life. They include sexual abuse or incest, physical abuse, severe neglect and serious emotional and psychological abuse[50].

Trauma-informed care (TIC) describes a program, organization or system that has three characteristics:

- Acknowledgment of the prevalence of trauma.
- The ability to recognize how trauma affects all individuals involved with the program, organization or system, including its own workforce.
- The capacity to put this knowledge into practice[51].

Increasingly, there is the expectation that service providers work from a trauma-informed perspective.

The key principles of a trauma-informed approach include:

Collaboration and mutuality

- There is true partnering and leveling of power differences between staff and clients and among organizational staff from direct care staff to administrators; there is recognition that healing happens in relationships and in the meaningful sharing of power and decision making.

Empowerment

- Individuals' strengths are recognized and validated and new skills developed as necessary.

Voice and choice

- Clients' and family members' experience of choice is assured with the recognition that every person's experience is unique and requires an individualized approach.

Peer support and mutual self-help
- These are integral to the service delivery approach and are understood as a key vehicle for building trust, establishing safety and empowerment.

Resilience and strengths based
- Providers believe in resilience and in the ability of individuals, organizations and communities to heal and promote recovery from trauma; builds on what clients, staff and communities have to offer rather than responding to their perceived deficits.

Inclusiveness and shared purpose
- The provider organization recognizes that everyone has a role to play in a trauma-informed approach; one does not have to be a therapist to be therapeutic.

Cultural, historical and gender issues
- These are addressed; services are culturally sensitive and move beyond past cultural stereotypes and biases, offer gender responsive services, leverage the healing value of traditional cultural connections, and recognize and address historical trauma.

Change process
- This is conscious, intentional and ongoing; providers strive to become a learning community, constantly responding to new knowledge and developments.

The principles of TIC are strikingly similar to those associated with person-centered care. This should really be of no surprise; both approaches are focused on the importance of understanding each individual and their history as unique and responding in kind with appropriate empathy and sensitivity as well as services and supports. Some experts in the field have identified person-centered planning as a strategy to assure that services are in fact trauma informed[52].

We have come to better appreciate the importance of understanding each person's story and the impact of trauma along with the imperative of person-centered responses. Now emerging on the horizon is the America Psychiatric Association's *Diagnostic and Statistical Manual* (DSM-5™) and with it the opportunity to be more person-centered in diagnosis and classification.

XI. DSM-5™

The American Psychiatric Association released the 5th edition of the *Diagnostic and Statistical Manual* in May 2013. While it was seen as a long overdue and much welcomed advancement in diagnosis and classification by many, it was met with skepticism, criticism and mixed reviews and outright rejection by others. After eight years of development, its publication rekindled long-standing arguments about the lack of biological markers for mental illness and the benefits and dangers associated with trying to classify the human experience of the mind, emotions and behavior[53]. As Hippocrates once observed, "It's more important to know what sort of person has a disease than to know what sort of disease a person has."

Some feel that DSM-5™ attempts to better integrate scientific and clinical evidence than previous versions. Diagnostic criteria were developed from extensive literature reviews and secondary data analyses to ensure that proposed changes have a clearly defined and defendable empirical basis. Consultation was also sought from experts in mental health as well as social work, neurology, pediatrics, forensics and beyond. For whatever its faults as well as its improvements over the DSM-IV and earlier editions, it will be the reference standard for diagnosis of mental and substance use disorders for years to come.

Surprisingly, there may be changes to this edition that actually help to promote more person-centered approaches to assessment, diagnosis and care. The DSM-5™ attempts to avoid overdiagnosing normal human experience by addressing more contextual issues—these include considering the effects of age, gender and culture on symptomatology. This could potentially counter, mitigate or, in some cases, confirm the diagnosis of mental disorder. For many diagnoses, there is descriptive information about gender, culture, age, functional consequences, associated features and more to help make diagnosis more sensitive to each individual. Hopefully these details will provide a clearer picture and facilitate each person's diagnosis. It would be hard to argue that this is not at least moving in the direction of being more person-centered and less arbitrary.

Another feature of the DSM-5™ is the Cultural Formulation Interview (CFI). This structured 16 item interview is designed to help providers understand the role and impact of culture and identity in a person's life and to understand symptoms and possible diagnosis informed by a better appreciation of the ways in which culture may impact the person's experience of illness and help seeking. Cultural competence and cultural humility are both highly correlated with person-centered approaches. Details about the use of the CFI can be found in Chapter 3 of this book as well as in the DSM-5™ itself.

There is one other noteworthy change in DSM-5™ that may also provide an opportunity to make the process of making a diagnosis a bit more person-centered[54]. The integration of dimensional assessments and patient- and clinician-completed questionnaires on symptoms and functioning with the more categorical approach to classification could improve the quality of care by offering a greater opportunity for patients to actively participate in their own diagnosis and treatment planning. However, the lack of consideration of a person's strengths and assets—a hallmark of person-centered approaches—as compared to the continued focus on symptoms, deficits and impairments in establishing a diagnosis is disconcerting. Only time will tell how these promising changes may in fact help to enhance person-centered approaches to diagnosis.

XII. READY TO GO

We have completed our scan of the health care landscape. We have looked at current and emerging trends in the environment that will create opportunities as well as challenges in our efforts to be more person-centered and use treatment/recovery planning as a tool to improve the experience of care as well as outcomes. This overview of the terrain is by no means exhaustive—rather we have tried to highlight some of the more prominent features that are likely to influence our journey and shape efforts to advance the quality of physical health, mental health and addiction treatment services as we move forward. Other smaller landmarks and points of interest will be highlighted throughout the text in the context of topics considered in each chapter and subsection.

The prep and the orientation are completed. We've checked the oil and kicked the tires. We're ready to hit the road.

REFERENCES

1. Berwick D. What "patient-centered" should mean: confessions of an extremist. *Health Aff.* 2009;28(4): w555–w565 (published online 19 May 2009; 10.1377/hlthaff.28.4.w555).
2. Institute of Medicine. *Crossing the Quality Chasm: A New Health System for the Twenty-first Century.* Washington: National Academy Press; 2001.
3. Committee on Crossing the Quality Chasm. *Adaptation to Mental Health and Addictive Disorders. Improving the Quality of Health Care for Mental and Substance-Use Conditions.* Washington, DC: Institute of Medicine; 2006.
4. New Freedom Commission on Mental Health. *Achieving the Promise: Transforming Mental Health Care in America. Final Report.* DHHS Pub. No. SMA-03-3832. MD: Rockville; 2003.
5. http://www.personcenteredmedicine.org/docs/pdf04.pdf.
6. Frank R, Glied S. *Better But Not Well: Mental Health Policy in the United States since 1950.* The Johns Hopkins University Press; 2006.
7. National Empowerment Center and the Recovery Consortium. *Voices of Transformation: Developing Recovery-Based Statewide Consumer/Survivor Organizations.* 2nd ed. MA: Lawrence; 2007.

8. http://www.wabusinessalliance.org/blog/post/the-american-sick-care-system.
9. http://www.integration.samhsa.gov/health-wellness/wham.
10. Prince M, et al. No health without mental health. *Lancet.* 2007;370(9590):859-877.
11. http://homeless.samhsa.gov/Blog/post/2013/04/22/I-Am-Not-My-Diagnosis.aspx.
12. Adams N, Grieder D. Person-centered care and planning. *Recovery to Pract.* 2008;13:2. http://www.cswe.org/File.aspx?id=48912.
13. Longhi D, Kohlenberg E. *Early Experiences in Service Integration: What We Can Learn from No Wrong Door Startups.* Washington: Department of Social and Health Services Research and Data Analysis Division Olympia; 2003.
14. Adams N, Grieder D, Nurney T. Models, principles and values of person/family centered planning. SAMHSA White Paper; 2005.
15. Tondora, et al. Implementation of person-centered care and planning: how philosophy can inform practice. www.psych.uic.edu/uicnrtc/cmhs/pcp.paper.implementation.doc; 2005.
16. Personal communication.
17. Shared Decision-Making in Mental Health Care. *Practice, Research, and Future Directions* HHS Publication No. SMA-09-4371. Rockville, w: Center for Mental Health Services, Substance Abuse and Mental Health Services Administration; 2010.
18. http://informedmedicaldecisions.org/library/?pt=imdf_sdm_pr_research.
19. Stanhope V, Ignolia C, Schmelter B, Marcus S. Impact of person-centered planning and collaborative documentation on treatment adherence. *Psychiatric Serv.* 2013;64:76-79.
20. Osborn R, Squires D. International Perspectives on Patient Engagement: Results from the 2011 Commonwealth Fund Survey. *J Ambul Care Manag.* 2012;35(2):118-128.
21. Bazelon Center for Mental Health Law & UPENN Collaborative on Consumer Integration. *In the Driver's Seat: A Guide to Self-Directed Mental Health Care.* February 2008.
22. Institute of Medicine (US) Committee on Crossing the Quality Chasm. *Adaptation to Mental Health and Addictive Disorders.* Washington (DC): National Academies Press (US); 2006.
23. Elwyn G, et al. *Br J Gen Pract.* 1999;49:477-482.
24. Stuart M, et al. *Patient-Centered Medicine: Transforming the Clinical Method.* 2nd ed. Radcliffe Medical Press; 2003.
25. Wagner EH, Austin BT, Davis C, Hindmarsh M, Schaefer J, Bonomi A. Improving chronic illness care: translating evidence into action. *Health Aff (Millwood).* 2001; 20(6):64-78.
26. *Behavioral Health/Primary Care Integration: The Person-Centered Healthcare Home and the Four Quadrant Model.* National Council Community Behavioral Healthcare; July 2008.
27. Hibbard JH, Greene J, Overton V. Patients with lower activation associated with higher costs; delivery systems should know their patients' "scores." *Health Aff.* 2013; 32(2):216-222.
28. http://www.improvingchroniccare.org/index.php?p=Model_Elements&s=18.
29. http://www.ihi.org/offerings/Initiatives/TripleAim/Pages/default.aspx.
30. http://www.ihi.org/IHI/Programs/StrategicInitiatives/TripleAim.htm.
31. Brookings Institute. *Bending the Curve: Person-Centered Health Care Reform.* Washington, DC; 2013.
32. Patient Protection and Affordable Care Act, P.L. 111–148, 124 Stat. 1025; 2010.
33. Feinberg L. *Moving Toward Person- and Family-Centered Care* Insight on the Issues 60. Washington, DC: AARP; March 2012.
34. Mahoney K. Person-centered planning and participant decision making. *Health Soc Work.* 2011; 36(3).
35. Parks J, et al. *Morbidity and Mortality in People with Serious Mental Illness.* Alexandria VA: National Association of State Mental Health Program Directors (NASMHPD) Medical Directors Council; 2006.

36. Collins C, et al. *Evolving Models of Behavioral Health Integration in Primary Care*. New York, NY: Milbank Memorial Fund; 2010.
37. Funk M, Ivbijaro G, eds. *Integrating Mental Health into Primary Care: A Global Perspective*. Geneva, Switzerland: World Health Organization and London, UK: World Organization of Family Doctors; 2008. Available at http://www.who.int/mental_health/policy/Men tal%20health%20.
38. http://www.mentalhealthamerica.net/go/action/policy-issues-a-z/integrated-care.
39. Macfarlane D. *Current State of Collaborative Mental Health Care*. *Mississauga: ON: Canadian Collaborative Mental Health Initiative*; 2005. Available at http://www.ccmhi.ca/en/products/documents/12_OverviewPaper_EN.pdf.
40. Harding C, et al. The Vermont Longitudinal Study of Persons with Severe Mental Illness, I: Methodology, study sample, and overall status 32 years later. *Am J Psychiatry*. 1987;144:6.
41. *The Evidence: Consumer Operated Services*. SAMHSA, Evidence Based Practices Kit; 2011.
42. Peer Specialists in State Hospitals. *Responses to Query of NASMHPD Medical Directors*. Pennsylvania: Mary Diamond; 2008.
43. Bluebird G. *Paving New Ground for Peers Working at Delaware Psychiatric Hospital. Peers Working in In-Patient Settings*; 2010.
44. Solomon P. Peer support/peer provided services underlying processes, benefits, and critical ingredients. *Psychiatr Rehab J*. 2004;27(4):392-401.
45. Position Statement 37: The role of peer support services in the creation of recovery-oriented mental health systems. Mental Health America, Washington DC. http://www.mentalhealthamerica.net/go/position-statements/37.
46. Smith DG. *Department of Health & Human Services, Centers for Medicare & Medicaid Services*. Baltimore: Centers for Medicare & Medicaid Services, Maryland letter to state Medicaid directors, Peer Support and Medicaid Services; 2007.
47. http://www.samhsa.gov/traumajustice/traumadefinition/.
48. Jennings A. *Models for Developing Trauma-Informed Behavioral Health Systems*. National Center for Trauma Informed Care, SAMHSA; 2008.
49. Terr L. Childhood traumas: an outline and overview. *Am J Psychiatry*. 1991;148:10-20.
50. Giller E. What is Psychological Trauma? *Sidran Inst*. 1999.
51. Gillece J. *Promoting Alternatives to Seclusion and Restraint through Trauma-Informed Practices*, SAMHSA; 2012.
52. Trauma Informed Treatment in Behavioral Health Settings. *Ohio Legal Rights Serv*. 2007.
53. Brooks D. Heroes of uncertainty. *New York Times*. 27 May 2013.
54. Kuhl E, Kupfer D, M.D., Regier D. State of the art and science: patient-centered revisions to the DSM-5. *Am Med Assoc J Ethics*. 2011;13(12):873-879.

Getting Started

We are now prepared to launch into the more technical details about the role of person-centered planning on the road to wellness. Section I, *Land of Opportunity*, described key features of the current health care environment and the terrain which our journey to whole health and recovery must cover. The environment is one that clearly fosters and promotes person-centered care and the important role of person-centered planning in helping individuals to fulfill their wellness vision—but it is not without mountains to climb and rivers to forge.

Section II will deal with the specifics of engaging the individual in a process of shared decision making and mapping out their personal journey.

Chapter 2 is focused on gathering information and assessment. It addresses the importance of finding a balance between collecting data and building a healing partnership. In it we find that information about the particulars of the journey is essential, but equally important is the bonhomie and collaboration between the person served and the provider as fellow travelers.

Chapter 3 examines the importance of understanding and integration of all the information gathered. It discusses the transition from collecting data to providing important understanding insights and knowledge; this begins to identify opportunities for success as potential barriers to achieving whole health. This will become the fuel that sustains the trip. We may know where we want to go, but without understanding, we do not have a good idea about how to get there.

These two linked steps are essential to setting the compass—together they begin to lay out the individual's route, to define the purpose of the journey, as well as identify the destination.

CHAPTER 2

Assessment

Knowing is half the battle.

G.I. Joe

I. STATING THE CASE

Ostensibly, the purpose of an assessment is to gather information; this is the essential first step in shared decision making and creating a person-centered plan. It has been said that any plan is only as good as the assessment. There are many books and references that consider the challenges and issues in assessment for mental health and addiction recovery services at a level of detail that is beyond the scope of this book—it is a rich and complex topic worthy of its own book and exploration. However, taking some time to understand the process of assessment is a worthwhile investment for success in providing person-centered recovery-oriented services. Identifying the unique attributes and needs of individuals and families is the essence of being person-centered.

The Process of Assessment

Providers have a responsibility to fully understand the individual and family, their strengths, abilities and past successes, along with their hopes, dreams, needs and problems in seeking help. Only this knowledge prepares the provider to promote shared decision making and help create a responsive, efficacious plan, which is consistent with the expressed values, culture and wishes of those receiving services.

But assessment is more than the mere gathering of information; it is the initiation of building a trusting, helping, healing relationship, and the forging of an alliance upon which to build a plan responsive to the individual's and family's needs. In terms of the road trip metaphor, this is the point of "getting started" on the journey and gathering the needed provisions in order to begin the trip. While there is no question that the accuracy and quality of information that we gather is important, *how* the information is gathered is perhaps even more critical. In many instances, it is easy to confuse the process of assessment with the requirements of paperwork and forms,

Treatment Planning for Person-Centered Care
http://dx.doi.org/10.1016/B978-0-12-394448-1.00002-0

but ultimately assessment is primarily about building a relationship. While forms and documentation need to be completed, *it may be better to pursue a natural conversation rather than follow a linear approach* to completing these forms.

This is akin to the metaphor of the road map. Following a decision to travel and the choice of destination, preparations begin, the route is laid out and the intermediate stops are selected. Simply beginning a journey without a destination should be avoided, to prevent heading in the wrong direction and having to double back. Without following these basic steps, reaching the destination is unlikely. Assessment is the "getting started phase," identifying what we need to bring with us, choosing the provisions, gathering the essentials and packing for the trip. In the process of creating an individual plan, information is the fuel that propels us.

Before continuing with the discussion on assessment, it may be helpful to clarify the terminology. The words "triage," "screening" and "assessment" are often used interchangeably, resulting in some degree of confusion. While they are related processes, they also represent distinct clinical functions.

Triage A process of assigning priorities for access to treatment based on urgency and risk, typically but not necessarily used in emergency or crisis situations.

Screening A cursory of the preliminary assessment process for determining the need and appropriateness of services, often used in the initial determination of eligibility, level of care, and so on.

Assessment An in-depth gathering of data and information, typically conducted at the initiation of treatment, needed to understand an individual's or family's needs as a prerequisite for developing a plan of care.

This chapter will focus on assessment.

Establishing a Relationship

Too often, initiating an assessment begins by asking and focusing on what is wrong. In a recovery-oriented, person-centered approach, the challenge is to think about more positive, inviting, as well as affirming ways of responding to and engaging individuals and families seeking help. The need to accept and "meet the person on their own terms" is an often recited phrase, but its real meaning needs to be examined in response to an individual's or family's request for assistance. Sometimes simply asking the neutral and inviting question "How can I be of help?" begins to realign some of the inherent and at times undermining power differentials in the relationship between the provider and the person seeking services. This helps to set the stage for a more positive and productive course. There are times when this process is framed as one of alliance building or engagement. While this may at one level be accurate, the importance of the tone, quality and experience of the relationship cannot be overestimated. Treating people with dignity and respect, and as experts in their own lives, should always be our standard of practice and guiding rule, regardless of the circumstance.

The importance of a strengths-based approach to assessment cannot be overstated. An immediate focus on problems and shortcomings all too often leads to feelings of shame, blame and failure. This does not promote openness or support engagement and partnership; it does not set the stage for a successful recovery endeavor. A deficit-based approach emphasizes a negative perspective and often leaves the individual and family feeling that they are the problem. Instead, there is an opportunity to be empowering and collaborative even in the process of gathering assessment information. In a strengths-based and person-centered approach, the focus should be on possibility and response rather than the identification of all of the problem areas[1]; this helps to build trust, cooperation and meaningful involvement by the individual and family.

Another approach is to actually begin to build the helping alliance with some form of an orientation to how services are provided and the process of assessment and treatment planning, rather than immediately engage in data gathering and assessment. There are multiple levels of orientation to consider: orientation to the larger concept of mental health and addiction, orientation to the planning process, orientation to the service organization and available services, and/or orientation to a particular program. Depending on the needs, experience, knowledge and sophistication of the individual and family, all four levels of orientation might be indicated. Although providers are themselves generally very familiar with the mental health and addiction services process, many of the individuals and families seeking help are not. For many people, each new experience in seeking services promotes anxiety and uncertainty. Both children and adults will frequently carry fears and misconceptions, not knowing what to expect. Beginning with an explanation or overview of the whole process can help reduce anxieties, begin to build the alliance and support the assessment.

Organizing the Steps

Figure 2.1 begins to show a hierarchy for the multiple sequential steps that lead to the creation of a plan. Each step in the pyramid builds upon the

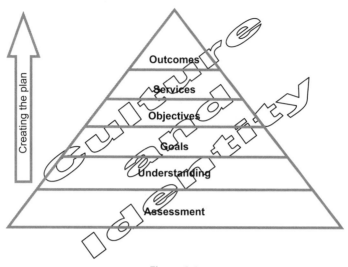

Figure 2.1

preceding one. Like the metaphor of building a house, creating the foundation is the essential first task. Each successive step must not only be completed in order, but must be done properly if the final result is to succeed. Skipping a step or jumping ahead will typically not work well. Perhaps not surprisingly, assessment is the first level of the pyramid. It is metaphorically as well as practically foundational and the start of the process in response to a request for help. The important underpinnings of culture and identity cannot be underestimated and, although often in the background, they influence the entire structure.

The pyramid itself can be a useful orientation tool that provides a simple graphic explanation of the various steps or phases in the process. Actually reviewing this diagram provides an opportunity to reassure individuals that the focus is on understanding their unique and individual needs and strengths as well as the importance of their role in making decisions about their care. Being person-centered in not only about *what* is done, but also about *how* it is done. In this way, individuals and families seeking help can be assisted in developing a plan for change that is reflective of their own expectations, priorities and goals. This is often in and of itself empowering and helps set the stage for successful outcomes.

Developing a plan typically begins with an assessment interview involving the individual and his or her self-defined family, and provides an opportunity for the provider to engage the person in treatment and begin building a successful alliance. From the data gathered in assessment, an integrated summary or narrative understanding is created. Next, long-term global recovery and outcome-oriented goals are identified; ideally, these are captured in the words and language of the individual receiving services and represent a potential endpoint or transition in the service delivery process. The objectives or the action steps the individual will need to take to lead to their goal should follow. In a person–centered plan, these time-framed and attainable near-term changes build upon the individual's needs, preferences, abilities and strengths. Services or interventions (also referred to as strategies and methods), which are culturally sensitive and appropriate, are then specified in a process of shared decision making and provided in support of the objectives and consistent with individual preference. Ideally these services help build the strengths, skills and capacities of the individual; whenever possible, interventions should include services utilizing and building on the natural supports available to the individual in the community. Ongoing reassessment and evaluation of timely progress and change are essential to keeping the recovery and wellness journey on track. This may also suggest the need for additional objectives or services to help the individual reach his or her goals and transitions.

In this hierarchical process, assessment is the base upon which shared decisions and the creation of the plan are built. In responding to a request for assistance, be it self-referral or some form of mandated treatment, the first step is to engage the individual as a partner in telling the story and gathering information.

There are always circumstances in which an individual or family will have only one visit—typically an assessment. Sometimes this is appropriate, but many times the lack of follow-up reflects a failure in our ability to adequately initiate or establish a relationship and engage people seeking help in the recovery process. Sadly, there are instances when individuals and families may experience contact with the mental health and addictive disorders delivery system as not merely unhelpful but rather as traumatic or re-traumatizing.

The relationship between childhood traumatic experiences and increased prevalence of mental illness throughout the lifespan is well documented[2]. For example, children experiencing trauma were 30 times more likely to have behavior and learning problems than those not exposed to trauma[3]. With this increasing recognition of the prevalence of trauma in people's lives comes the need to create "trauma informed" systems of care that include consideration and assessment of trauma as part of standard practice[4]. This is a particularly critical issue in serving diverse multicultural multi-ethnic communities where the issues of poverty, stigma, avoidance and the ability to trust mental health professionals may be even greater. This makes the task of conducting a good assessment even more challenging. However, with careful attention to each person, and sensitivity to his or her unique cultural and ethnic background, success in creating a physically and emotionally safe environment, building a relationship and learning about their needs can be achieved.

The Cycle of Assessment

Assessment is often described as being both "initial and ongoing." Assessment should never be considered a one-time event. At every step along the way we should be conducting an assessment or reassessment, evaluating the impacts of services and the changes that occur in people's lives and circumstances over time. Achieving a personal vision of recovery and wellness is inevitably a dynamic process in which we must attend to the new and different information that is generated in each individual's journey. Responses to services and interventions shed new light and have the potential to set new directions and priorities. People's lives and their environments are not static and changes are occurring apart from the provider's efforts to assist. Figure 2.2 describes how the planning and service processes have both linear and circular elements. Beginning with an effort at outreach, or a

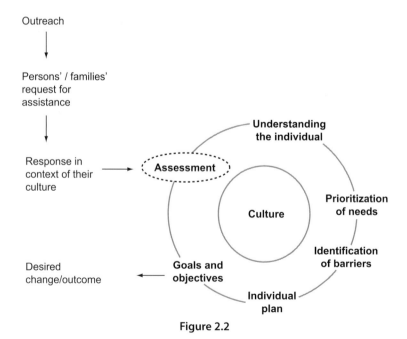

Figure 2.2

self-initiated request for assistance, all the way to the desired change, it can be viewed as linear. At the same time, assessment is a focal point in the overall process and part of a loop which is circular and repeated until the intended outcome is achieved. The cycle from assessment to plan to services and back to assessment revolves around a central theme: understanding the individual and family in the context of their culture.

A common problem in many service-delivery systems and settings is the lack of documentation of formal, regular and periodic reassessment. Providers will frequently claim that they have in fact been conducting an ongoing process of assessment and reassessment consistent with good practice. Both here and throughout the service-delivery process, the old adage applies: "If it's not written down, it didn't happen." While many providers often feel that they are crushed by the burden of paperwork and documentation, creating an accurate record is inevitably as much a part of the helping process as any other activity. Above and beyond the requirements of regulatory authorities, payers and the like, our ability to assure continuity, consistency and coordination is greatly enhanced by recording thoughts and observations as the recovery journey progresses; often, the information gathered proves to be useful for the individual and other providers in the future. Properly recording our assessment data helps to assure continuity of care over time.

Although there are no standard rules or instructions for the proper period of review and update of an assessment, it should be timely and relevant to the provision of services. Oftentimes, regulatory agencies and funding sources will establish criteria for reassessment. In evaluating actual practice in a wide range of settings, it is not unusual to find current service plans based upon assessments that are quite old. As a guiding principle, a formal and comprehensive outpatient reassessment should be considered in the provision of long-term services at minimum every year; in all likelihood, briefer and focused reassessments will occur more frequently, particularly in the inpatient or residential setting. In more short-term or acute service settings, the period of reassessment should correspond to the timeframes in each individual's and family's plan and be related to the anticipated or average length of services. Midpoints are often convenient times for some formal reassessment. Individuals who continue beyond the customary duration of services are also good candidates for reassessment. Quarterly reviews of treatment plans are considered by many to be a maximum interval for evaluation of recovery progress and also provide an opportunity for reassessment.

What to Collect

If assessment pertains to gathering information, then it is reasonable to ask a few questions: How much information is enough? What is the right volume of data? What is the right level of detail? Ultimately the answer is this: an amount of information sufficient to adequately understand each individual and family. In practice, the service setting often shapes this amount. Long-term services responding to long-standing needs and problems will likely require more detailed assessments, while more short-term programs and plans will require less. External demands from accreditation organizations, licensing bodies and funding sources may require certain types of information to be included, domains to be addressed or even standardized assessment instruments, such as the Child and Adolescent Needs and Strengths (CANS)[5] for children or the Addiction Severity Index (ASI)[6], to be utilized. A person-centered assessment does not have to exclude these requirements, nor is it necessarily in conflict with such requirements; a person-centered assessment is a matter of focus, emphasis and approach more than any specific or particular data elements.

As we consider the scope of our assessment and the range of topics to address, perhaps one domain is more important or essential than all of the rest: identifying the individual's and family's strengths. Not only is this information important in and of itself, but the message communicated in efforts at recognizing and validating the individual is also engaging and healing as well as supportive of the larger recovery process. Knowing about a person's hopes, dreams, accomplishments and self-esteem helps us to better understand that person's challenges and needs. This becomes the essence of the experience of dignity and respect for the person seeking services, and ultimately it is these attributes upon which we will build a successful plan to address the individual's challenges and needs.

Conducting a structured comprehensive assessment is often aided by organizing the data gathering into domains or broad topic areas to minimize the risk of overlooking critical information. People's lives are unique and complex. An individual is far greater than his or her presenting symptoms and whatever challenges they may cause. For many people, it is not easy to be immediately forthcoming about every detail of their lives—particularly at a time of distress. Assuring that an assessment is organized and comprehensive means that no important facet is overlooked and the individual seeking services is given ample opportunity to identify his or her needs and strengths. This does not, however, mean to suggest that the assessment should be a virtually scripted long list of questions or boxes on a form to be ticked off. Sometimes this approach requires a conversation that extends beyond one assessment appointment; admittedly, this can challenge the flexibility and creativity of providers as well as organizations and systems.

What does it mean to be comprehensive? How is an assessment tailored to the needs of each individual and family? Individual characteristics such as age, gender, ethnicity and disability may provide some initial guidance. For example, it is typically appropriate to inquire about educational issues for a child and work issues for an adult. Health concerns are an issue across the lifespan but may be more critical in understanding the needs and circumstances of an older adult.

Detail and depth should not be confused with breadth. While being broad or comprehensive is a general criterion, the depth or detail of an assessment may vary depending on the immediacy and severity of an individual's circumstances and the treatment setting. Although it is important to touch on and consider a broad range of life areas, not all require the same depth of inquiry or detail. Many accrediting organizations, licensing bodies and other standard setting groups will generate long and exhaustive lists of items to be included in a comprehensive assessment—but clearly not all of the items are always relevant or appropriate to an individual or family and there is no substitute for good judgment and thoughtful consideration.

Tailoring an assessment to each individual is part of being person-centered. There may be times when this impacts the depth of exploration in any one particular area more than the breadth of the assessment overall—particularly when there are licensing or accreditation standards proscribing domains or topics that must be addressed. However, the recognition of the need to be flexible and less proscriptive or absolute is reflected in the Joint Commission on Accreditation of Healthcare Organization's (JCAHO) Behavioral Health standards[7]. This new approach requires that "the organization defines in writing the data and information gathered during the psychosocial assessment," without a proscriptive emphasis on specific or required domains.

Attention to mental health or addiction treatment needs should always include consideration of the individual's and family's general/physical health, drug and alcohol use, nutrition, health habits, etc. The essential connection between mental and physical well-being has historically been minimized if not overlooked in many mental health and substance abuse treatment settings[8]. Truly integrated approaches to care require that basic medical information, including identification of the individual's primary care provider, as well as information about known illnesses and medications, is part of the behavioral health assessment. In many instances, the general health care provider is an important source of information and support in each person's pursuit of wellness and recovery, and their perspectives and information about general health status should be incorporated as much as possible into a behavioral health assessment.

From What to Why

It cannot be repeated too often that collecting information is but a first step. Weaving that data into understanding is a separate but closely linked, critical and often-overlooked task. Chapter 3 on the role of the integrated summary in understanding needs will discuss this in greater detail. For now, it is important not to confuse *what* and *why*. In general, assessment describes *what*, and hopefully with sufficient detail we can use that information to begin to understand *why*. The why of an individual's or family's needs is often the critical factor in developing a successful plan of response. Without this, there is a risk of not truly addressing the issues and problems. Ultimately, the measure of an adequate assessment is its ability to support a meaningful level of understanding.

For example, knowing that an individual does not take their medicines as prescribed is a simple bit of information—and a not uncommon issue in both mental health and general health care services. That fact alone may suggest the need for all kinds of support and supervision to assure adherence to the prescribed regimen, even to the point at times of suggesting the use of long-acting injections. However, there may be many reasons an individual does not take prescribed medicines. A list of possible reasons might include the following items:

- unwanted side effects
- lack of apparent benefit
- forgetfulness and disorganization
- a belief that they are cured
- lack of financial resources
- religious beliefs
- lack of understanding the purpose of the medication
- family opposition
- preference for alternatives, such as vitamins and homeopathy
- auditory hallucinations with negative commentary about treatment
- lack of trust in the physician
- trauma associated with past treatment

Research studies have found that not taking medications as prescribed is often a conscious decision by individuals based on adverse effects, price or personal choice[9].

Depending upon the reason, i.e., the understanding of the "why" lying behind the simple fact of non-adherence, a provider's response is likely to be quite different. For example, the response to unwanted side effects should be quite different than the supports and assistance provided to address financial burden, and different yet again from the psycho-education initiatives needed to address family opposition. It is easy to see how the data alone, without an accurate understanding that goes beyond the mere facts, are not sufficient for preparing an effective helping response.

Dual Diagnosis of Co-Occurring Disorders

In their many articles and training sessions, Minkoff and Cline[10] have posited "dual diagnosis is the expectation, not an exception." Research has proven them correct: 55% of individuals in treatment for schizophrenia report a history of substance use disorders, and 60% of individuals with substance use disorders have an identifiable psychiatric diagnosis[11]. The message should be clear—when assessing individuals who present at either a mental health or an addictive disorders program, providers need to be prepared to view them as whole persons, with multiple needs and issues not necessarily fitting into one diagnostic or service category! Using an integrated assessment instrument to conduct a single biopsychosocial assessment (not having the individual separately assessed by the mental health "experts" and the addiction "experts") is recommended. There should be "no wrong door" and individuals and families should be able to receive a complete assessment regardless of where they seek services. Minkoff has recently developed practice guidelines that can be useful and relevant for providers in developing integrated approaches to assessment[12].

Cultural Issues in Assessment

With the changing demographics of American society and the increasing diversity of our communities, attending to the issues of language and culture in the process of assessment is also critically important. The lack of equity in access and health status of ethnic and racial minorities in the US and other countries is a well-established serious concern. Removing barriers—linguistic, cultural, physical, psychological and others—and promoting equity has increasingly become a mandate for health and human services delivery systems. If assessment initiates the process of responding to need, then assuring the cultural competence of our assessment is essential. In many respects, a person-centered approach that is culturally informed and focuses on the unique needs of each individual and family is the essence of a culturally competent approach.

The importance of cultural awareness, sensitivity and competence, not just in assessment but also in the entirety of mental health and addictive disorders services, cannot be overstated. Culture does not refer only to matters of race and ethnicity but rather to the myriad ways in which people self-identify and affiliate; these factors may strongly influence each person's definition of wellness and recovery. Understanding this is central to any notion of being person- and family-centered. Individuals and families must be understood in the context of their culture and experience with full awareness of the ways in which culture can create barriers to an appropriate response.

Assessment must include recognition and appreciation of the person's culture as a crucial part of developing an integrated summary and should include cultural considerations that can influence diagnosis and care. These are essential elements in creating a service plan that includes culturally appropriate interventions and can lead to better outcomes for individuals.

It is useful to have a working definition of the concept of culture. A simple but effective approach is to recognize culture as a shared set of beliefs, norms and values in which language is a key factor. Other factors that play an important role include ethnicity, race, sexual orientation, disability and other self-defined characteristics. Equally important is to remember that culture is not fixed or frozen in time but rather exists in a constant state of change that is learned, taught and reproduced. A framework for considering human diversity can be thought of using the ADDRESSING pneumonic and includes the following factors:

- **A**ge and generational influences
- **D**evelopmental and acquired **D**isabilities
- **R**eligion and spiritual orientation
- **E**thnicity
- **S**ocioeconomic status
- **S**exual orientation
- **I**ndigenous heritage
- **N**ational origin
- **G**ender

While this list is not exhaustive, it provides a handy tool to help assure that providers remember to consider those qualities that make every individual unique.

Issues of culture, ethnicity, race and other attributes which individuals use to self-identify impact the quality of interactions with providers and thus the assessment. Cultural tradition, experience and bias—by both the individual as well as the provider—are all part of an often unstated but powerful dynamic in the helping relationship that impacts how information is provided and received. Providing a psychically comfortable and emotionally safe environment for disclosure and to allay the fears, anxieties and preconceptions of those seeking help is critical to success in assessment. Understanding and being sensitive to the roles of status and power should also be a part of our approach. Knowledge about other cultures, awareness of one's own limits and a willingness to seek help and consultation when necessary are also key ingredients for success.

Assessment must also consider how culture and social contexts shape an individual's symptoms, presentation and meaning, as well as coping styles. In addition, family influences, attitudes towards help-seeking, stigma, autonomy and individuality, as well as the willingness to trust helping professionals, are all influenced by culture. The relationships between the provider and the individual and family are also potentially shaped by differences in culture and social status. Our efforts at assessment are impacted by factors including styles of communication, capacity for rapport, comfort with disclosure, the perception of safety and privacy, and the experience of power, dignity and respect, all of which are to a degree culturally determined. The impact of a number of other factors including acculturation and immigration stress, identity, racism, marginalization, trauma history or discrimination, all affect help-seeking and successful engagement, and must also be considered. Issues of assimilation, alienation and cultural trauma can also affect the experience of seeking and receiving services.

Ultimately, efforts at assessment should result in providing the information necessary to develop a cultural formulation as specified in the American Psychiatric Association's *Diagnostic and Statistical Manual of Mental Disorders* DSM-5™[13]. In this context culture refers to

- The values, ordinations, knowledge and practices that individuals gain from membership in diverse social groups
  - may include ethnic groups, faith communities, occupational groups, and so on.
- Aspects of the individual background, developmental experiences and current social contexts that may affect his or her perspective
  - may include geographical origin, migration, language, religion, sexual identity and race ethnicity.

- The influence of family and friends and other community members, i.e., the person's social network, on his/her illness experience.

It has been said that awareness of the role of culture in the individual's life and its potential influence on diagnosis, understanding the individual experience of illness and care along with service planning is the essence of being person-centered. Efforts at understanding the individual and family will inevitably be limited without the completion of a cultural formulation.

Much like the DSM-IV, there are five key elements or sections to the Cultural Formulation. They have been modified slightly from the DSM-IV and now include:

- cultural identity of the individual
- cultural conceptualization of distress
- psychosocial stressors and cultural features of vulnerability and resilience
- cultural features of the relationship between the individual and the provider
- overall cultural assessment

The DSM-5™ also includes a 16 item structured interview, the Cultural Formulation Interview (CFI) that includes guides for its administration. The 16 items are organized into four domains of assessment that include:

- cultural definition of the problem
- cultural perceptions of the cause context and support
- cultural factors affecting self-coping and past help-seeking
- cultural factors affecting current help-seeking

Developers of the CFI have strongly recommended that it be used routinely at the initiation of any psychiatric diagnostic interview or assessment regardless of the cultural background of the individual or the provider; understanding the rest of the data to be gathered within the context of a cultural formulation is critically important. International field trials suggest that the CFI can be completed in approximately 20 minutes in a wide range of settings[14].

Standardized Assessment Instruments

Commonly used, scientifically reliable and valid assessment tools for mental health and/or addiction treatment include any number of standardized instruments. A partial list, including some examples of commonly used instruments and tools, is as follows:

- AC-OK screen for co-occurring disorders (mental health, trauma-related mental health issues and substance abuse), a five-minute screen.
- Addiction Severity Index (ASI).

- Adolescent Drinking Index (ADI), for adolescents using alcohol, ages 13 to 17 years.
- Adult Needs and Strengths Assessment (ANSA).
- Alcohol Use Disorders Identification Test (AUDIT), brief screening designed by WHO for use in primary care practices.
- Beck Depression Inventory-Second Edition (BDI-II), for adults and adolescents with life functioning and behavior problems.
- Behavioral and Symptom Identification Scale (BASIS-32), for adults with risk factors/symptoms/life functioning issues.
- Brief Psychiatric Rating Scale (BPRS), for adults with major psychiatric disorders.
- Child and Adolescent Functional Assessment Scale (CAFAS), for children and adolescents experiencing life functioning, family, behavior and/or risk factors.
- Child and Adolescent Needs and Strengths (CANS).
- SF-36 Health Survey, for adolescents and adults with severity and/or risk factors and life functioning problems.
- Minnesota Multiphasic Personality Inventory (MMPI).
- Michigan Alcoholism Screening Test (MAST), for identifying adults who potentially abuse alcohol or are alcoholic.
- Personal Health Questionnaire PHQ-9 for Depression.
- GAD-7 for Generalized Anxiety Disorder.
- Screening and Brief Intervention Referral and Treatment (SBIRT).
- Substance Abuse Subtle Screening Inventory (SASSI), for adults who may be abusing substances.
- Stages of Change Readiness and Treatment Eagerness Scale (SOCRATES), for adults presenting with alcohol and other drug issues.
- University of Rhode Island Change Assessment (URICA), for drug-using adults.
- World Health Organization Disability Assessment Scale, WHO-DAS 2.0.
- Biological methods, including breath tests, urinalysis and blood tests, to determine substance use.

An important change from the DSM-IV to DSM-5™ is the elimination of the 5 Axis diagnostic protocol. This means that the Global Assessment of Function (GAF) scale, previously Axis V, is no longer required. Instead DSM-5™ has recommended the use of the World Health Organizations Disability Schedule 2.0 (WHO-DAS 2.0) as a replacement for the GAF. Information about the WHO-DAS 2.0 and its use can be found at http://whqlibdoc.who.int/publications/2010/9789241547598_eng.pdf.

These and other standardized data-gathering tools may be helpful in terms of assessing the individual's severity of symptoms, life functioning abilities, problem behaviors, domains of impairment, degree of alcohol-related problems and alcoholism, and so on. However, standardized assessment tools may not always be culturally sensitive or competent, and they are often too proscriptive and not sufficiently flexible to be useful in a person-centered approach. While there is some value in standardization, this must be balanced with a need for appropriate modification—through supplementation or editing—to ensure that each assessment is truly responsive to the individual's and family's unique attributes and circumstances. In comparison, standardization in terms of breadth or comprehensiveness is less of a problem than the use of structured assessment tools that limit our ability to individually explore the important topic areas in detail.

In summary, assessment is the first and, therefore, most important step in initiating a person-centered plan. It is the gathering of the provisions needed (the data), packing them into a suitcase (the formatted documents of the clinical record), selecting the destination (as described in the integrated summary) in order to support a process of shared decision making and creating individualized person-centered recovery and wellness plans. There are many barriers within existing practice that make gathering information, developing understanding and creating a person-centered plan difficult. Yet changing current practice to be more person-centered and creating the information and understanding needed to better serve individuals and families is quite doable within existing systems and resources: it is about changing the *how* of assessment as much as it is a matter of changing the *what*.

II. CREATING THE SOLUTION

Ironically, thinking about how to be more person-centered in assessment seems perhaps more difficult than in other phases of developing individual plans. This may be the case because assessment should be far more about process than about product—so much so that it is difficult to think about how to evaluate the "person-centeredness" of an assessment. Yet, in many service delivery settings there is often a strong focus on the written product and documentation. What is the written demonstration of a person-centered assessment? How is it different from other assessment styles or approaches?

Gathering Data

The objective of assessment is to gather information about the individual and family—something that on the surface would appear to be the essence of being person-centered. However, there is a real need to shift the focus away from an emphasis on the quantity of information. Instead, more importance ought to be placed on the experience of the individual and family in the course of the process as well as the quality and type of information gathered. With a greater concern about the process employed in gathering information, there is some assurance that assessment will be person-centered. This is not meant to suggest the need for a radical transformation of many providers' current practice. Rather, it is about a shift in emphasis, focus, approach or style that has the potential to have a powerful effect on how providers as well as individuals and families experience the process of seeking and receiving help.

However, it is not entirely unusual that in the effort to meet a whole host of regulatory, accreditation, payment, productivity and other standards—not to mention the demands of a full schedule and much-too-large caseload—the preferences, needs and values of the individual and family can be overlooked. At that point, assessment is not about the individual and family; rather, it is driven by the obligation to gather all of the necessary information in a specified (and oftentimes too brief) period of time. The following pages contain some tips and tools that can assist providers in their efforts at being more person-centered in assessment and data gathering as a first step in the journey towards creating a meaningful and relevant individual plan.

Welcoming

It has been suggested that the welcoming attitude of the provider, expressed in terms of empathy, respect, warmth, genuineness and concreteness, is the key to the practice of person-centered assessment. This approach provides the individual and family with a comfortable and assuring environment in which they can explore, understand and benefit from the assessment process. Two essential elements of the provider's attitude have been identified. It can be said that assessment is person-centered when

- each person is viewed as a person of worth and is respected as such, and
- each individual's right to self-direction is honored, i.e., the right to choose their own values and goals and to make their own decisions.

In this framework, the assessment provides the individual and family with an opportunity to learn about potentially desirable changes in their lives and to better participate in the planning process. It is not for the benefit of the provider.

Steps to Collecting Data

Reordering the process of collecting information in the assessment can help a provider to be person-centered. There are often a host of administrative requirements that determine the elements of a comprehensive assessment and often unreasonably shape the assessment process. This domain-based and structured approach can unwittingly lead to an approach that overemphasizes shortcomings, deficits and problems. This can leave the individual and family seeking help feeling exposed, judged and criticized. Instead, a person-centered approach places emphasis and focus on understanding the goals, hopes, wishes and strengths of the individual and family in terms of their own self-defined identity and related cultural concerns.

A recognized text on treatment planning suggests that "A semi-structured [interview] format is recommended as the best means of gathering information from the patient [*sic*]…this ensures that all interview information that is generally helpful or needed in formulating a clinical picture of the patient is obtained"[15]. Instead, a "conversational and less formal" approach, which fosters a relationship with the individual and family rather than merely collecting information or promoting a particular service, is more likely to succeed in being person-centered[16]. Experience shows that one of the best ways to engage individuals is to focus on their goals, hopes, wishes and dreams. This is primarily and closely tied to a strengths-oriented approach that is at the heart of recovery, wellness and resiliency.

Domains

While every individual and family is unique and different, there are unifying concepts or concerns that can help to organize an assessment. These are frequently called domains. These broad categories are a useful framework by which to organize the collection of data. The following list is offered as an illustration of commonly considered domains:

- Identity
  - may include issues of culture, race, ethnicity, sexual orientation, spiritual beliefs, etc.
- Health and medical status
  - including identification of the primary care provider along with any medical disorders and treatment, diet and nutrition, efficacy of current or previously used medications, medication allergies or adverse reactions, risk-taking behaviors (e.g., intravenous drug use, sexual transmission of diseases, and so on), dental, hearing and eye care needs.

- Psychiatric and psychological status and history
  - may include mental status exam, identification of urgent needs, issues of personal safety, history of abuse and concerns (either as a victim or the perpetrator), co-occurring disorders identified.
- Alcohol and other drug use (present and past)
  - including alcohol and misuse of prescribed medications, as well as illegal drugs, caffeine, and tobacco.
- Treatment history
  - may include past hospitalizations, outpatient encounters for both mental health and addictive disorders.
- Family life
  - including history, present status, family members with mental illness/addiction issues.
- Community participation
  - may include all types of relationships, including use of natural supports, need for and availability of social supports, recreational pursuits, use of transportation.
- Housing status
  - including independent living, homelessness, incarceration, shelter living, group homes, and so on.
- Education and employment
  - including level of education attained as well as level of functioning
  - may include present and previous employment, vocational aptitude
  - financial status and ability to manage funds.
- Legal status
  - may include both civil and criminal current legal situation, conviction history, incarceration.
- Developmental history (particularly for children)
  - including developmental age factors, motor development and functioning, speech, visual and hearing functioning, learning ability and intellectual functioning, prenatal exposure to alcohol, tobacco or drugs, and so on.
- Levels of functioning
  - cognitive, emotional, behavioral functioning, including living skills.

This list is only a starting point. In particular settings and in response to specific individual and family needs, other assessment information may be indicated or even required. For instance, additional assessments for individuals in criminal and juvenile justice programs or hospital settings will likely require additional information and consideration. Regardless, content must always be balanced with process.

Strengths

The importance of strengths-based approaches is often invoked, but how to translate that into practice is not necessarily well understood—in part because there are many definitions or interpretations of "strengths." Focusing solely on shortcomings or deficits in the absence of a thoughtful analysis of strengths disregards the most critical resources an individual has on which to support their recovery journey. Therefore, the assessment of strengths and resources, including how they might inform the plan, is an essential component of person-centered recovery planning.

Moreover, many providers are not well trained in identifying strengths given the traditional focus in clinical training programs on diagnosis, symptoms, problems and deficits. One approach to understanding individuals' strengths lies in the concept of recognizing each person's "core gifts." This language is important in its implicit valuing of individual attributes. By not emphasizing deficits and problems, providers create an opportunity to see possibilities, options and opportunities for partnership change and improvement. Focusing solely on deficits in the absence of a thoughtful analysis of strengths disregards the most critical resources an individual has on which to build his or her efforts to advance his or her recovery. Therefore, the assessment of strengths and resources, including how they might inform the plan, is an essential component of person-centered recovery planning. This strengths-based assessment should be completed through in-depth discussion with the individual and (with the individual's permission) through conversations with collateral contacts with the individual's family and natural supports[17]. By not emphasizing deficits and problems, providers create an opportunity to see possibilities, options and opportunities for change and improvement.

A basic inventory of strengths should at minimum include consideration of:
- abilities, talents, competencies and accomplishments in any range of settings from home
- to school and work or other social settings
- values and traditions
- interests, hopes, dreams, aspirations and motivation
- resources and assets, both monetary/economic, social and interpersonal
- unique individual attributes (physical, psychological, performance capabilities, sense of humor, and so on)

- circumstances at home, school, work or in the community that have worked well in the past
- family members, relatives, friends, and other "natural supports" (both formal and informal relationships) within the community
- physical health status

For youth, it might be helpful to use the Resiliency Scales for Adolescents (RSCA) as described below, to determine the person's particular areas of strength/resiliency[18]. The RSCA assesses three areas of perceived strength and/or vulnerability related to psychological resilience. The RSCA Personal Resiliency Profile may be used as a screening tool for prevention programs and for referral; in combination with the Beck Youth Inventories (or other symptom-based measures) to link characteristics of resiliency with specific symptoms for more targeted treatment planning. The three Resiliency Scales may be used together or as stand-alone global scales as follows:

- Sense of Mastery Scale measures optimism, self-efficacy and adaptability.
- Sense of Relatedness Scale measures trust, support, comfort and tolerance.
- Emotional Reactivity Scale measures sensitivity, recovery and impairment.

Another tool to consider using for assessing both strengths and culture within families and youth is the strengths and discovery tool developed by Stacey Cornett[19]. The provision of services from a strengths-based and culturally informed framework has been identified by many researchers as best practice[20–22]. The Strengths and Cultural Discovery Tool Box 2-1 offers clinicians a way in which to think about the wide range of questions that can illicit insight into both of these areas. The tool is intended to assist a clinician to consider the types of questions that can be useful in learning how families think about their strengths as well as cultural influences. Both of these areas are often difficult for individuals to describe. Frequently the best way in which to embark on a discovery is by listening to family members describe one another and identify everyday routines. The tool is structured to consider the perceptions of caregivers as well as youth about themselves as well as one another. This information should be used to inform the service plan to ensure that services are strengths based and culturally informed.

The DSM-5™ introduced several assessment tools in Section III— Emerging Measures and Models. These include a Cross Cutting Symptom Measure for adults and one for children ages 6–17; these are based on the individual's and family's self-perception and report. Also included in

BOX 2-1   Strengths and Cultural Discovery

A strengths and cultural discovery best takes places in a conversational nature. The following list is examples of questions to facilitate this conversation with both caregivers and youth. Sections include the discovery of strengths and culture related to both youth and caregivers. Seeking the input of both youth and caregivers is essential.

Caregiver Questions Related to Their Child

- What stands out in your mind about your child's strongest points?
- What are some behaviors you have seen in your child that help in coping or dealing with a challenging event?
- Are there adults and peers that your child has good relationships with outside the family?
- Are there special activities that come easy for your child or that they especially enjoy?
- Does your child deal well with change?
- What is your child's mood most of the time?
- Would you describe your child's reactions as intense or calm most of the time?
- Does your child participate in any activities in the community?
- Does your child seem to have a strong ability to cope with stressors?
- Tell me a story about your child that makes you smile.
- When you find your child easiest to care for, how would you describe their behavior and interaction with you?
- In what situations or circumstances do you find your child behaves or functions at their best?
- Is there a year in school that your child did better than others? What are your thoughts about what made that happen?

Questions to Caregivers Related to Their Strengths

- In what situations with your child do you feel most competent?
- Describe what you're most proud of in your role as a parent?
- When do you have the most fun with your child?
- Do you have activities that help you relax?
- Do you have friends and family that you can turn to for support?
- What strategies do you have to calm down when you're overwhelmed as a parent?
- What do you think are the most important things you do for your child as a parent?
- In what ways do you feel alike or different from your own parents?
- Do you have certain strategies that work when your child is very upset or in crisis?

BOX 2-1   Strengths and Cultural Discovery—*cont'd*

- Do you feel comfortable asking others for help?
- What strategies do you have for talking to others about your child's needs?
- Are you able to predict situations that your child will have difficulty with?
- Can you describe a time when you felt really close to your child?

Child Questions

- What are you most proud of?
- What area in school do you feel best at?
- What would you like to be when you grow up?
- Are there things that you especially like to do?
- If you could plan your future, what would happen?
- What would your friends say about you?
- What are some skills that you feel especially proud of?
- What are some things that others believe you do well?
- What are some activities that you find enjoyment in?
- What would be the things that your friends would say you are good at?
- What types of tasks come easy for you?
- Are there some adults in your life that are helpful to you?
- Who do you like to spend time with?
- What do you do when you need to calm down?

Child Questions Related to Their Caregiver

- Can you describe a time when you really had fun with your caregiver?
- What is the best thing about your mom or dad?
- When is it easiest to listen to your mom or dad?
- What do you count on most from your mom or dad?
- What does your mom or dad do to make you feel better when you're upset?
- What would your mom or dad tell us they like most about you?
- Do you have special activities that you only do with your mom and dad?

Cultural Discovery
Questions to Caregivers

- Who are the people that you consider your family?
- How would you describe your ethnicity?
- What are you most proud of regarding your ethnicity?
- How do you share with your children ideas about their ethnicity?
- Do you feel others understand your views, values and traditions?
- Do you have trouble understanding other's views, values and traditions?
- What is your preferred language?
- Is communication ever a barrier for you?
- How would you describe the most important roles of a parent?

Continued

BOX 2-1   Strengths and Cultural Discovery—*cont'd*

- How would you describe how children should behave in the home, school or community?
- What is your preference for how I offer you information? Verbal or written? Language?
- What are your favorite activities?
- What family activities are most enjoyable?
- How does your family celebrate holidays and birthdays?
- What do you want most for your children?
- How do you interact with extended family?
- Does your family have friends that are a big part of your life?
- Are others at your house often?
- What are special rules that your family has?
- Does your family belong to a faith community?
- What does your family do in times of stress?
- Who do you call in times of need?
- How would you describe family routines?
- How would you describe your beliefs about relationships with professionals?
- How would you feel most comfortable sharing concerns or needs?

Questions for Child

- Who would you describe as your family?
- Do you have friends that spend a lot of time with your family?
- When is it easiest or most difficult to share your ideas with adults?
- Is it comfortable for you to talk about what you do well?
- How does your family spend time together?
- Does your family have certain ways of doing things at mealtimes?
- Do you feel your family has ways of doing things that are different than other families?
- What language do you like to speak in?
- Do you ever have a hard time understanding how others do things?
- Does your family have an identity or ethnicity that is talked about?
- How would you describe your family?
- How does your family expect kids to act?
- What are the jobs of the parents?

DSM-5™ is the Clinician Rated Dimensions of Psychosis Symptom Severity assessment. Time will tell the extent to which these measures become incorporated into standard practice, but their inclusion in the DSM-5™ is noteworthy and significant.

Stages of Change and Recovery

The idea of stages or phases in the recovery process can often be useful in understanding an individual's or family's responses and ability to participate in a person-centered assessment. Townsend et al. have proposed a model in which individuals are placed in one of four stages of recovery, as detailed in Table 2.1[23]. Often providers will report feeling overwhelmed by the number and severity of an individual's needs and their reluctance to engage. Recognizing that the individual may be at Stage I, dependent and still unaware of their own potential for recovery, can help guide the assessment and work towards assisting the individual, and enhance their ability to articulate a vision for their own recovery.

Staff at Boston University's Center for Psychiatric Rehabilitation have proposed another schema for staging, which describes individuals as being in one of the following states with regard to their challenges, disabilities or illness[24]:

- overwhelmed by
- struggling with
- living with
- living beyond

This model is useful in understanding that a hopeful progression and course exists for individuals and families to follow.

Osher and Kofoed have proposed a "stages of treatment" model for integrated mental health and addictive disorders service[25]. This is an adaptation of Prochaska's stages of change model[26], which was developed for the

Table 2.1 Stages of Recovery: Ohio Model

Stage I dependent and unaware	The individual is dependent on the mental health and disabilities system and unaware of the potential for their own recovery.
Stage II dependent and aware	The individual is dependent on the mental health and disabilities system but is aware of the possibilities and potential for their recovery.
Stage III independent and aware	The individual is not dependent on the mental health and disability system, and is able to make choices about his/her life and aware of additional opportunities.
Stage IV independent and aware	The individual is interdependent, involved in the life of the community, and aware of the possibilities for themselves and others.

addiction-treatment field. The stages of treatment parallel the recovery process:

- engagement
- persuasion
- active treatment
- relapse prevention

In the engagement stage, the alliance between the provider and the individual is established. The focus of the persuasion stage is to develop the person's awareness of problems and challenges in order to motivate change. The active treatment stage has its focus on reducing substance abuse, with an ultimate goal of abstinence, and the relapse prevention stage has stability, further recovery and the prevention of relapse as its goals. Understanding the individual's stage at initiation of services (either voluntarily or under duress) is helpful in assisting the individual to succeed in plan development and ultimate outcomes.

Level of Care

Another component of assessment is helping to determine the breadth and intensity of services or level of care the individual and family will likely require to address their needs and concerns. This is a component of person-centered planning and medical necessity and utilization management as well as an element in quality of care. Assessment data are the critical starting point in determining the appropriate level of care.

In the mental health arena, the Level of Care and Utilization Scale (LOCUS)[27] developed by the American Association of Community Psychiatrists (AACP) for adults as well as children and adolescents (CALOCUS)[28] has gained wide acceptance as a tool to support medical necessity determinations. The six domains of assessment for the adult LOCUS include:

- risk of harm
- functional status
- medical and psychiatric co-morbidity
- recovery environment
- treatment and recovery history
- engagement

The CALOCUS for children and adolescents effectively uses the same domains with age-appropriate modifications and an emphasis on resiliency rather than recovery.

In the addictive disorders field, the American Society of Addiction Medicine's (ASAM) level of care tool, the *Treatment Criteria for Substance-Related,*

Addictive, and Co-Occurring Conditions, has become a virtual standard for level of care determinations[29]. The ASAM criteria are based upon an assessment of multiple biopsychosocial factors to help support consistent and objective, clinically based placement decisions and to determine the appropriate level of care for adults and adolescents (e.g., outpatient, residential, inpatient, and so on) requiring addictive disorders treatment. Six domains or dimensions are considered in the ASAM schema:

- intoxication and withdrawal
- biomedical conditions
- emotional/behavioral conditions
- treatment acceptance/resistance
- relapse/continued use potential
- recovery environment

Based upon the findings in each of the six domains, guidelines are provided to suggest an appropriate level of care, for example intensive outpatient or medically monitored residential treatment. There are striking similarities between the LOCUS and the ASAM criteria in their design and logic. Both of these systems use a matrix of criteria or domains and the individual's status or symptoms in each domain to guide decision making. However, each of these tools or instruments includes its own specific decision rules to help determine the most appropriate level and location of services. While much of the required data can be routinely included in the assessment process, it is useful to be aware of some of the specific elements and how they are integrated into these decision support tools.

Culture

How can providers be culturally sensitive and competent? The answer lies in learning to understand how culture and social contexts shape an individual's and family's mental health symptoms, presentation, meaning and coping styles along with attitudes towards help-seeking, stigma and the willingness to trust helping professionals—all of which are factors in assessment influenced by culture.

As a first step, providers should become familiar with and routinely use the Cultural Formulation Interview included in the DSM-5™. To use this interview tool well, it is helpful for providers to be aware of their own cultural experience and orientation as well as limitations and biases. Generalizations, stereotyping and making assumptions based upon culture are unacceptable, dangerous practices that are the essence of discrimination. Within any ethnic or cultural group there is a tremendous amount of heterogeneity. Thus, a person-centered approach that focuses on understanding and appreciating the role that culture and ethnicity plays in the life of each individual and family is so important. In this way we can build an effective trusting relationship that helps to ensure an accurate assessment. Sadly, service providers are not immune to racism, either overt or covert. Systems may have institutional barriers to full access by all individuals. Honesty, self-awareness and a willingness to confront these issues by providers as well as supervisors and administrators are important first steps towards assuring cultural competence in person-centered services and reducing disparities.

Language is a key factor in removing cultural and ethnic barriers to access and services. Understanding the fluency of the individual and family is necessary but not sufficient. For example, if English is a second language, it may not be the preferred language. In addition literacy may be different than verbal fluency in a language. Conducting an assessment in the language that provides the greatest comfort and ability in expression and communication for the individual becomes the prerequisite of conducting an effective assessment. Providing written materials in the language of literacy, and remembering that literacy may be a problem even for native-born English speakers is also important.

Provider Competencies

We can perhaps begin to identify a minimal set of competencies required for providers to succeed in assessment, particularly in their work with diverse multicultural communities. Providers need to have awareness, knowledge and skills. Table 2.2 provides a brief but more detailed summary of some key competencies.

Table 2.2 Cultural Competencies

Awareness of . . .	their own culture and social status
	power differentials in relationship
Knowledge about . . .	how theory and practice are culturally embedded
	history and manifestations of racism
	sociopolitical influences on lives of persons served
	culture specific diagnoses
	differences in family structures and roles across cultures
Skills to . . .	understand the person's conceptualization of their illness
	self-assess their own cultural competence/bias
	modify assessment techniques/tools so that they are culturally sensitive and appropriate
	design and implement non-biased effective service plans

As a complement to the DSM-5™ Cultural Formulation Interview (CFI), or for those who choose not to use it, we have identified some key elements or considerations in understanding the roles of culture and identity for both individuals and families:

1. Conducting a culturally competent assessment begins by clarifying the identity of the individual and family. Oftentimes the simple question *How do you see yourself?* helps to provide vital information about race, ethnicity, sexual orientation, religion, color, disability reference group and other factors important to the individual's and family's sense of self and place in society.

2. Language is another set of important concerns that shape the entire assessment process. Inquiring about language fluency, literacy and, perhaps most importantly, preference is essential. Conducting an assessment in the individual's and family's preferred language is always ideal; the use of an interpreter is second best. Family members should be used as interpreters only as a last resort when it is clear that no other resources are available.

3. Understanding the individual's and family's experience and history of immigration, the country of origin and possible trauma is important. Did they leave voluntarily or were they victims of persecution or even torture? Were they refugees? Did they seek political asylum? Similarly, understanding attitudes and perceptions of acculturation, assimilation, discrimination and alienation are equally important.

4. Evaluation of family composition, relational roles and dynamics along with cultural factors in individuality and identity should be considered.

5. Considering the impact of culture and language on the description of distress and symptom expression is important. There are times when somatic concerns may represent emotional distress. Awareness of possible culture-bound syndromes is essential along with idioms of distress. Inquiry about the experience of symptoms in relation to cultural group norms may help to explain the cause of the problem. Preferences for and experiences with professional and "popular" or traditional providers should also be explored. It may be advantageous to involve racially/ethnically/culturally specific providers, when possible and appropriate, to assist in gathering and understanding data either directly or through consultation.

6. If formal assessment tools and forms are used, they must be normed and validated for the specific cultural group as well as be linguistically appropriate.

7. Providers should consider the individual's and family's preference for linkages with their identified racial, ethnic or cultural community.
8. Evaluation of the psychosocial environment, the interaction and multiplicity of stressors and availability of supports along with levels of functioning and disability are often revealing of important data.
9. Understanding the individual's and family's beliefs and practices with regards to mental health and substance abuse, including attitudes about stigma and shame, is essential. Also important is an appreciation of any gender bias in help-seeking behavior that may be culturally determined or influenced.
10. Consideration of the possible impacts of poverty, discrimination based upon race ethnicity and/or sexual orientation, and spirituality and religious affiliation should also be included as part of the assessment.

This set of information provides the database necessary to ensure that the overall planning process is culturally sensitive and informed, by supporting DSM-5™ diagnoses informed by a cultural formulation as part of the overall process of assessment.

III. MAKING IT HAPPEN

Three specific techniques and tools are presented in the following pages of this chapter. They include (1) understanding the individual's stage of change, (2) using motivational interviewing, and (3) some sample interview tools that can help draw out the individual's recovery goals and concerns. These represent but a few of the many strategies available to ensure a person-centered approach to assessment. Without a doubt there are others, but these three build on many providers' existing knowledge and can be easily mastered as possible ways to enhance skills and current practice. This section concludes with four examples of person-centered assessments.

Stages of Change

In an attempt to better understand the process of recovery, rehabilitation and wellness, Prochaska, DiClemente and Norcross[26] described five basic stages of change. Most if not all people pursuing recovery seem to move through these stages, but the process is not always linear or direct. These stages are not unlike those described earlier in the *Creating the Solution* section above, but here the focus is largely on the issue of motivation for change.

Understanding the stage of motivation of an individual and family is not only a product of the assessment; it is important information that guides and structures the assessment and the entire planning and service process. The five stages are as follows:

- pre-contemplation
- contemplation
- preparation (determination)
- action
- maintenance and relapse prevention

This approach derives in large part from the experience and tradition of practice in the addictive disorders field but has much broader applicability in helping to support a person-centered approach. It provides insight into people's awareness, fears, anxieties and ambivalence, as well as their drive for change. Identifying an individual's current stage, and the provider's role in helping them, is empowering for everyone involved.

In the *pre-contemplation* stage, the individual has not yet considered the possibility of change and seldom presents voluntarily for treatment. This is different than the historical notion of "being in denial" which has negative connotations and does not tend to foster collaboration. In this circumstance, the provider's job is to increase the person's perception of risks and problems with his or her current behavior. In the *contemplation* stage, the individual is ambivalent, vacillating between motivations to change and justifications for not changing. At this stage, the provider should strengthen the person's ability to change his or her current behavior by heightening awareness of the risks of not changing. *Determination or preparation* occurs when the individual experiences the motivation to change and the provider helps the person determine the best course of action to pursue. The *action* stage is the point at which the individual seeks services and the provider helps the person take the necessary steps toward services. *Maintenance* is when the individual attempts to sustain the change and the provider helps to identify strategies to prevent relapse and promote ongoing recovery.

The stages-of-change framework also helps to explain the individual's or family's current view or outlook on their situation. The entire construct offers a positive perspective and allows for reframing problems and circumstances in a way that leads to alliance, hope and success. For example, instead of using language that may sound harsh or critical, the provider can help the person to understand that they are in a pre-contemplation stage and are in the earliest phases of the change process. This also supports the idea of mapping out what lies ahead.

This perspective invites the question: What will it take for the individual to get to the next stage? The answer, once learned or discovered, can play an important role in shaping and directing the individual plan. Using the stages-of-change framework, along with motivational interviewing, embodies respect for the individual, a true person-centered approach to assessment, the development of a trusting and helping relationship, and a style of orientation that will hopefully produce better information and outcomes.

Motivational Interventions

A complement to this model is the practice of motivational interviewing largely developed and refined by Miller and others at the University of New Mexico[30]. This approach follows the stages-of-change model and is useful for improving efforts at person-centered assessment. In this approach, providers use their skills and understanding to encourage individuals to analyze their own behavior and derive their own conclusions. Responsibility for change remains with the individual, while the provider is non-judgmental and does not assume the role of the "expert." The individual, with the provider directing the assessment interview, identifies any reasons to change and the goals of the treatment episode. Through a discussion about the findings of the assessment, the authors contend that this dialog helps the individual to explore his or her decisions and, therefore, the process of decision making is the foundation for change. Assessment then is the understanding of the individual and the meeting of his or her needs as well as recognition of his or her strengths and abilities.

The acceptance and recognition of the value of motivational approaches has expanded and is continuing to grow beyond its historic popularity in the addictive disorders field because it offers an alternative to traditional techniques and is consistent with the values of a person-centered and recovery oriented approach. This is particularly useful in working with individuals who are required to seek services linked to the civil or criminal justice systems and are not truly ready to make life changes. That said it is not unusual to find that, even highly motivated individuals seeking mental health and addictive disorders service do so with some ambivalence and anxiety about change.

Tools

There are other techniques that can be used to promote a person-centered assessment. Some providers and programs utilize self-report questionnaires that the individual and family complete independently in order to describe their needs, desires, preferences and goals. Others may use a worksheet that is completed in conjunction with a more traditional interview.

A very simple approach to eliciting the individual's own sense of recovery is demonstrated in the following example. For some individuals, expressing these thoughts and feelings in writing provides another opportunity and alternative to verbal communication that allows them to feel more in control. These are a few semi-structured questions that can serve as their self-assessment of strengths and resources:

> **Recovery Planning Worksheet**
> - What are your greatest stressors?
> - Are there any signs/triggers of wanting to use substances or feeling like you are not doing well?
> - What has helped your recovery in the past?
> - What are your goals for yourself?
> - What can the staff do to help?
> - What can you do to help?
> - Who else can help?

Peer specialists at Austin State Hospital have developed a Recovery Inventory which they use to interview all patients. It includes questions such as:
- What does recovery mean to you at this time?
- Do you believe it is possible to overcome your current challenges?
- What are your strengths and interests?
- What are your goals?
- Where do you want to live?
- Where do you want to work?
- For my family and social life, I want…
- For health and recreation, I want to be able to…
- In the community, I want to be able to…
- I want my follow-up care to include…
- Which goals do you want to focus on right now?
- What barriers to those goals do you identify?
- Which recovery tool(s) is most appropriate at this time?
  - Wellness journal
  - Recovery support group
  - Community resources
  - Substance abuse services
  - Talking to someone living in mental health recovery

Trauma is an important but sensitive issue. It has been suggested that we adopt "universal precautions as a core trauma informed concept"[31]. Given the high prevalence of trauma histories among individuals seeking help with mental health and addiction problems it is important to begin any assessment with the assumption that every person has been exposed to abuse, violence, neglect or other traumatic experiences. Questions about a history of trauma should be a standard part of assessment for both children and adults. The importance of therapeutic engagement during an interview cannot be overemphasized, and for children assessment can be made through play and behavior observations.

An assessment of trauma should include the following inquiries:

Type

Was it sexual, physical, emotional abuse or neglect and/or exposure to disaster?

Age

When did the abuse occur?

Who

Was the perpetrator of the abuse?

Symptoms

Is the individual experiencing dissociation, flashbacks, hyper-vigilance, numbness, self-injury, anxiety, depression, poor school performance, conduct problems, eating problems, etc.?

It cannot be overemphasized that results and "positive responses" to questions about trauma must be addressed in treatment planning or assessment is useless.

At the beginning of this chapter, it was suggested that a simple question such as "How can I be of help?" could provide a powerful alternative to the usual approach of "Tell me what's wrong." The process and approach used in data gathering can make a big difference in assuring that assessment is person-centered. Below are nine suggested action steps and fresh approaches that providers can use to facilitate a person-centered assessment:

- *Ask* the person
  - what they are seeking
  - what services they want
  - what they hope to accomplish from this treatment episode/this particular service experience
  - what his/her hopes and dreams for the future are
  - if he/she has any preferences in receiving services or assistance.
- *Listen* to the individual's concerns before interrupting with an opinion.
- *Assist* the person to understand reasonable alternatives.
- *Use* the assessment interview to begin to engage the person in services, even if they are a reluctant participant or coerced into treatment.
- *Help* the person identify his/her strengths and resources.

- *Include* the family member and other members of the person's support network in the interview process and elicit their feedback.
- *Respect* the individual's preferences, needs and values.
- *Determine together* the individual's current stage of recovery.
- *Share* the findings from the assessment with the individual.

In implementing these steps, the provider can become an effective partner with the individual and family, use the assessment process as an opportunity to clarify the individual's expectations of the provider, and better collaborate with their decisions and choices.

Examples

Ultimately, *Making it Happen* is about translating theory into practice and examples are always useful for helping learners to consolidate the information presented and transition into developing their skills. In this chapter, and each to follow, concepts and principles will be translated into a review of the sample assessments, narratives and plans included in the Appendices.

Four examples of individuals and families with various needs and challenges have been collected from actual clinical practice, and the documentation for each is included in his or her respective appendix. A presentation and commentary on each, to highlight certain issues, begins in this chapter and follows throughout the book at the end of the *Making it Happen* section. These sample scenarios address a variety of settings, populations, diagnoses, lengths of stay, cultural influences and situations that require different goals, objectives and interventions.

These examples are drawn from real people and circumstances, but each story may well include elements from several different instances and individuals. These examples are by no means intended to be all encompassing. However, they will hopefully serve to illustrate the principles presented in the chapters about data gathering, formulation and planning services. They are not necessarily intended to be clinically correct; the examples do not reflect the one and only diagnosis, proper mental status exams, perfect conclusions via the integrative summary or the only way to "fill in the blanks." This book was never designed to be a "how to" on providing treatment or matching diagnosis to treatment interventions. Rather, the intent is to use real-life stories to illustrate how to develop a person-centered individual plan.

The scenarios presented are those of the following four people:

- *Appendix 1: Diana* is a 12-year-old child with mental health needs who has some natural supports, including a family with their own struggles.

- *Appendix 2: JR* is a transition age youth (TAY) who represents a person with active psychotic symptoms, religious conflict and a non-supportive family.
- *Appendix 3: Keisha* is an adult with long time mental health and addiction challenges and is fortunate to have some natural/community supports.
- *Appendix 4: Roberto* is an adult veteran with co-occurring illnesses receiving inpatient services.

The presentation of these examples is not intended to suggest the perfect or ideal comprehensive biopsychosocial assessment document. Instead, they are merely vignettes that provide enough data for the purpose of developing a serviceable integrative summary and the creation of a sample plan. These examples were selected to provide a range of different histories and circumstances across cultures and phases of life. No particular approved or recommended planning form is utilized for any of these examples; instead the integrative summary/formulation and the recovery plan forms included have been developed for training and teaching purposes.

Diana

The summary of the assessment data identifies Diana's barriers to achieving goals, strengths to build upon, developmental issues, an in-depth description of the family environment, family relationships and cultural factors, along with a review of her school functioning—the basic information that ought to be gathered in assessing a child's needs. With Diana, there are many issues that arise; they may or may not be ultimately addressed in the individual plan. For example, the mother's trauma history may not be part of the recovery plan, depending on her mother's willingness to address it. The challenge for the provider will be to synthesize the data, which includes barriers/needs to achieving goals, strengths, developmental issues, an in-depth description of the family environment, family relationships and cultural factors, and school functioning—all of the information that is needed for assessing a child.

JR

Although brief, JR's assessment gives us an insight into what his experience of psychosis has been like and how much distress he is experiencing. The history about the onset and course of his difficulties is helpful in terms of diagnosis. Clearly JR is experiencing significant psychosocial impairment and loss as a result of his mental illness. The assessment also brings forward

JRs strengths and makes sure they are not overshadowed by his symptoms. The nature of JRs psychotic symptoms and religious conflict provides a sense of what's important to him and some of this may well shape the plan as it develops. The assessment also helps us to determine his stage of change which will be important in thinking about how to successfully engage him in recovery-oriented services.

Keisha

The assessment of Keisha provides a very comprehensive look into the details of this woman's life. It describes a woman who has been able to function fairly independently in the community using mental health supports for many years, but who has experienced a recent crisis and relapse of her symptoms that resulted in her being hospitalized. In reading the story one gets a vivid picture of who she is and a clear understanding of what she has been experiencing as well as why she is now seeking help. The challenges she faces along with her receptivity to help in overcoming these problems are well described along with the supports and resources she can draw upon in her recovery efforts.

Roberto

Roberto's story is not all together unusual and he is representative of the challenges and needs faced by many veterans returning from war. Especially given that he is in a crisis and receiving inpatient care, the assessment is comprehensive and thorough and provides insights into the many facets of his life which will all likely impact his recovery. Knowing about his general health needs and his substance use is essential and we could not really begin to understand Roberto without this information. The assessment also provides important information about his cultural background and how that may impact his help-seeking and receptivity to services.

REFERENCES

1. Wagner R, Clark HB. Strength Discovery Assessment Process for Transition Aged Youths and Young Adults. University of South Florida. http://tip.fmhi.usf.edu/files/StrengthDiscoverModule.pdf.
2. Watts-English T, Fortson BL, Gibler N, Hooper SR, De Bellis MD. The psychobiology of maltreatment in childhood. *J Soc Issues*. 2006;62:717-736.
3. Burke N, et al. The impact of adverse childhood experiences on an urban pediatric population. *Child Abuse Negl*. 2011;35(6):408-413.
4. http://www.tn.gov/mental/policy/best_pract/Pages%20from%20CY_BPGs_46-76.pdf.
5. http://www.praedfoundation.org/About%20the%20CANS.html.
6. http://pubs.niaaa.nih.gov/publications/AssessingAlcohol/InstrumentPDFs/04_ASI.pdf.

7. www.jcaho.org.
8. Integrated Behavioral Health Project. *Mental Health. Primary Care and Substance Abuse Interagency Collaboration Toolkit.* 2nd ed. 2013; www.ibhp.org.
9. Murray M, Harrison J. Prescription abandonment: another path to medication nonadherence. *Ann Intern Med.* 2010;153(10):680-681.
10. Minkoff K. *State of Arizona Service Planning Guidelines: Co-occurring Psychiatric and Substance Disorders*; 2000. Draft.
11. National Institute on Drug Abuse (NIDA). *Topics in Brief: Comorbid Drug Abuse and Mental Illness: A Research Update from the National Institute on Drug Abuse*; 2007.
12. http://www.kenminkoff.com/ccisc.html.
13. American Psychiatric Association. *Diagnostic and Statistical Manual of Mental Disorders.* 5th ed. DSM-5™; 2013.
14. Aggarwal N, et al. *Barriers to Implementing the DSM-5™ Cultural Formulation Interview: A Qualitative Study.* In press.
15. Maruish ME. *Essentials of Treatment Planning.* New York: John Wiley and Sons; 2002.
16. Hodge MS, et al. *Practical Application of Recovery Principles in Clinical Practice—The Ohio Experience.* Unpublished manuscript; 2003.
17. Tondora J, Miller R, Guy K, Lantieri S. *Getting in the Driver's Seat of Your Treatment: Preparing for Your Plan.* Yale Program for Recovery and Community Health; 2009.
18. Prince-Embury S. *Resiliency Scales for Children & Adolescents – A Profile of Personal Strengths (RSCA)*; 2005.
19. Adapted from: Cornett SM. *Home-based Services with High-Risk Youth: Assessment, Wraparound Planning And Interventions.* Kingston, New Jersey: Civic Research Institute; 2011.
20. Cross T, Bazron B, Dennis C, Isaacs M. *Towards a culturally competent system of care: a monograph on effective services for minority children who are severely emotionally disturbed.* vol. 1. Washington, DC: CASSP Technical Assistance Center, Georgetown University Child Development Center; 1989.
21. Rapp CA, Goscha RJ. *The Strengths Model: Case Management with People with Psychiatric Disabilities.* 2nd ed. New York: Oxford University Press; 2006.
22. Stroul BA, Friedman RM. *A system of care for severely emotionally disturbed children and youth.* Washington, DC: Child and Adolescent Service System Program (CASSP) Technical Assistance Center, Georgetown University; 1986.
23. Townsend, et al. *Emerging Best Practices in Recovery.* Ohio Department of Mental Health; 2003.
24. Farkas M. The vision of recovery today: what it is and what it means for services. *World Psychiatry.* 2007;6(2):68-74.
25. Osher F, Kofoed L. Treatment of patients with psychiatric and psychoactive substance abuse disorders. *Hosp Community Psychiatry.* 1989;40(10):1025-1030.
26. Prochaska JO, DiClemente CC, Norcross JC. In search of how people change: applications to addictive behaviors. *Am Psychol.* 1992;47:1102-1114.
27. www.communitypsychiatry.org/publications/. clinical_and_administrative_tools_guidelines/LOCUS%20Instrument%202010.pdf.
28. www.communitypsychiatry.org/publications/. clinical_and_administrative_tools_guidelines/calocus.aspx.
29. Mee-Lee D. *The ASAM Criteria: Treatment Criteria for Substance-Related, Addictive, and Co-Occurring Conditions*; American Society of Addiction Medicine; 2013.
30. Miller W, et al. *Motivational Interviewing: Preparing People for Change.* 2nd ed. New York: Guilford Press; 2002.
31. http://www.slideshare.net/CrimePreventionCouncil/docs-admin-1297952v2 cplaurierrobinsontraumainformedpractice.

CHAPTER 3

Understanding Needs: The Integrated Summary

We All Face Problems and Challenges; the Way We Frame Them is the First Clue to Our Ability to Deal with Them.

C. Tollett

I. STATING THE CASE

The gathering of information in the assessment is only the beginning of the recovery journey. Integration and summary of data and clinical formulation are essential but often-overlooked steps in the process of developing a person-centered individual plan. The assessment data are about *what*, while the integrated summary and formulation is about *how* and *why*. Understanding the problem from the perspective of the individual and family, as well as understanding their needs, strengths and resources, is the foundation for identifying barriers and developing personal goals.

Following the data collection efforts of the assessment, preparing an integrated summary is the next step in moving towards creating an individual plan. The integrated summary, alternatively referred to as the formulation, interpretive summary, diagnostic summary, clinical impression, and so on, is more than a mere compilation and retelling of the assessment data. Rather, it involves integration or synthesis of the data and it draws upon the provider's insights and interpretation. It is similar to weaving a whole cloth from a collection of threads; out of the bits and pieces of the assessment data, we can create a holistic understanding of the individual and family that extends beyond the mere facts.

Provider Role

Creating an integrated summary draws upon the skill, intellect, training, clinical orientation, experience, intuition and creativity of the provider. This step in the overall planning process is where the provider has a unique if not essential contribution to make. If the individual and family understood their problems and needs, then they might not require assistance to address them.

It is often because they do not understand the issues, or cannot envision a solution, that they seek help. From this perspective, the value of the provider's contribution is very apparent.

The ability of the provider to integrate data into understanding, and the sharing of this insight and perspective with the individual and family, is often in and of itself a powerful intervention. It is the essence of empathy, a key ingredient of successful helping relationships. The provider is not merely a sponge absorbing facts and detail but rather a skilled partner working in collaboration with the individual and family. Sharing the understanding and formulation that emerges provides an opportunity to further that alliance and promote shared decision making about treatment options. How is their request for assistance understood? What does all of the information gathered mean for this individual and family? What has been learned about them to help prepare an effective response? In a person-centered approach, this understanding brings forward the unique abilities, talents, skills and strengths that serve as the cornerstone in development and implementation of the plan.

The written integrated summary documents the rationalization and justification for the provider's recommendations and suggestions as well as promotes shared decisions about how best to proceed. It creates the platform from which the individual and the team/provider launch into creating the individual plan and charting the course for recovery and wellness. The summary explains the goals, identifies the barriers as well as strengths, orders the priority of tasks and objectives, describes the level of care, clarifies the diagnosis, explains the role of culture and ultimately provides a foundation for the interventions or services provided to each individual and family.

The skilled and seasoned provider's special contribution to the individual's recovery journey is his or her capacity to interpret the data. While other less-trained and less-experienced members of the staff might be able to help collect the data, they typically have difficulty with synthesis and integration; it is the experienced provider's clinical leadership that vests them with the ability and responsibility to develop formulations and prepare an integrated summary. At the same time, that responsibility is not solely theirs—the person-centered collaboration with the individual and family is only truly realized when the individual's and person's perspectives as well as expertise in their own life and recovery are acknowledged and incorporated into the summary.

In this way, the individual and family are fully informed partners who are given an opportunity to contribute their own viewpoints, to add to the provider's understanding and to make sure that their personal vision of recovery and wellness is truly understood and appreciated. Sharing the integrated summary with the individual and family, and modifying it based on their input, also supports motivation, builds trust and enhances engagement. This creates yet another opportunity for dialog and discussion about the individual's and family's goals, hopes and dreams along with the barriers and challenges they face, and the resources they can hopefully draw upon. In the recovery journey, the provider cannot be working towards one set of goals based upon an understanding that is not shared by the individual, the family and any other members of the team. The integrated summary helps to assure that there is "common ground," mutual understanding and shared purpose.

Requirements and Standards

For many years, CARF—the Rehabilitation Accreditation Commission's standards for behavioral health—have emphasized the importance of the integrated summary[1]. The standards state that for each person served, an "interpretive summary" should "integrate and interpret all history and assessment information collected." The CARF guidelines identify some key components or elements to be included in an integrated summary. The guidelines suggest that the summary should include:

- a central theme about the individual
- the findings from history and any assessments conducted, including medical, psychological, vocational, and so on
- the perception of the individual's needs, strengths and abilities as well as their ability to engage "natural resources" within the community
- the provider's perspective about what might affect the course of treatment
- recommended treatments and the level of care
- anticipated duration of services
- goals of the treatment encounter

Other elements to add might include the following:

- the provider's insights into the underpinnings of the problem in terms of psychodynamics, family systems, cognitive behavioral styles, personality traits or any other relevant perspective/framework
- a hypothesis for an effective response plan
- speculation or understanding about the success and failure of past treatment efforts
- identification of barriers to the individual's goals
- anticipated outcomes and transition or discharge options

This summary is derived from all of the data gathered about the individual and family, not just the results of the face-to-face interview and the completion of a biopsychosocial assessment instrument. If the individual has had any standardized testing, or there is medical information, discharge summaries from previous treatment experiences, referral source information, and so on, these documents should be reviewed in order to gain a broader perspective to help in the interpretation of the data. The integrated summary also provides an opportunity to integrate the data from several disciplines (e.g., MD, PhD, MSW, MFT, etc.) and contributions from their respective multidisciplinary team's assessment into a coherent and comprehensive synthesis of data and understanding.

In order to foster a whole health approach, the summary should attempt to examine the interrelationship between co-occurring medical, substance abuse and mental health disorders, and social needs whenever appropriate and indicated. Typically, there is a powerful interaction between co-occurring conditions both in their onset, course and impact. When there are multiple issues and needs that challenge the individual's recovery journey, addressing them in an isolated if not fragmented way tends to undermine success in all arenas. A truly integrated summary that takes a whole health perspective and examines the interrelationships between co-occurring conditions is essential for the coordinated and integrated care and plan which is essential for achieving recovery goals.

Current Practice

Despite the importance and value of the integrated summary in individual planning, our experience working with providers and individuals seeking services makes clear that adequate attention to this task continues to be perhaps the most problematic part of the entire planning process. A few of the more common difficulties encountered in completion of this important step include:

- In the community setting, the integrated summary is only written from the perspective of the provider who actually conducts the psychosocial assessment or intake interview. All too often, meaningful and important data gathered by other members of the team are ignored simply because the writer has not personally collected the additional information, such as the medical history and physical, psychological testing or vocational evaluation. If the provider does not utilize all of the information available, it is not possible to reach an accurate conclusion and write an integrated summary that can truly support a person-centered approach to planning.

The underuse of all available data is also a common occurrence in the inpatient setting, where multiple assessments conducted by a range of clinical disciplines (per standards and regulations) can provide a rich array of perspectives, focus and details; however, here, too, integration of all that potentially valuable assessment information is often less than optimal.

- The provider lacks the skill and sophistication necessary to prepare an integrated summary. In some settings, the integrated summary is one more form that is left to the case manager or intake worker to complete. These tasks are often assigned to para-professionals and others who have not had sufficient education, training or experience, and lack the skills to create a meaningful summary. The question of who is actually able to interpret all the data raises an important issue of provider training, skill and competency.

- Sufficient time and resources are not provided to prepare a proper integrated summary. A specific team meeting in which all of the data and information resources are brought together, and a shared hypothesis is generated, is a particularly effective way of benefiting from the rich talent and perspectives of a multidisciplinary team. This requires a commitment to the value of formulation and the expectation that this task is an essential part of the overall planning process. Sometimes, a team approach to preparing the integrated summary is just not feasible, so decisions need to be made by the hospital or the community-based program as to which staff member is responsible for actually gathering all the assessment data and writing the summary. Adjusting the workload so that designated staff actually have the time required is essential.

- In most state Medicaid plans, or Medicare/CMS requirements, there is no regulatory requirement for an integrated summary to be completed as part of routine practice; accordingly, it has just not been done as a matter of practice. Clinicians are often hesitant to write the summary, even a paragraph or two, since they already feel overburdened with paperwork/data entry into the electronic health record and its completion is not critical to regulatory compliance and/or payment.

All of these examples involve the issue of time and human resources necessary to complete an integrated summary. There is no question that this task requires an effort and investment of resources in systems that often seem to be already limited and stretched. However, the alternative is really unacceptable. To proceed without understanding carries the risk of doing the right things for the wrong reasons or vice versa. That would be a waste of resources that no individual, provider or system of care can afford.

It is not uncommon to hear providers express discomfort in making an interpretation of the data. They question their qualifications, fear drawing the wrong conclusions based on limited assessment data, and worry about the impact of incorrect interpretations. Providers are often concerned that they might be held liable in some way for the impact of their determinations, and at the same time report that they are uncomfortable sharing their findings with the individual and family. This overlooks the opportunity to use the integrated summary as strategy for promoting engagement along with fostering collaboration, and as a basis for establishing common ground between the persons served and the provider. There cannot be true shared decision making or person-centered planning without this shared understanding

Providers need to be reminded that assessment and formulation are not one-time events, but rather part of an ongoing process of successive approximations and refinements leading to ever improved understanding and provider/client collaboration. In the process of helping the individual and family, there should be ample opportunities to clarify information and make corrections as needed. The emphasis should be on involvement, transparency, candor, honesty, sharing and empowerment—not on precision.

At times it seems that formulation and preparation of an integrated summary has become a lost clinical art. Historically, the critical thinking involved in formulation has been at the heart of most clinical training programs across the range of clinical disciplines. Regardless of the theoretical framework, providers were taught analytic skills and trained to look beyond the mere facts for understanding to shape their helping responses. Perhaps it is the pressure of time and the limited availability of resources over the past 10 to 20 years, or an unbalanced emphasis on behavior and outcomes, that have seemingly relegated this kind of understanding to the past. Whatever the reason, it is time to revive and renew the practice and once again make formulation and the preparation of an integrated summary a central part of what providers do in response to a request for help. This can be revitalized with a true commitment to shared decision making and person-centered approaches accompanied by the active involvement of the individual and family in refining the formulation.

Prioritization

The integrated summary also supports the important task of prioritization. Even the best at multi-tasking can only manage so much activity at one time, and deciding what comes first is often a challenge. This is true for both the provider as well as the individual and family. Ordering and organizing the problem-solving and task completion inherent in the individual plan is a valuable contribution that helps promote success. Maslow's hierarchy of needs can be a useful schema for helping to establish priorities[2]. For example, Maslow pointed out the primacy of health and safety concerns and the impact of psychosocial factors that can determine health and well-being. There should be little argument that if an individual is homeless, ill, unemployed or lacking money, the immediate objective, even if the individual is currently abusing alcohol and other drugs, is probably not lifelong recovery and abstinence from drugs. The first priority for the individual is probably to obtain shelter and medical care. All too often, however, the goal on that individual's plan is merely abstinence, commonly because it is a program requirement.

As previously noted, there are times when agreement on priorities is not obvious or easy. A provider may have an understanding of the goals based on professional experiences and perspectives only to find that the individual or family may have their own understandings, priorities and needs. Sometimes people simply feel unprepared or reluctant to address particular problem areas in their lives. This often occurs when drug and/or alcohol use is a part of the individual's and family's problems, but for a variety of reasons they are not yet able or willing to acknowledge the impact of their drug use on their physical and/or mental health and social well-being. Our efforts at formulation captured in the integrated summary should help us to understand their perspectives and support continued work with the individual and family. Unfortunately, providers often experience these differences as a virtual roadblock to further progress and a crisis in the treatment process that precludes development of an individual plan.

A recovery-oriented person-centered approach offers an alternative. Building on the philosophy and skills of motivational enhancement therapy, the work of Patricia Deegan, PhD, in her Intentional Care[3] framework for promoting recovery and wellness, the provider can find a workable solution: embrace the reality that decisions about the recovery plan ultimately lie with the individual and family. This is not to suggest that such differences should lead the provider to abandon the individual and family to "the natural consequences of their choices." Nor does it suggest that the provider violate their own sense of professional duties, ethics or, in some circumstances, legal obligations. By utilizing motivational interviewing and focusing on the importance of engagement, providers can encourage individuals to examine their own behavior and reach their own conclusions. In this way the person-centered recovery-oriented provider can remain non-judgmental, while supplying a combination of information and encouragement intended to help the person move to the next stage of recovery. These techniques are particularly effective during the early trust-building phases of the recovery journey.

If there is not mutual understanding of the needs and problems, or the priorities and goals to address them, how can there be shared decision making? How can an effective and meaningful plan be developed? Recognition of those differences, followed by discussion and in some instances negotiation between the provider and the individual, and sometimes the family, can play an important role in clarifying the goals and priorities. Unresolved differences and disagreements between the provider and the individual can be viewed as "grist for the mill" and just another issue to discuss, a means to enhance understanding and opportunity to build a collaborative alliance based upon mutual respect.

All too often providers shy away from this type of engagement and dialog and in a variety of ways reject the individual and family seeking help. There are times when the effort to create an integrated summary and achieve a shared understanding with the individual and family results in a mutual decision not to proceed further. Instead, hopefully, a conversation about these differences can ultimately lead to shared understandings, establish common ground and foster collaboration that reflects an appropriate balance between the concerns of the individual, family and the experience and perspective of the provider.

Clearly it is difficult to develop an effective and meaningful plan without shared understanding. Yet, the need for a plan and the pressure to move on can result in a provider creating a plan that is not meaningful or relevant for the individual and family. Sadly, there are many times when services are provided on this basis with everyone simply going through the motions. A high level of frustration, dissatisfaction and disappointment with outcomes is inevitable in such circumstances. If the provider or service organization has admission criteria that the individual does not meet, if a provider does not have expertise in the identified areas of need, or if the program has treatment expectations that are not individualized to the person, the most ethical and considerate person-centered response may need to include a facilitated referral to another program or provider.

Strengths

The integrated summary should begin with a description of the person based upon their life role and accomplishments along with the strengths identified in the assessment process. For youth, this can include the strengths identified utilizing the Resiliency Scale for Adolescents (RSCA) or similar assessment strategy (see Chapter 2). This strengths approach sets the tone for the understanding of the individual from a holistic and person-centered perspective; it is also a means to recognize each individual's personhood beyond their problems and disorders and can be a source of hope for both the person receiving services as well as the provider. This approach can also foster and promote engagement. People usually respond much more positively and are likely to experience a sense of partnership and collaboration with a focus on their strengths rather than a description based upon their challenges and barriers! A focus on strengths also helps to establish a context for the person's identified goal(s). Awareness of the individual's strengths and resources can help the provider team in crafting objectives for the plan that lead to success in attaining goals.

Barriers

The integrated summary also helps to identify the barriers that the individual and family may face in efforts to achieve their goals. Typically the barriers are associated with the symptoms and functional impairments associated with the diagnosed health/MH/SU problem, but may include personal needs, family issues, resource needs and other challenges. The identified barriers, whether a need for skills and supports, the resolution of interpersonal conflict or the lack of access to transportation, should be articulated in the integrated summary. This is an essential step towards developing a responsive plan with appropriate objectives and interventions. Identifying and addressing barriers that are an immediate result of the mental health or substance use problem is an important part of explaining the "medical necessity" of services to payers. The impact of barriers on shaping the individual plan is so great that it warrants its own more detailed exploration and discussion. The issue of barriers is discussed in greater depth in Chapter 5.

Stage of Change

The integrated summary should also include some consideration of the assessed stage(s) of change, as discussed in Chapter 2. The stage of change can be dynamic and not static, and regular and ongoing reconsideration is clearly in order. This is as applicable for mental health and substance abuse treatment as it is for providing a way to better understanding health-related behaviors in the primary care setting. There appears to be some universal truth in understanding how people—as well as even organizations—approach recognizing the need for change and committing themselves to the process.

Understanding the individual's stage of change has significant implications for engagement and collaboration along with the rest of the planning and service delivery process. By definition, a person who is in the "pre-contemplative" stage of change will regard the entire process of assessment, goal setting and services very differently than someone in the preparation or active stage. Not only is an appreciation for each individual's stage of change at the heart of person-centeredness, it can help set the stage for tailoring our response to a request for help to each person's unique needs.

Understanding the individual's stage of change toward their mental health issues, or perhaps their substance use or even physical health concerns, will help the provider team in offering the appropriate interventions on the plan. As part of sharing the entire integrated summary with the individual and family, a discussion about the team's understanding of the person's current level of motivation as well as desire and readiness for change can be quite powerful and productive. One useful tool to facilitate this conversation is the Readiness to Change ruler[4]. Considering readiness or stage of change can become a motivational intervention in and of itself, as well as provide further insight and understanding about how best to assure the person's sense of safety and comfort as well as inform the best approach towards goal setting and goal attainment. Part of this understanding and dialog may include a determination that people are at different stages of change with regards to different aspects of their lives. Someone might be highly motivated to improve their self-management of diabetes and reduction of their hemoglobin A1c, but pre-contemplative about considering how their feelings of depression and tendency to self-medicate with alcohol interfere with their physical health.

Diagnosis

The assessment and formulation process should provide the clinician with the information necessary to determine and support at least a provisional or working diagnosis. Much of this information is derived from the mental status exam and its inherent focus on symptoms but should also include other relevant biopsychosocial data about the individual's general health as well as other concerns. The integrated summary offers an opportunity to link the report and observations of symptoms and behaviors with everything else that is known about the individual and family and their needs— including an appreciation for the individual's experience of their illness and what meaning it may hold.

An emphasis on diagnosis may seem contrary to the principles of person-centered recovery—it evokes images of being "pigeon-holed" or labeled and classified rather than understood as a unique individual with strengths and resources in the context of his or her culture and community. However, the reality is that diagnosis is so ingrained in existing clinical practice, as well as systems of payment and accountability in both public and private care settings, that it is unavoidable. Although a person- and family-centered approach to the development of the plan is not necessarily driven by diagnosis, it is often necessary to establish a diagnosis for purposes of reimbursement, identifying possible evidence-based practices, prescribing medication and utilization management.

Mezzich and his colleagues have attempted to address these concerns with the development and promotion of the Person-Centered Integrative Diagnosis (PCID)[5]. In this approach, diagnosis is tentatively defined as the description of the positive and negative aspects of health, interactively, within the person's life context. The PCID includes the best possible classification of mental and general health disorders as well as the description of other health-related problems, and positive aspects of health (adaptive functioning, protective factors, quality of life, etc.), along with attending to the totality of the person (including his/her dignity, values and aspirations). The PCID employs categorical, dimensional and narrative descriptive approaches as needed, to be formulated and applied interactively by clinicians, patients and families.

The American Psychiatric Association's *Diagnostic and Statistical Manual of Mental* DSM 5™, as well as the International Classification of Diseases (ICD)-9/10 diagnostic systems, have their value and utility as well as their limitations. All too often a diagnosis is reached or recorded without much insight into the clinical thinking and reasoning to support that decision. The integrated summary provides an opportunity for the provider to sort through a differential diagnosis and record the rationale for a working if not definitive diagnosis. In addition, by sharing the summary with the individual and family, a diagnosis can be a tool to help them better understand the nature of their needs and challenges. This can often help build support for decisions about priorities, goals, objectives and interventions. Historically, there has been provider reluctance about sharing a diagnosis with individuals and families. Withholding such information, however, would be contrary to the principles of a person-centered approach in which information is transparent and readily accessible to the individual seeking services. As stated earlier, this sharing of understanding tends to build and strengthen the collaborative partnership with the individual, family and provider.

At the same time, it should be evident that an individual's preference not to receive such information should always be respected.

Diagnosis should inform but not drive the development of the individual plan. There is substantial literature on treatment planning that proceeds from the notion that a somewhat standardized plan with prescribed goals, objectives and interventions can be generated primarily from the diagnosis or type of service[6]. However, this is not a particularly person-centered approach and can alienate the person seeking help rather than further engage them. Increasingly, treatment-planning functions in electronic clinical record systems are based on this approach and philosophy; they often include a drop-down menu of selected goals and objectives for each diagnosis. But this needs to be used carefully if at all. While there may be some utility and efficiency in such an approach, it does not embody the spirit of person- and family-centered planning and is generally not helpful in creating the plan.

Ashra Misha, MD, a psychiatrist and associate professor at Virginia Commonwealth University, emphasizes the importance of a "person-first" style[7]. The person is not the illness; rather, "the illness is a part, but not the whole part, of the person." Regarding diagnosis, she says, "the burden should be on the professional…not to go in with preconceived notions about a diagnosis. Labels stick…I stay away from labels in general." Therefore, a diagnosis may be needed to meet administrative and regulatory requirements, but the integrated summary should truly reflect the provider's thoughtful understanding of the individual and family as a step towards creation of the plan.

Co-Occurring General Health, Mental Health and Addictive Disorders

It seems to matter little whether individuals and families initially identify their needs in one area or another—assessment frequently reveals that physical and behavioral issues and needs coexist. Based upon epidemiological studies and surveys, it appears that mental disorders, addictive disorders and general health problems are more often than not co-occurring—and each complicates the other[8]. The problem is not necessarily limited to immediate circumstances. For example, given the crossover between physical and behavioral problems, the individual with a current addictive disorder is significantly at risk of future mental health problems and vice versa.

There is increasing attention being paid to integrated approaches to care in which behavioral and general health concerns are understood and treated in a coordinated fashion. There are numerous local, state and federal initiatives to promote integrated treatment of co-occurring mental health and addictive disorders as well as efforts to improve the identification and treatment of behavioral health conditions in the primary care setting. A "no wrong door" approach has been advocated at a systems level with a focus on organizing funding and services to better integrate services[9]. Regardless of larger systems issues, it is important that all three areas—physical health, mental health and substance use—be addressed in an integrated summary. This should include consideration of not only past and present needs but also potential future concerns and risks and as well as issues of prevention and promotion of protective factors.

Experts in the field[8] have proposed a two-by-two matrix for considering the co-occurrence of mental health and addictive disorders needs in a dynamic model (Figure 3.1)[10]. This diagram illustrates how co-occurring mental health needs, addictive disorders needs (MH/SA in the figure) and physical health needs can be sorted into four categories based on the severity of each of the disorders. This matrix and its interpretation in the integrated summary can be used as a guide for service planning. Assignment to a quadrant on the matrix can help inform the most appropriate level and locus of care for an individual as well as establish service priorities.

Service needs can be divided and recognized as ranging from low to high severity for each disorder. Individuals with high mental health and addictive disorder treatment needs often have complicating physical health problems and require continuing integrated care in a multidisciplinary behavioral health/primary care system or setting. The greatest challenge is often in responding to the needs of those individuals in Quadrant IV with high physical health and behavioral health needs. The integrative summary provides an opportunity to consider the interrelationship of these conditions and circumstances and should raise questions about how these multiple conditions interrelated and the implications for treatment. It has been said "there is no health without mental health"; the obverse is equally true.

Health care reform, also referred to as the Affordable Care Act (ACA), implicitly acknowledges the significance of co-occurring conditions and the importance of coordinated integrated treatment. This has become part of how person-centered care is conceived, and the ACA includes incentives for the creation of Person-Centered Medical Homes. This principally refers to the elaboration of primary care clinics and service delivery systems that assume responsibility for meeting the full continuum of a person's needs—including co-occurring medical and behavioral health conditions. There is also growing interest in the idea of Person-Centered Health Homes so that

The Four Quadrant Clinical Integration Model

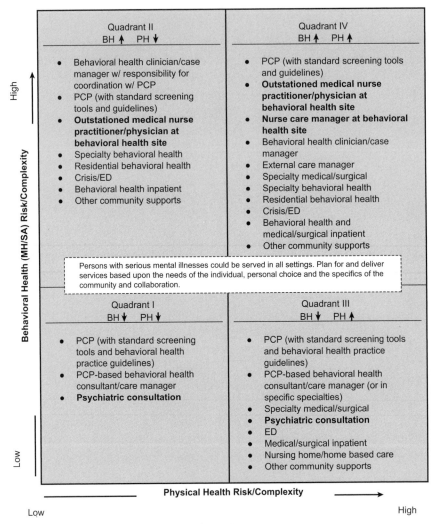

Figure 3.1

the same notions of centralized comprehensive and accountable care can grow out of behavioral health care settings and include primary care. Regardless, it is increasingly clear that notions of person-centeredness are key to health care reform implementation and the development of accountable integrated care systems that are capable of addressing both behavioral and general health needs.

Cultural Formulation

If the integrated summary is about assuring that we are person-centered in our understanding of the individual and their seeking help, then accounting for the role of culture and ethnicity is critical to a true appreciation of the individual and how best to respond to their needs. It is essential that information gathered during the assessment from the DSM-5™ Cultural Formulation Interview (CFI) and other sources be routinely included in the integrated summary and consideration of diagnosis if the commitment to being person-centered is to be consistently respected, honored and fulfilled. Given the emphasis on sharing the integrated summary with the individual and family, the inclusion of an understanding of the role of cultural factors in the diagnosis and formulation opens additional opportunities for dialog, understanding and partnership. Cultural sensitivity and cultural humility are key components of cultural competence and person-centered practice.

Transition and Discharge Planning

Transition and discharge planning is another essential part of the clinical process that is often overlooked or minimally addressed during assessment and treatment planning—in both community behavioral health care as well as inpatient settings. Having an identified and agreed upon end point for services can be very empowering and motivating. Accordingly, the integrated summary should also include consideration of the appropriate level and setting for care, the anticipated length and intensity of services, and ideally some notion of when the individual may be able to transition to another level of care or be discharged. It should also begin to anticipate the level of care and if aftercare needs are likely to be required.

Accrediting and other standard setting organizations commonly call for early transition/discharge planning. In addition, there have been landmark court decisions such as the Olmstead ruling that focused on the importance of transitions to lower level and less restrictive settings for care[11]. Preparation of the integrated summary creates an opportunity for providers and individuals and families together to identify the criteria for transition/discharge, even if the individual may ultimately require long-term services. There is hope and power in thinking about some sort of end point and defined accomplishment or change as compared to a more open-ended process. Understanding the individual's needs and likely destination at discharge plays a key part in determining the anticipated length of stay. This is especially important in situations where length of stay is predetermined by diagnosis or treatment protocol as is still commonly seen in residential treatment settings. Instead of expecting everyone to "complete the program"— the antithesis of individualized services—the type and duration of services and appropriate level of care must be organized and tailored to meet the unique needs of each individual.

In practice, the anticipated discharge or transition shapes the individual plan's objectives and helps to identify the barriers as well as clarify the strengths and resources available. Specifying the criteria for discharge or transition is crucial. In doing so, the idea of a journey becomes more than a metaphor—a destination has been determined. By integrating all of the information gathered and creating an integrated understanding, the trip is launched and the resources are set in motion. The individual plan becomes the map and the integrated summary becomes the tour book.

II. CREATING THE SOLUTION

If many providers are uncomfortable with formulation, and the creation of an integrated summary has become a lost art, it is reasonable to ask: What knowledge, skills, abilities and competencies do person-centered, recovery-oriented providers need to develop a formulation and integrated summary? A common error is to consider a succinct summary or restatement of the assessment facts as satisfying the need for an integrated summary. Instead, the integrated summary should go beyond the facts and provide analysis, understanding and insight that have the potential to provide unique creative and effective solutions for each person and family seeking help.

Below are several suggestions for provider activities and competencies that can help support a person-centered approach to assessment, formulation and the documentation of an integrated summary. They include the ability to:

- be empathic and non-judgmental in reviewing assessment data, and developing summaries with an inclusive approach that promotes an open and frank dialogue about the conclusions
- work collaboratively with the individual and family to create and sustain a helping partnership—and not assume an all-knowing, authoritarian role implying that "I'm the expert and I'm going to tell you what you need to do"

- use respectful person-first language that avoids jargon or labels; examples of person-first language include speaking of a "person with a diagnosis of bipolar disorder," not "a bipolar," or someone with a "history of depression," not "suffering from depression"
- engage the individual and family through motivational interviewing
- consider the individual's stage of change as well as motivation and how that impacts their readiness for engagement and active treatment
- encourage the individual to determine who should be included in the assessment and planning meetings as well as take into consideration information and perspectives from all of the participants
- be culturally competent and sensitive to the influence of cultural factors in understanding the needs of individuals and families
- implement a team approach that includes the individual, family members and providers in reaching agreement about a formulation
- actively support the individual's and family's choices even with the realization that some choices will likely be unattainable
- seek feedback on his or her performance through focus groups and surveys completed by individuals receiving services
- participate in regular peer/supervisory review of the records to
  - receive feedback about the integrated summary
  - evaluate whether goals established on the plan are in reasonable alignment with the conclusions of the integrated summary

An integrated summary that appropriately describes the individual's and family's needs, stage of change, strengths, abilities, as well as barriers and challenges, facilitates the creation of an individual plan that is actually relevant and helpful in achieving their desired outcomes. The outcomes that are identified in the plan—self-management, improved quality of life, symptom reduction, overall recovery goals, meaningful activity/work, and so on—comprise what is in essence a treatment or social contract between the individual and the provider. It becomes almost impossible to accurately identify those desired outcomes for each person if a shared understanding of the individual is not included in the integrated summary. The competencies previously described include important skills and abilities that can truly promote providers' success.

Coordinating the Team

How is an integrated summary actually created? What is the analytic process? How is the data integrated? How does the team collaborate? Below are three approaches or models for creating an integrated summary. Each of these gives the provider prompts and helps structure the task. Not every item is appropriate in all cases, and each area of response may be only a few sentences, but length and verbosity are not what is important. Rather, it is all in the interpretation of the data! These models need not be rigidly applied; embedded within each approach are tools that can be mixed and matched to help providers improve their skills in formulation and preparing integrated summaries.

Regardless of the model, thinking about how to actually coordinate and integrate the multiple inputs from the perspectives of the various members of a team is time well spent. For the team that is simply a dyad of provider and individual, this is a relatively easy task, but it does require the commitment of time by the provider, individual or family to develop and review. However, for a six- or eight-member multidisciplinary team, finding the time, integrating and coordinating the various assessments, and developing a consensus process can be a real challenge. One approach is as follows:

- Each provider conducts a discipline-specific assessment, prepares summary conclusions and forwards a copy of the assessment to the team leader prior to the team meeting.
- The team leader or another designated team member integrates the assessment data from each of the disciplines and prepares a draft integrated summary including a proposed formulation.
- At the team meeting, each team member presents a brief (two- to three-minute) summary of their key assessment findings.
- The team leader presents the draft integrated summary and formulation for consideration and discussion by the team and helps the team to reach consensus on a final summary and formulation.
- The team leader or another team member shares the summary and formulation and key findings with the individual and family as part of the individual planning process.

Clearly this workflow will not apply or be useful in every setting. It is, however, an example of the kind of organization, task assignment and coordination that can help to make creating an integrated summary a manageable, meaningful and relevant task.

Model I: the 10 Ps

This approach identifies 10 components to consider and include in creating an integrated summary. The first edition of this book included only six "Ps." Based on training experiences and working with providers since then, an additional four "Ps" have been suggested. Conveniently, each focus begins with the letter "P." In each category there are a number of factors to bear in mind. However, the suggestions below are by no means intended to be exhaustive; neither should each category be considered mandatory. The list includes consideration of the following items:

1. *Pertinent history*

   Some of the details included in this section may include age, marital status, children, educational history, work history, cultural affiliation, languages spoken, history and duration of mental illness, first hospitalization, number of hospitalizations, reasons for hospitalizations, longest hospitalization, medication history, therapy history, suicide, violence, arrests, addictive disorders, and so on.

2. *Presenting symptoms*

   A succinct description of major or significant symptoms that helps to support the diagnosis and may explain in part why the individual and family are seeking help at this time. This may include the experience of hallucinations, delusions, depression, anxiety, trauma, personality disorders and/or other behaviors, and should include information about the onset, duration and course of these symptoms.

3. *Precipitating factors*

   This helps to answer the often critically important question: "why now?" The answer typically includes consideration of psychosocial life events and stressors, e.g., losses (death of a loved one, job, home, pet, and so on), poverty, immigration, trauma and lack of support from family or significant others, community and friends. Possibly relevant biological concerns such as substance use, medical conditions or physical trauma, non-compliance with medication, and so on, should also be included. The list is only suggestive and by no means complete.

4. *Predisposing factors*

   Biological factors predisposing an individual to challenges and the need for assistance might include genetics (i.e., family history), medical needs (trauma, seizures, general health conditions), alcoholism and other addictive disorders, and medications along with other medical concerns. Psychosocial factors could include early family dynamics, abandonment, loss, neglect, abuse, traumatic experiences and exposure to violence.

5. *Perpetuating factors*

   A number of issues play a role in perpetuating an individual's or family's needs. This might include the nature of mental illness or addictive disorders problem, a persistent medical problem, a history of not following through with medications, difficulty with engaging in psychosocial treatment and services, a lack of outside support or poor support structure or the lack of a relapse prevention plan, as well as many other factors.

6. *Previous treatment and response*

This section should include a description of what services and interventions the individual has previously received, their effectiveness and any problems associated with the services. This may include consideration of acceptability, preference, tolerance, culture, risk and benefit or outcome.

7. *Prioritization*

What's important to and for the individual at this point in time? What comes first? There is a practical need for prioritization and determining priorities can then help define the overall goal for the person-centered recovery plan. People receiving services may have multiple dreams/ goals/desired results, but it may not be feasible for them to work on them all simultaneously. At the same time, personal and family values need to be considered and cultural influences may prove to be significant. Legal mandates and basic health and safety issues also need to be considered.

8. *Preferences*

What does the individual feel would be most helpful? Are there particular preferences around types of services, such as the gender/age group of a practitioner? A few simple sentences describing preferences can help with crafting of the plan, especially in considering and choosing interventions and action steps.

9. *Prognosis*

What do we think is a likely outcome for this person? How and where do we expect them to be functioning/living in the future? Clinical judgment is inherent in the notion of prognosis; however, obtaining the individual's input throughout the assessment process will contribute to the practitioner's understanding of the person and thinking about their future. Having these insights may particularly help determine the objectives on the recovery plan, since these are often about overcoming symptoms and functional impairments and may inform the discharge and transition criteria.

10. *Possibilities*

What do we (and/or the individual) see as possibilities for his/her future? What do we think would best contribute to the individual's recovery? What opportunities are available within the community? Part of partnering with people is to help them see their strengths as well as possibilities for their lives. If one is "stuck," it is difficult to "think outside the box" and envision a different future. Our role as recovery-oriented clinicians is to communicate hope by considering a range of possibilities.

This (re)organization of the assessment data helps set the stage for creation of the narrative summary. The 10 Ps is a useful framework to help bring forward the most relevant and compelling information collected and supports the process of understanding. These 10 factors or areas of focus and consideration, and the specific details in each, should be the basis upon which the formulation is built.

This approach anticipates the phrase "And in conclusion…" which should then lead to some interpretation or finding of significance and meaning embedded within the facts. For example, if perpetuating factors seem to be the most compelling part of the individual's story, then the circumstances that sustain the individual's needs or challenges should inevitably become a focus of the individual plan. On the other hand, recognition that the individual's needs are situational will direct the focus and the plan to the precipitating factors. Often an understanding of the impact and benefit from previous treatment and services is essential.

Knowing what has or has not worked in the past can and should inform current plans. Revisiting what has been helpful previously simply makes good sense; conversely there is generally little if any justification for repeating efforts at change that have not worked in the past. In other instances, the individual's and family's priorities and preferences may be absolutely critical in understanding how best to respond. This does not mean to imply that only one factor must be the identified focus—several may inform our understanding and plan development. The ability to extract that kind of knowledge from the assessment is the real value of the integrated summary.

Model II: Integrated Outline

In this approach, the integrated summary is less structured and more narrative, but still works to integrate all of the assessment data as well as abstract several appropriate, dominant and explanatory central themes. It should also begin to suggest strategies for response and issues to consider in the creation of a plan. The summary can begin to describe the person and what has led to their seeking help along with identifying their hopes and aspirations. The value of a more story-based presentation lies in its ability to help the listener feel as if they really know the person beyond the problems and conditions they present with.

Typically, the integrated narrative begins with a brief description of the individual or family and typically includes consideration of:

- The reason(s) the individual and family is seeking services
- The individual's and family's acceptance or understanding of the problems/needs which should include consideration of the stage of change
- Strategies for relapse prevention
- The individual's strengths as well as challenges and limitations
- Potential barriers to community inclusion/integration
- Successful attainment of goals and movement toward recovery
- Complicating co-occurring conditions/disorders including substance use and serious medical conditions
- Diagnosis and rationale as appropriate
- The choice of goals
- The balance between appropriate risks and choice
- Needs at transition/discharge

This model is an outline with prompts for including and considering several important topics; once again the clinician's judgment about what to include or emphasize is essential. Although organized somewhat differently, it is not entirely unlike the 10 Ps and leads to a similar outcome. Perhaps the first item is the most significant: the reason for seeking services. The word *reason* could simply imply the individual's and family's accurate explanation of their needs. However, there are times when it is important to go beyond the individual's description and develop a deeper explanation of how the problems came to be and why the individual and family need help in addressing them. This is the essence of an integrated summary and creating a platform from which to build an effective plan.

Model III: Eclectic

This approach is called eclectic because it builds from and includes the successful experience of a number of different providers and settings. It is a blending of several approaches and is a complement to the models previously described. In this approach, the integrated summary should include the following steps:

1. A summary of the individual's mental health needs and substance use problems, along with a clear statement of their goals (with appropriate consideration of other life concerns and issues) using the full scope of assessment data.
2. An evaluation of the stage of recovery based upon a summary of the individual's and family's perception of their behavioral health needs, including consideration of other life problems as well as a description of motivation and commitment to resolve these problems.

3. An explanation of the source of the problem or needs and an under-standing or hypothesis about the barriers that prevent the individual and family from attaining their goal(s).
4. A summary of both the positive and negative factors likely to affect the course of treatment and outcomes after discharge that includes but is not limited to consideration of identified strengths, assets and abilities, skills and supports needed, previous successes, relapse issues and cultural factors.
5. A realistic description of mental health and addictive disorders service goals that will be the focus of the individual plan including antici-pated transition or discharge criteria and needs, the type and range of services (or level of care) required, and the estimated length or inten-sity of services.
6. Identification of additional services and/or referrals that the individ-ual and family will likely need to improve their quality of life, pro-mote community inclusion and facilitate recovery.

In this approach, item 3, the explanation of the source of the problem, should never be overlooked.

Removing Barriers

If we reconsider the schematic in Figure 3.2, identifying the barriers to progress at points *B, C* and *D* that keep the individual from moving from *A* to *E*, informs and structures the successful individual plan, helps to establish objectives, and is an important part of the integrated summary. Developing a plan and specifying objectives relies heavily on understanding the factors that cause and perpetuate a particular need. An integrated summary and formulation should provide the insight and understanding required to create a map like this simple but effective diagram.

A novel alternative approach to reaching this kind of understanding is to borrow from the problem-solving techniques of quality improvement and the use of a tool alternately referred to as an Ishikawa diagram, cause-and-effect diagram, fishbone diagram or root cause analysis. Figure 3.3 provides an example of such a diagram.

The basic concept in the diagram is that the goal or need is entered on the left side of the diagram at the end of the main "bone." The factors leading to

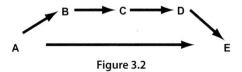

Figure 3.2

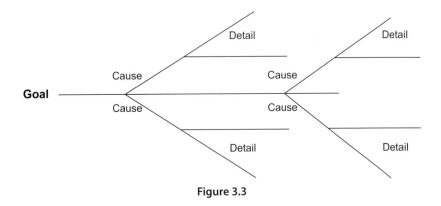

Figure 3.3

the need and the barriers to its resolution are then drawn as bones off of the main backbone. Brainstorming among members of the team, including the individual and the family, can help to identify possible causes and barriers to the goal. This subdivision in terms of increasing specificity continues as long as the challenge areas can be usefully explored and subdivided. The practical maximum depth of this tree is usually about two, or at most three, levels.

When the fishbone is complete, a rather comprehensive picture and understanding of the possible factors leading to and sustaining the need emerges. The Ishikawa diagram provides a powerful visualization and can also serve as an organizational tool. Arranging the ideas and insights of the team in this graphic and systematic way facilitates the understanding of the issues. This in turn can support the planning process by focusing attention on causes and removing the barriers towards reaching the goal. Ultimately, the objectives of the plan will help to resolve the identified problems and the description of the underlying issues and causes will help inform the selection of services and interventions necessary to remove the barriers.

This exercise can empower the whole team—it is the essence of creating the roadmap. The real value of the integrated summary is its ability to identify and explain the underpinnings of the needs of the individual and family. By understanding the barriers that have made the issue irresolvable for the individual and family, the provider is able to be strategic and effective in planning and providing services. Actually creating a fishbone diagram and including it in an integrated summary—with a bit of explanation—is a practical way of satisfying many of the planning process requirements and giving the treatment team the tools and directions needed to plan for the individual's recovery journey.

III. MAKING IT HAPPEN

A written integrated summary must be part of every assessment and should be updated and modified as necessary during regular and periodic reassessments. At minimum this should be done once a year, or more often as circumstances warrant. It may be documented in the individual plan itself, be attached to the assessment documents, or be included in the general notes section of the record. It does not need to be lengthy, but it must be complete.

There is no substitute for experience in learning to prepare an integrated summary. A relatively small number of essential criteria to use in creating and evaluating the quality of an integrated summary can be articulated and be useful in routine practice. A checklist to use in reviewing and evaluating an integrated summary will be discussed in the following text. This is designed to give providers, peer reviewers and supervisors a tool by which to evaluate an integrated summary and identify areas for improvement. Not every box will or should for that matter be checked off—there are many times when a particular issue is not relevant or appropriate.

There is no such thing as a perfect integrated summary—inevitably even a document that meets all the criteria stated could have room for improvement. But an adequate integrated summary can be described and modeled. This is especially important for clinical supervisors who *de facto* provide substantial on-the-job training to staff in their routine work. The very fact that the summary is integrated and not a matter of checkbox forms and simple data fields can create significant anxiety and discomfort with some providers. Hopefully the models in the *Creating the Solution* section above, along with the following examples, can make a difference. They are intended to give providers the tools and confidence they need to be more person-centered and effective in their work with individuals and families.

Sometimes an outline can be helpful in crafting the integrated summary. Many providers have found the following prompts to be especially helpful. The summary should address the following:

Identity
consider age, culture, spirituality/religious affiliation, sexual orientation, etc. Focus on how cultural identifications/preferences may impact recovery and/or treatment preferences
Explanation of illness/presenting issues
why is the person here, why now?

Psychosocial environment
consider housing, employment, support system, acute/chronic stressors, and so on
Strengths, preferences and priorities
personal talents/interests/coping skills as well as natural supports and community connections
Stage of change/stage of recovery
Summary of priority needs/barriers to goal attainment
with a focus on how symptoms are interfering with functioning in community settings
Hypothesis
central themes, insights, understandings, *not* a repetition of the data

Figure 3.4 is a useful checklist tool that providers and supervisors can use to review and evaluate integrated summaries. Providers unfamiliar with the task of writing integrated summaries may need to simply dive in, while seasoned practitioners may find some of the tools and prompts included helpful in refining and improving their skills. Providers are encouraged to self-evaluate their integrated summaries against the checklist. While the principal source of feedback should be the individuals and families seeking help, supervisors and staff peers can also offer valuable input. Providers should not be afraid to share their work (with appropriate protections of privacy and confidentiality) with colleagues for review and comment. Although it is not commonly done, it is a very useful, if not powerful, strategy for changing and improving practice. Merely reading texts such as this is not likely to change practice; taking risks and being open to constructive criticism, as well as praise, can greatly help to develop new clinical skills and habits.

Examples

Four examples of integrated summaries based on the learning examples previously introduced are provided, with an important caveat: They are not necessarily clinically perfect! Rather they are intended as samples of at least one *reasonable* interpretation of how data can be integrated to support individual planning. Readers may well come to different conclusions from their review of the assessment data. Each case is illustrative and instructive in its own way; accordingly, important aspects of the integrated summary are highlighted in conjunction with each example.

Far more important than the specific formulations, however, are the organization and thought processes reflected in these examples. No doubt there are many different possible interpretations of the data presented in the sample

NARRATIVE SUMMARY CHECKLIST

☐ Moves from what (data) to why (understanding) with
    ☐ clear formulation or explanation of meaning
    ☐ description of a central theme for the individual and family
    ☐ identification of stressors/precipitants
☐ Integrates and summarizes the data collected to include
    ☐ results from standardized tests
    ☐ previous treatment experiences
    ☐ discharge summaries
    ☐ school evaluations and reports
    ☐ face-to-face psychosocial interviews
    ☐ psychiatric and psychological
    ☐ mental status evaluations
    ☐ at least a tentative or initial diagnosis
☐ Summarizes the perceptions of the individual
    ☐ describes choices and prioritization
    ☐ explains what's most important and what comes first
      consistent with the individual's and family's
      concerns/perspective
☐ Identifies
    ☐ the individual's strengths
    ☐ personal/family values
    ☐ cultural nuances
    ☐ abilities and past accomplishments
    ☐ interests and aspirations
    ☐ resources and assets
    ☐ unique individual attributes
☐ Provides
    ☐ the foundation for developing treatment plan goals and
      objectives by setting the stage for prioritizing needs and
      goals
    ☐ behavioral descriptions of the needs and problems
☐ Identifies the barriers to achieving desired goals
☐ Reflects a balance between the understanding of the individual and the
provider
☐ Identifies co-occurring disabilities/disorders
☐ Recommends a course of treatment and determines the levels of care
    ☐ specifies the stage/phase of recovery
    ☐ anticipates transition/discharge (length of services)
    ☐ recommends referrals, tests, special assessments, as indicated
    ☐ documents the recommended intensity of services

Figure 3.4

biopsychosocial assessments. Without knowing the individual or having their direct input into the process, the preparation of an integrated summary example requires a bit of conjecture. Examples removed from the real world of practice are inherently limited. However, for learning purposes they can serve to illustrate how a meaningful transition from data to understanding can be accomplished without a mere repetition of the assessment. The real test of their adequacy will be clearer as the subsequent elements of an individual plan for each of these four examples, built upon these summaries, are introduced and the process is examined in the chapters to follow.

Diana

The integrated summary for Diana gives us a rich sense of the complexity of her needs as well as her strengths and does so in the context of her culture and her age-appropriate development along with her efforts at establishing her own identity and her affiliations to her family and her cultural background. The integrated summary also makes clear that as much as we know about Diana there remains some things about her situation that need further clarification. The summary does a nice job of helping us to understand Diana in the context of her family and begins to suggest that engaging the family will become important in helping her to achieve her goals.

JR

The integrated summary for JR incorporates some additional information and insights that we did not gain from the initial assessment. The detail of the summary feels as if some time has passed between the creation of this document and the initial assessment. Presumably the provider was able to get additional information from JR as well as some collateral information from his family to help them better understand JR, his strengths and his needs, as well as his problems. The summary describes JR as someone who remains uncertain and hesitant about seeking help and perhaps that others see JR's circumstances as more problematic than JR himself. At the same time, the integrated summary demonstrates an openness, honesty and thoughtfulness that hopefully create an opportunity to engage in further dialogue with JR about his use of alcohol and other drugs and its impact on his life.

Keisha

The integrated summary for Keisha flows from the assessment data. It is far more than a recitation of the facts; rather, it gathers the salient details and important nuances that help explain Keisha and her current needs. It starts by highlighting what is important, significant and different at this time in contrast to past experiences in seeking help—the fact that Keisha has come voluntarily as compared to fulfilling an external mandate is extremely important. The integrated summary focuses on strengths and past accomplishments with a balanced acknowledgment of her past problems and failures. This integrated summary helps to provide guidance and justification for the medical necessity of services and the appropriate level of care. The use of a stage-wise model helps to clarify the impact and significance of the current contemplative phase—especially as compared to her historical pre-contemplation and difficulty in sustaining active treatment.

Roberto

Roberto's integrated summary provides an example of the multidisciplinary team at the hospital coming together to share their current understanding of Roberto; it might well have been written by the psychologist or the treatment team coordinator for that particular unit. The summary is fairly brief and to the point, and it effectively integrates the information from the many assessments conducted by the various disciplines at the hospital: nursing, psychiatry, psychology, social work, education/rehabilitation. It nicely serves the function of being a conceptual and written transition between the assessment and the creation of the plan. By synthesizing all the assessment data, the summary really begins to map out the journey for Roberto and his family—particularly in its clarification of the inpatient treatment goal and its anticipation of treatments issues and modalities.

Perhaps most importantly, the summary provides a formulation and a hypothesis for understanding the issues and precipitants that lie behind Roberto's apparent depression, trauma and anxiety. As objectives are identified, this will be critically important in framing the plan and selecting appropriate interventions. The linkage of his symptoms and diagnosis to cultural factors, and the speculation about the role of culture in his experience of the illness, are also key to successful engagement, treatment and outcomes.

REFERENCES

1. CARF. *Behavioral Health Standards Manual.* 2012.
2. Maslow A. *Motivation and Personality.* 2nd ed. Harper & Row; 1970.
3. http://www.intentionalcare.org.
4. http://www.adultmeducation.com/AssessmentTools_3.html.
5. Mezzich J, Salloum I. Towards innovative international classification and diagnostic systems: ICD-11 and person-centered integrative diagnosis. *Acta Psych Scand.* 2007;116:1-5.
6. Jongsma AE. *The Complete Depression Treatment and Homework Planner.* New Jersey: Wiley Publishing; 2004.
7. Changing the Face of Mental Illness in Virginia. The Alliance for Increased Mental Health Awareness, p. 5.
8. Institute of Medicine (US) Committee on Crossing the Quality Chasm. *Adaptation to Mental Health and Addictive Disorders. Improving the Quality of Health Care for Mental and Substance-Use Conditions.* Washington (DC): National Academies Press; 2006.
9. Sterling S, Chi F, Hinman A. Integrating care for people with co-occurring alcohol and other drug, medical, and mental health conditions. *Alcohol Res Health.* 2011;33(4):338-349.
10. Collins C, Hewson D, Munger R, Wade T. Evolving Models of Behavioral Health Integration in Primary Care. Milbank Memorial Fund; 2010.
11. Olmstead v. LC, E.W. Supreme Court decision; 1999.

On the Road

The three chapters of this section cover the core elements of any plan: goals, objectives and interventions. We are about to begin our journey, the final destination is clearly specified, and at least some of the early signposts are identified. What we need to get there, the obstacles we may need to overcome and the tools and resources to assure our safe, successful passage are all part of being on the road.

The road movie is a favorite Hollywood genre, often filled with wonderful scenery and bits of humor, and sometimes fraught with peril as the characters run or drive in pursuit of some dream. It focuses on the human spirit being quickened by the thrill of motion and change—new vistas, new challenges and new opportunities. Ask people about hobbies, interests and pastimes, and they often pick travel first. The opportunity to make a change and experience something different and new seems to be part of human nature.

Some trips can be aimless—the journey is the destination itself. However, the road to recovery seems to benefit from a bit of forethought and planning. The goals, objectives and interventions are the implements of a complete expedition.

Setting Goals

If you Don't Know Where You are Going, You Will Probably End up Someplace Else.

Lawrence J. Peter

Goals are Dreams with Deadlines.

Diana Hunt

I. STATING THE CASE

In setting the goal for the individual plan, the real creation of a map begins. The goal should reflect the individual's and family's clearest articulation of the destination—the optimal outcome from seeking help and receiving services. Goals reflect the individual's and family's strengths and resources. Their motivation for a better future and their ability to articulate a vision of health and wellness is an important first step towards health and wellness.

A properly conceived and written planning goal should be a broad general statement that builds on and reflects strengths as well as expresses the individual's and family's desires for change and improvement in their lives, ideally captured in their own words. A goal should be long term and reflect a personal vision of health, well-being and accomplishment. It is a simple statement of the individual's and family's anticipated changes and benefits that will result from receiving services—it is typically linked to their motivation in seeking help and reflects the resolution of their problems and needs. Some describe it as the "reason to get up and get going in the morning." The goal statement should encompass the individual's and family's hopes and dreams, not only for resolution of their immediate problems and needs, but also to possibly address another major life area that needs attention.

Goals are not necessarily measurable. At the same time, however, their achievement or realization should be something easily recognized and readily apparent to all. Goal statements may be reflective of the individual's and provider's "meeting of the minds" about what can be reasonably achieved within the context of the helping relationship and service setting.

109

The goal statement often reflects the implicit or explicit point of engagement with the individual and family and becomes the focus of further collaboration with the care provider. If the plan is thought of as a contract between the individual and the provider, the goal is the ultimate or overall "deliverable" specified in the contract.

For the most part, goals are not necessarily time framed, but may be if including a target date is meaningful and relevant by anchoring its attainment to some defined point in the future. This is often influenced by a number of factors ranging from the service setting (e.g., inpatient or residential as compared to outpatient), the acuity of the individual's and family's needs, externally imposed time factors, deadlines or requirements, and the specificity of the goal itself. When there are multiple goals, clarifying priorities and sequencing by setting timeframes can help to provide clarity and organization to the development of the plan.

Types of Goals

Two different levels of goals might be identified, depending on the service setting: life goals and service or treatment goals; however, not every plan has to specify both types. Often these two goals are closely related, if not one in the same, depending in part on the circumstances and service setting. Goals described as *life goals* may include aspects of the individual's life where they have hopes for overall improvement and may include aspirations such as "I want to be married" or "I want a job." Such goals may or may not appear to have an immediate relationship to service needs and are less likely to be time framed. Yet the difference in the power and momentum of the plan that occurs when "I want a job" becomes "I want to be working full-time within nine months" cannot be ignored. Regardless, the recognition and acknowledgment of the individual in identifying and setting life goals can be a critical part of building and maintaining an effective collaboration.

Service or treatment goals address the resolution of the needs and concerns that are a barrier to discharge or transition from services. These goals are often closely linked to the issues and needs that prompted the individual and family to seek help and are responsive to the immediate circumstances. Because of the frequent linkage or interplay of general health concerns with mental health and substance abuse challenges, goals may reflect a vision of a life framed by overall wellness and health.

Treatment goals may be setting specific or address concerns for a particular episode of care or a particular level of service. In an inpatient or residential care setting, these goals are typically the positive reframing of the discharge criteria and the removal of the barriers for a transition to a lower level of care. These goals are often quite succinct and may be more specific or measurable. For example, an individual may have a life goal of a career as a teacher, but is currently living in a clean and sober housing program. The life goal might be: "I want to become a teacher" while the treatment goal in the current setting is "I want to return to living with my family."

In some settings or circumstances, as in the previous example, treatment goals may be a subset of larger and broader life goals. The more non-specific and larger the life goals, the greater the likelihood that there will be important, more specific or immediate service goals to identify and achieve. Admittedly, this can be confusing and blur the distinction between objectives (short-term intermediate steps) and goals. At some level, the distinction between the two is qualitative and subjective and needs to be considered in the context of a specific individual plan. One could argue that returning home from a clean and sober housing program could be viewed as a short-term goal or objective—an intermediate step on the road to getting one's life back on track and pursuing the dream of becoming a teacher.

This is part of the *art* of individual planning—knowing how to organize a strategy that is most effective in helping the individual and family. Typically there are barriers or challenges that need to be resolved in order to achieve a goal; in a plan this is addressed through a series of very specific objectives that resolve those obstacles to success. This is reviewed in greater detail in Chapter 5. In contrast to the goal(s), an objective is one of several efforts to focus on a measurable and targeted change in behavior or capacity within a specified timeframe that helps the individual and family to move forward. In a well-crafted plan, there may even be just one goal but multiple objectives. Goals are tied to discharge and transition; objectives are tied to the attainment of goals.

The complexity of people's needs and challenges will often be reflected in the complexity of the plan and the number of goals that are identified. There are times when life goals and treatment goals may be one and the same. This is most likely to occur when needs are time limited and acute, and the individual is not working to overcome a disability or other significant and long-standing challenge. In more long-term rehabilitation, a significant and meaningful life goal may provide an organizing principle for a series of more short-term, focused and sequential goals leading to fulfillment of the individual's dreams. There is no absolutely right or wrong way nor a set formula or proscription for how best to organize these elements of the plan. Plans vary from individual to individual and provider to provider and this tailoring of a plan is at the heart of being person-centered.

Respecting Goals

There is perhaps no greater expression of respect, understanding, hope and empathy by the provider than the ability to elicit, acknowledge and accept the individual's and family's goals. In many respects, this is where individuals may feel most vulnerable—sharing their hopes, their fantasies, their desires. Goals are often a reflection of a sense of one's "best self" and a life lived in health and well-being. Individuals and families often seek help because they feel overwhelmed, frightened and defeated by their needs and challenges. Rekindling a connection with their dreams and aspirations can be an essential first step in engaging the individual and family, establishing a helping partnership and creating a successful and effective plan. The standard should not be whether or not the goals are realistic. Rather, the criteria for success in this crucial planning step is whether or not the goals help to build the sense of trust, safety and collaboration necessary for successful alliance and achievement in pursuit of wellness and recovery.

There are times when individuals and families will bring forward goals that, in the moment at least, seem utterly unattainable. The provider must resist any impulse, albeit it well intended, to challenge, dismiss or diminish them as unrealistic. This is not a time for "reality testing"—if necessary, that can come later. Inevitably, there is tremendous meaning and significance in the goals that are identified. The provider's task is to accept and understand. There was poetic insight in the lyrics of Crosby, Stills, Nash and Young when they sang in their well-known and prophetic song *Teach Your Children*:

> You, who are on the road
>
> Must have a code that you can live by
>
> And so become yourself
>
> Because the past is just a goodbye.
>
> Teach your children well,
>
> Their father's hell did slowly go by,
>
> And feed them on your dreams
>
> The ones they pick, the one you'll know by.

Don't you ever ask them why, if they told you, you will cry,

So just look at them and sigh and know they love you.

And you, of tender years,

Can't know the fears that your elders grew by,

And so please help them with your youth,

They seek the truth before they can die.

Teach your parents well,

Their children's hell will slowly go by,

And feed them on your dreams

The ones they pick, the one you'll know by.

Don't you ever ask them why, if they told you, you will cry,

So just look at them and sigh and know they love you.

This acceptance can prove to be empowering for both the individual and the provider. It is the essence of being person-centered.

Clarification of treatment goals can follow from the individual's and family's identification of life goals. The provider's question then becomes: How can I be of help? What is in the way, what is keeping you from those dreams? What can I do to assist you in your journey? Plans can and should recognize life goals while at the same time creating a focus on more immediate service goals.

Common Problems

There are common problems encountered by providers in attempting to identify and incorporate goals into the individual plan. These pitfalls include selecting goals that are not sufficiently:

- directed towards recovery
- responsive to need
- strengths based
- broad or global

In addition, it is not unusual to see plans with too many goals. It is often if not almost always appropriate to have only one goal that captures the essence of the individual's and family's vision of their recovery and pursuit of wellness and health. Having too many goals or goals that are too specific can seriously undermine the rest of the planning process. Getting this right is perhaps the most frequently identified problem or hurdle to effective planning.

A goal is broad and captures the big picture, while an objective is focused, specific and incremental. A goal stated in the individual's own words might be "I want a job." While health providers cannot assure employment, they can help the individual be physically as well as emotionally able and ready to secure and maintain work. However, a goal written as "I will be able to complete employment applications" is probably best treated as an objective. Obtaining a job may well be the end point of an episode of treatment, but the inability to complete a job application is likely a barrier to successful job seeking and ultimate employment.

If getting the job is the goal, then helping the individual and family to overcome the barriers that result from a medical or behavioral health problem should be considered the objective. This is not a trivial distinction and can lead to the creation of plans with limited utility if not addressed correctly. If "successful job application" becomes the goal, then writing an objective for this goal can quickly become a tedious exercise and the plan soon becomes a tangled web of unnecessary details that confounds rather than facilitates the individual's recovery. If there are too many goals, managing the plan (for both the individual and the provider) becomes overwhelming and renders it a fairly useless process. Providers are encouraged to carefully evaluate any plan that contains more than one goal and to question whether or not the plan is enhanced and strengthened by having multiple concurrent goals.

The other most common problem in goal setting is the inclusion of goals that reflect provider concerns and needs rather than those of the individual and family. Sometimes this is driven by the provider's own sense of values and what is correct, most urgent or most important. Other times this reflects a lack of meaningful engagement and involvement by the individual and family in the problem-solving and identification processes; it can be an early sign of trouble in the individual/provider partnership. The standard of good practice is that goals are expressed and documented in the individual's own words.

Goals developed by a provider should not be subsequently "translated" into the individual's words in an attempt to give them authenticity. Rather, as much as possible, goal statements should capture in a short phrase or sentence what individuals and families seeking services see as their needs and expected outcomes from the plan. It is perfectly acceptable for the provider to suggest language or ideas to facilitate the process. If an individual or family is unable to articulate goals, then the first task in the service process is to provide them the comfort, safety, tools and supports necessary for them to be able to identify a goal. After all, it is their journey, their destination—the provider merely serves as guide, facilitator and mapmaker along the way.

There are service-delivery systems that continue to have requirements—oftentimes tied to provider reimbursement for services—for specific or multiple goals; sometimes these are linked to each domain of a structured assessment tool or protocol. This is often seen in addictions treatment where the expectation is that every individual and plan will specify sobriety as the goal. All too often, however, what the individual wants is a satisfying life, health and wellbeing and their substance dependence thwarts their ability to achieve and sustain success. In this instance, it may be best to regard the need for sobriety as an objective and a barrier to a better life. Somewhat ironically, there is perhaps no better relapse prevention strategy than a life of accomplishment, meaning and purpose.

Specific requirements for goal setting run the risk of creating detours on the road to successful planning; they are not built on the understanding of the individual captured in the integrated summary and create unnecessary complexity that confounds the service process and potentially dilutes the effectiveness of the plan. Yet, in many settings and circumstances, these expectations and regulations cannot be ignored. If multiple goals are required, one practical solution is to identify some goals as active or inactive, or as primary and secondary, allowing the team to focus on a few of the more immediate and critical needs. Another strategy is to link sobriety to meaningful life changes so that the goal becomes, for example, "I want to (get clean and sober so that I can) be a better parent."

Developing Goals

Goals are developed from the information gained in the assessment and the understanding derived from the integrated summary. The assessment process helps to identify the unique attributes of each individual and family—including needs and problems, strengths, resources, barriers and priorities in reaching the goals. In a person-centered approach, the provider's responsibilities are (1) to help the individual and family identify and express those issues and needs, and (2) to help to frame the resolution of those needs as goals to be included in the individual plan. Providers must guard against the temptation to step in and assert their experience, wisdom and/or values in stating goals that reflect the provider's concerns or priorities rather than those of the individual and family. The provider's obligation is to create an emotionally safe environment, respect the individual's and family's choices and preferences, as well as assist them in articulating and achieving those goals. Sensitivity to a history of trauma and the ways in which it can impact the process are critically important and is why trauma-informed care is so important. Without sensitivity to these concerns, a replication of trauma dynamics can occur in the process of goal setting. The values of trauma-informed care include: trustworthiness, choice, collaboration and empowerment. Effective goal setting involves maximizing the individual's and family's control and enhancing the person's skills in the context of being a recovery-oriented, gender-responsive and culturally competent process.

The link between goals and anticipating transition or discharge from services is an often neglected but essential part of the overall planning process. Goals should reflect the resolution of the problems or needs that initially led the individual and family to seek services. The treatment goals specified in the plan can be used as a yardstick to measure readiness for discharge or transition from services. If the individual achieves the goals, and there are no other goals that emerge, it is probably time for transition or new goals need to be identified.

However, clarity about discharge or transition criteria is often missing from mental health and addictive disorders service plans. In many instances it seems not even to be a consideration; often the implication is that the relationship with the provider is forever and there is no exit for the individual and family. This can lead to fostering a codependency and a process with no end that lacks any accountability. Especially in managed care environments, the ability to identify specific end points, and with that accountability to the payer as well as the individual and family, is increasingly a requirement. It is no accident that health care reform is known as the ACA—the Accountable Care Act. An important function of the individual plan is the identification of goals and the articulation of discharge or transition criteria that begin to create mutual accountability and describe success in the attainment of desired outcomes.

The true power of the goal statement is often captured in its simplicity. It is not necessary for goal statements themselves to reflect a sophisticated or highly developed understanding of the problem and needs—this typically occurs in the task of identifying barriers, developing objectives and specifying interventions. Oftentimes the most effective statements of goals reflect the everyday basic concerns, wants and needs of individuals and families. For adults, they might include such things as:

- managing one's own life and being free of external control
- wanting a better quality of life with greater comfort or ease

- improved housing
- improved access to transportation and mobility
- the ability to work
- pursuing an education
- access to specific activity or accomplishments
- social opportunities and more satisfying relationships
- sexual satisfaction
- spiritual fulfillment
- better health and well-being
- wanting to feel better and be happy
- the ability to have fun and enjoy things

For children and adolescents, goal statements may be something like:

- having friends
- getting a driver's license
- graduating school
- playing on a sports team
- doing better in school
- getting off probation/drug court

In a hospital setting, treatment goals might revolve around

- reducing the impact or burden of symptoms
- reducing the risk of harm
- returning to a previous home/placement
- improved capacity for self-care of high risk behaviors

While these are goals that may well be facilitated by general health, mental health and addictive disorders services, they are not treatment or disorder specific. Recovery and rehabilitation are concerned with helping people lead their lives to the fullest potential. These concerns and needs are at once mundane and profound. However, it is important not to lose sight of the need to understand and link these challenges to the barriers created by the medical, mental health and addictive disorders that have led the individual and family to seek help.

Culture can also play a role in identifying goals and can affect both real and perceived priorities. The interplay of personal experience, culture, society and the service delivery system is complex. Awareness of and sensitivity to this interaction is critical. Stigma and culture are often linked in intricate ways and may also play a role and shape help-seeking behaviors and expectations. The potential for an individual or family to self-limit their hopes for a better life, in the face of the challenges resulting from mental illness and addictive disorders, is real. Providing education about the potential for recovery, resilience and wellness is part of supporting the process of goal identification and definition. The provider's task is to help people to see beyond what was to what can be by removing the blinders of fear, ignorance and misunderstanding.

Culturally sensitive and informed mental health recovery peers can oftentimes succeed in this effort when providers cannot. Because of the power of their lived experience and natural capacity for empathy, peers are increasingly seen as essential members of the treatment team. The role of a peer specialist can be integral to a treatment team. A key differentiating factor in the peer's role from other members of the team is that in addition to traditional knowledge and competencies in providing support, the peer specialist draws upon their lived experience and experiential knowledge[1]. Peer specialists are uniquely qualified to assist individuals in identifying goals and objectives that form the context of the peer support relationship[2]. Some commercial managed care plans now actively promote the role of peers and pay for peer-based services[3].

For example, individuals and their family members may have a limited vision about an individual's employment potential because of a mental health or substance abuse problem. They are resigned to a life of disability and unemployment based on old beliefs about benefits, treatment options, prognosis, and so on, or they are unaware of the established success of supported employment programs and peer supports for individuals with even the most severe challenges. Providers need to inform the individual of options, and share their professional judgment about what they believe would be most effective. Providers, including peers, need to help the family and individual move beyond disability labels (e.g., "can't work," "low productivity," "won't stay on task"), and instead build on their hopeful vision for a different future.

Priorities

Priorities are an important consideration both for establishing goals as well as for setting objectives, but they differ in significance for each individual and each phase of the service process. Priority in goal setting is really driven by the wishes and desires of the individual and family—with appropriate help from the provider, as needed, in clarifying those preferences and priorities. If multiple goals are identified, it is important that their priority, order or sequence be considered and specified.

Addressing the issue of priorities is perhaps one of the more difficult and potentially conflictual aspects of the planning process. There are times when the priorities of the individual and family are very different than those of the provider. Sometimes this is simply a matter of values and perspectives. At other times providers must give priority to protecting and preserving the basic health and safety of the individual, family or community. Abraham Maslow elaborated a hierarchy of needs that helps to shed some light on the perspective of many providers[4]. Maslow identified five levels of human need as follows:

Physiological needs: These biological needs are the strongest needs because if a person were deprived of all needs, the physiological ones would come first in the person's search for satisfaction.

Safety needs: When all physiological needs are satisfied and are no longer controlling thoughts and behaviors, the needs for security can become active. Adults have little awareness of their security needs except in times of emergency, while children often display the signs of insecurity and the need to be safe.

Needs of love, affection and belongingness: When the needs for safety and for physiological well-being are satisfied, the next class of needs for love, affection and belongingness can emerge as people seek to overcome feelings of loneliness and alienation. This involves both giving and receiving love, affection and the sense of belonging.

Needs for esteem: When the first three classes of needs are satisfied, the needs for esteem can become dominant. These include needs both for self-esteem and for the esteem a person gets from others. Humans have a need for a stable, firmly based, high level of self-respect and respect from others. When these needs are satisfied, the person feels self-confident and valuable as a person in the world. When these needs are neglected, the person feels inferior, weak, helpless and worthless.

Needs for self-actualization: When all of the foregoing needs are satisfied, then and only then are the needs for self-actualization activated. Maslow describes self-actualization as a person's need to be and do that which the person was born to do: "A musician must make music, an artist must paint, and a poet must write." These needs express themselves in feelings of restlessness; without some outlet, the person feels on edge, tense and has a sense of lacking something. If a person is hungry, unsafe, not loved or accepted, or lacking self-esteem, it is very easy to know what the person is restless about. It is not always clear what a person wants when there is a need for self-actualization.

Provider Perspectives

When the individual or family has significant physiological and/or safety needs, providers may have both moral as well as legal mandates and obligations that guide or direct their sense of priorities. In some instances, the provider may have requirements to file reports with various welfare or law enforcement agencies, warn potential victims of the risk of harm or violence or seek the involuntary confinement and treatment of the individual. When the provider sees the individual and family as being at risk in a manner not recognized or acknowledged by them, an impasse that threatens trust and the recovery alliance can occur.

This circumstance of irresolvable differences seems to occur most frequently when there are differences between the provider, individuals and families in the recognition of the impact of substance use and dependence on their needs. The challenge for the provider in such instances is to find a way to remain true to their professional, moral and legal obligations and at the same time prevent a rupture or breach in the relationship. This often requires the most artful negotiation and ability to compromise, and some willingness to take risks. There is much in the literature to suggest that these are risks well worth taking[5].

For example, numerous past efforts to help people who are mentally ill and homeless, whose problems are complicated by substance use, have not succeeded because they have made shelter and housing a reward conditioned on good behavior, drug and alcohol abstinence, and compliance with medications. This is an instance of providers placing their own priorities above and beyond those of individuals—the antithesis of being person-centered. A substantial number of initiatives and programs in a range of settings/environments have demonstrated success with a different model[6]. The alternative approach is to offer and provide food, clothing, and shelter without the expectation of sobriety or treatment acceptance. This has not only helped to remove individuals from living on the streets, but it has often been a first step in building a trusting empathic relationship that respects an individual's dignity and over time has fostered the individual's ability to feel safe and consider their medical, psychiatric and addictive disorders treatment needs. This is an excellent example of how critical the issue of priorities can be, and how success can be achieved when the individual's and family's priorities are allowed to be expressed, acknowledged and included in a truly person-centered planning process.

Children and Adolescents

The process of identifying and agreeing upon goals raises some issues unique for working with children and adolescents and their families as compared to adults. Sometimes, the goals that are identified are more those of the family member(s) than the child or adolescent. Too often, the child's or adolescent's voice gets lost in the crowd of other interested parties: parents, teachers, social service personnel, guidance counselors, probation officers, and so on. If the goals of the plan do not reflect the child's or adolescent's views, input and desires in a significant way, the plan is not likely to succeed. Children and youth are people too and in a person-centered approach, their perspectives must be heard and addressed and not dismissed.

Children and adolescents deserve care that is both family- and person-centered. Providers working with youth need to spend the time necessary to build a trusting relationship that allows children and adolescents to engage and express their own perspectives about the issues and concerns that have brought them to the service setting. For the child too young or otherwise unable to understand, it is often appropriate for the provider to play a more active role. Suggesting that the provider is there to help the child or adolescent improve their relationship with their parents, succeed at school, stay out of trouble with the law or help them overcome a painful loss or trauma is quite appropriate. Offering and suggesting goals that the child can agree upon, acknowledge and accept often helps to assure success in planning and services.

It is not entirely unusual to find that parents and children—especially adolescents—have very different understanding of the problems that have brought them to seek help and the goals/resolution. In these instances, the provider must recognize and affirm the authority and responsibility of parents and at the same time acknowledge the youth's desire for autonomy and self-direction. In these circumstances it is not unusual for an adolescent to identify emancipation as a goal which the provider and parents may find difficult to accept or endorse. It would be unrealistic to say that resolving these differences and conflicts are easy, and in some instances efforts at goal setting *de facto* become family therapy sessions. Finding a shared and common goal between the child and the parent may be as difficult as achieving lasting peace between Israelis and Palestinians, but finding sufficient resolution to support establishing goals is still an essential step towards progress. In some instances, acknowledging and including both the parents' as well as the child's goal on a recovery and wellness plan is an effective resolution that helps to promote the engagement of the entire family.

Even if the youth is a reluctant participant in the planning process and service program, as may be the case when schools, welfare agencies, and so on refer children and adolescents, the provider can use the principles of motivational interviewing to help build the youth's commitment to change.

During the initial assessment phase, the child may not be able or willing to accept responsibility for the behaviors leading to the referral and will tend to blame others. Sometimes the provider's task is to help the child begin to simply acknowledge the consequences of their behavior without assigning responsibility. Even the smallest agreement can help to establish a goal and become the start of meaningful engagement and the beginning of a positive change process.

II. CREATING THE SOLUTION

The solution to establishing person-centered goals, the heart or focal point of the individual plan, lies in the provider's ability to put aside his or her own needs and desires to be helpful and resist the impulse to be paternalistic or even judgmental[7]. The task instead is to listen and understand the individual and family and to help them reveal their hopes and dreams. The successful plan is built upon the creation of a shared vision between the individual, family and provider.

Reaching agreement on the goal is extremely critical—the entire process could be at risk without that alignment. If the provider is unable to understand, appreciate and capture the goals of individual and family, then the plan is inherently limited in its utility or value. The individual and family are essential members of the team, and a team cannot succeed without a shared goal and common purpose—it is the essence of the power and success of a team. Every team member must ultimately embrace that goal or difficulty—if not, failure will inevitably ensue. In the words of John O'Brien, an innovator in person-centered planning for individuals with developmental disabilities, "To put it simply, I do not see person-centered planning as the cause of change. I see it as a way to improve the odds that purposeful change will happen"[8].

The provider's job is to help the family feel comfortable, safe and sure enough about the process that they are able to share their goals. Sensitivity to issues of past trauma, culture and failed efforts at help-seeking can often be critical factors in success. The goals that are established in the plan must have immediate meaning and relevance for the individual and family. They must speak to their strengths along with their concerns and motivation in seeking help. This may be contrary to what the provider thinks is the appropriate goal for the individual, but agreement in setting the goal is where the provider must be the most accepting and accommodating.

In addition, the provider must be aware of the distinction between life goals and treatment goals. It is perfectly acceptable to ask the individual and family about what they see as their goal in each category. Helping to clarify what goals the individual and family are hoping will be addressed facilitates the process of agreeing upon goals to be recorded in the plan document. It can be useful to have a place on the forms or in the electronic record system to document both types of goals.

Some organizations have used the tool of having a "goal sheet" wherein the individual is asked to write his or her hopes, dreams or goals in their own words (if they are capable of doing so). This worksheet is then utilized during the planning meeting as a mechanism to further define and prioritize. A worksheet with topical headings such as "What I want to do," "Where I want to work," "Friends I'd like to make," "These are my hobbies/favorite activities," and so on, may provide be useful prompts for some people in helping them identify their goals. Also, the evidence-based practice of Illness Management and Recovery (IMR) for individuals receiving services includes a strong focus on goal setting[9].

The Power of Peers

As mentioned earlier throughout this text, peer specialists can be critical to helping individuals identify their goals. One effective approach we have observed at Austin State Hospital in Texas and other facilities is for a peer to meet with the person prior to a formal "planning meeting" with the team and conducting a "recovery inventory"[10]. Another strategy is for peers specialists to facilitate ongoing groups that are focused on goal setting in order to help individuals think about and formulate goals prior to meeting with the treatment and developing or reviewing a plan. At Bluebonnet Trails Community Services, also in Texas, the peer specialist-led group *Destination Recovery* is a billable service under the state's rehab option plan, and focuses on helping individuals receiving services develop skills that help them to better participate in the goal setting and planning process[11]. This goal setting group is based on the toolkit developed by Janis Tondora and her colleagues at Yale, *Getting in the Driver's Seat of Your Treatment: Preparing for Your Plan*[12]. This toolkit is rich in resources for people receiving services, and includes ideas on how to prepare for the planning meeting, selecting supporters, as well as questions to reflect on regarding goal setting.

Goal discovery in WRAP (Wellness Recovery Action Planning) is important to planning and can reduce the amount of time taken to develop the goals to be worked on in the plan[13]. Certified WRAP specialists who are typically persons with lived experience lead wellness planning groups and individual sessions. Although a WRAP plan is owned solely by the individual, versus the treatment/recovery plan which is shared with the provider team, the WRAP can be an essential step in preparing the individual to be thinking about personal goals, wellness strategies, etc.

Discharge and Transition Planning

It is commonly said that discharge or transition planning begins at admission, but common experience is that this adage is often forgotten or overlooked in mental health and addictive disorders service-delivery systems. However, given the link between goal setting and discharge/transition planning, it is a step in the process that cannot be skipped. Discharge or transition criteria should be clearly stated in the plan and shared with the individual and family.

Setting discharge and transition criteria can be a straightforward task. The provider simply asks the individual and family to describe what would need to change so that they could manage on their own and not be in need of mental health and addictive disorders services. The answer to this question often holds both the criteria for discharge or transition as well as the basic elements of a treatment goal. Life goals and quality of life enhancements may extend beyond the treatment goal. However, in creating the plan, the expectations of the individual and family and the role of the provider in attaining those goals should be made clear.

Asking this question will inevitably make some providers uncomfortable; it often challenges their deeply held beliefs about mental illness and addictive disorders, the provider's authority and each individual's potential for recovery and wellness. Sadly, some persons seeking services experience significant stigma and discrimination from providers and this can be very hurtful if not (re)traumatizing[14]. Providers must embrace recovery and join with individuals and families to envision a time when they might not be in need of or dependent on services in the same way. Embedded within this process is the essence of hope.

Reconnecting with the Past

Another practical approach to helping individuals and families identify goals is to help them reconnect with their past. There are times when people are so overwhelmed or even defeated by their problems, challenges and needs that it is impossible for them to imagine how things might be different. In such an instance, asking the individual and family to recall an earlier and easier time, before their difficulties began, can be helpful. Using suggestion, guided imagery, empathy, support and other techniques, it is often possible for people to reconnect with an earlier sense of hopefulness and purpose in their life. When they were in high school, for example, what were their goals and how did they see their life unfolding? What happened that prevented attaining the goal? What would it take to resume, even with some modification, that original dream?

Within the answers to these questions may well lie the goals of the person-centered plan. Revisiting this history can in some instances be painful, but it can also communicate a message of hope. Joining with the individual and family in acknowledging what was special, exciting, compelling and satisfying about their earlier vision can be empowering and has the potential to carry with it a message of caring, hope and possibility. In this way, creating a recovery and wellness plan is not just the completion of a form and satisfaction of a burdensome administrative requirement for the provider. Rather, it can be a powerful healing intervention that assures a person-centered approach to planning and providing services and sets the stage for successful outcomes.

The Challenge of Addictions

Prioritizing and agreeing upon goals is when working with individuals and families whose needs and concerns are complicated by ongoing substance abuse or dependence can be especially challenging for any number of reasons. Often the most pressing issue or question is whether or not abstinence and sobriety should be the goal. While sobriety might be desirable, simply the presence of a substance dependence should not dictate that his must be the goal of the plan—whether an addiction is the only issue or it is complicated by a co-occurring general medical or mental health concern.

There are some circumstances wherein sobriety becomes an externally imposed condition of treatment instead of an outcome. In other words, treatment is withheld or denied unless sobriety is the goal. This may occur especially when mental health and addictive disorders services are not provided in an integrated fashion. Regardless, this is not acceptable and not reflective of a person-centered approach. Such actions unnecessarily force a set of priorities that often push the individual away rather than engaging them. Given the circumstances, what are the individual's wishes? Following Maslow's hierarchy, some form of harm reduction and assurance of safety should be a priority over demands for sobriety. Meeting the person "where they're at" is the person-centered approach.

This is particularly a problem when individuals come seeking services in a "less than voluntary" fashion. It is not unusual for many people to initially seek addictive disorders services under a court order or other legal mandate. They often feel victimized or unfairly picked on, angry, resentful and lack awareness or acceptance of the negative impact of alcohol and/or other drugs on their lives. As a result, they have little real interest in being abstinent from these substances. In these instances, a goal of abstinence, even in the face of a judicial mandate, will not likely succeed. It fails to recognize that successful and enduring treatment for recovery and effective addictive disorders ultimately requires self-derived motivation and an understanding that real change often requires a stage-wise approach. If the individual is in the pre-contemplation stage, then the provider should focus on contemplation and engagement. Setting goals that have meaning and relevance to the individual and their stage of change, rather than imposing someone else's goals, are part of creating a successful person-centered plan.

Goal setting, especially for seeking help with a problem of substance use or dependence, should be informed by an understanding of their stage of recovery and their treatment readiness as well as their needs and preferences. Questions that help to assess the person's willingness to change and to participate in the planning process and treatment setting include: What is your motivation for treatment? What is your definition of addiction? What experiences have you had with treatment programs (either for yourself or family members)? Do you see any connection between your use of alcohol and/or other drugs with this referral?

Rarely are sobriety and abstinence the clearly stated goals of the individual at the outset of seeking help. Many if not most individuals struggling with addictive disorders have tremendous ambivalence about relinquishing what has been at times a source of pleasure and enjoyment, a connection to friends and a way of life. Rather they want relief from the chaos and turmoil in their lives that is at least in part a result of the substance use. Engaging the individual and family by agreeing to help them resolve the problems and challenges in their life is an appropriate approach to setting goals—abstinence and sobriety will likely become objectives in the plan as the individual comes to better understand that their goals cannot be realized if their substance use continues.

Every person with an addictive disorder problem is a unique individual with his or her own issues and needs. Yet in practice, it is not unusual to see sobriety become a one-size-fits-all goal with "the program" as the universal solution or service. Instead, each individual should have their own goal responsive to their life circumstances and needs. Even the individual involuntarily referred for services will be hard pressed to deny or rebuff the team's interests in his or her strengths, preferences, interests, gifts and competencies. Sobriety, or even an initial reduction in use, may be an objective along with several others, and "the program" may be one of several services or interventions to help the individual attain the objective.

The Language of Goals

Whenever possible, goals should be expressed in the words of the individual and written in the person's primary language. Some criteria for evaluating the appropriateness of goals are included in Table 4.1.

Table 4.1 The Language of Goals

Criteria	Possible goals
Provide a focus of engagement/life changes as a result of treatment	• *I want to withdraw from drugs* • *I want to have a boyfriend/ girlfriend*
Are consistent with a desire for recovery, self-determination and self-management	• *I want to learn how to…* • *I want to be able to drive a car* • *I want to open my own bank account*
Reflective of the person's values, lifestyles, and so on	• *I want to work as a…*
Culturally relevant, in consultation with individuals and their families	• *I want to live with my family* • *I want my family to accept me*
Appropriate to the individual's age	• *I want to stop getting into trouble with my parents* • *I want to be able to stay at home with my family* • *I want to get through the school year*
Based upon the individual's strengths, needs, preferences and abilities	• *I want to find out why I keep relapsing* • *I hope to live in my own apartment*
Written in positive terms, which embody hope, not negative in focus	• *I want to keep my job*
Appropriate to the stage of recovery	• *I want to get the judge off my back (pre-contemplation)*
Alternative to current circumstances	• *I want to feel better by stopping grieving over my husband's/wife's death*

Obviously not all criteria apply at all times, nor is the list in Table 4.1 intended to be complete. Rather these suggestions are offered to provide a handy reference to use in developing goals statements.

Parsimony

Simplifying goal setting, and resisting the temptation to elaborate too many goals, is one of the secrets to success in developing effective individual plans. It is possible that some plans will have multiple goals—especially when it is appropriate to have a life goal as well as a treatment goal. However, there are many instances in which having only one will suffice. The intent of the plan is to make change a manageable process, and identifying too many goals can complicate and confound the efforts of individuals, families and providers. Having too many goals in the plan is simply overwhelming for everyone and undermines the entire process.

Encouraging parsimony in setting goals for individual plans is one of the important points of departure from common practice today. Providers are encouraged to have only one or perhaps two goals at a time. It is questionable whether having more than one or two goals adds to the value of the plan and the effectiveness of service. First, goals should be global and expansive—having too many is an inherent contradiction. Second, goals linked to discharge and transition criteria should be a stable element of the plan as the recovery process unfolds—having multiple goals that are short term and narrow in focus means that this element of the plan will likely need frequent revision and render planning a burdensome chore. Instead, the focus for short-term change should be found in the objectives.

It follows that prioritization of goals is a necessity. When it appears that there are multiple goals, the provider should try to help the individual identify different approaches and options, or choose the areas that are most immediately important and educate the person about the possibilities. Simply stating, "let's try and focus on one or two things that are most important to you for starters" and explaining how focusing on one thing at a time can be a strategy for success can be enormously effective. All of these activities are strategies for developing a partnership with the individual.

Evaluation of the Process and Outcomes

How can one tell if the goals on an individual plan are truly person-centered? The following criteria are useful for evaluating individual plans. Upon review it should be clear that:

- the findings from the assessment and integrated summary have been shared with the individual and family
- a planning meeting has occurred with the individual (and perhaps others) to set goals and further develop the plan
- goals are aligned with the information gathered in the assessment and described in the interpretive summary
- there is a connection between what are identified as strengths, needs, abilities and preferences, and what are actually stated as goals
- the individual and family have been given useful information about services and treatment options to help them establish goals
- questions have been asked to help elicit goals
  - "How do you want your life to be in the future?"
  - "What is important to you?"
  - "What are your hopes and dreams?"
- the goals on the plan are actually written in the words of the individual
- the individual and family member receiving services can articulate the goal(s) on their plan
- the goals relate to the discharge and/or transition criteria

Outcome measures for a recovery-based service system are not the same as for traditional mental health programs because recovery-oriented services are based on rehabilitation principles, focus on improving the overall quality of life and are driven by each person's goals. Ideally our approach to measurement is also person-centered so that success is based on our ability to know how consistently we help people attain their individual desired outcomes. Goal attainment scaling has been suggested as a way of evaluating the effectiveness of person-centered plans in helping individuals attain individualized outcomes. However, this approach is fraught with methodological problems and is not commonly used[15]. As an alternative, the use of person-centered survey tools such as the Personal Outcome Measures program, developed by the Council on Quality and Leadership, help to look at a person's quality of life by examining indicators[16] rather than goal attainment.

In addition, Chapter 7 includes the *PCP Quality Indicators for Chart Review Sub-Scale* as a tool for evaluating plans, including goals as well as other elements of the plan. While reviewing records has an important quality assurance and quality improvement function, it tells us little about the process of engagement, assessment, goal setting and creation of the plan. Ultimately, the person served's experience of the process of creating a person-centered plan and setting individual goals is the truest measure of quality care. Surveys such as the Consumer Assessment of Healthcare Providers and Systems (CAHPS) program, a nationally standardized survey system to examine patients' experiences, and the Experience of Care and Health Outcomes Survey (ECHO™) are designed to collect consumers' ratings of their behavioral health treatment. The PCP Quality Indicators sub-scale for people in recovery does just that as well. It asks people receiving services seven simple questions about their recovery planning experience, including if their plan has goals that are their own hopes and dreams. The information from these surveys can be very informative and useful in efforts to enhance the overall process of care, advance the person-centeredness of services and improve outcomes[17,18].

III. MAKING IT HAPPEN

In practice, goal setting is not as easy as it might appear to be on the surface. There are many things that get in the way of people clarifying and declaring their life goals, even when that is not complicated by health, mental health or addiction problems. In the process of developing a person-centered plan, establishing goals is the essential first step and the foundation of the plan itself. Hopefully the information gained in the assessment, and the understanding that comes from the integrated summary, can help make goal setting a less painful and more productive process than it might otherwise be. It's important to remember that in person-centered planning, the goal belongs to the person served and not the provider team.

Let's consider the four learning examples and see how the assessment and integrated summary do in fact set the stage for elaborating and clarifying goals for each individual.

Examples

Diana

Diana's goal is "I want to be happy (stop fighting with my mother)." Diana has many strengths as identified by the CANS assessment as well as clinician observation; they include getting along well with others (except her mother with whom she has a conflictual relationship), bright and friendly affectionate, etc. It is reasonable to assume she would want to be happier and get along with her mother as a goal. From a cultural and developmental perspective it's only natural that she would want a better and less conflictual relationship with her mother. She is moving from childhood to adolescence, trying to make sense of what it means to be a Latino girl in her family, and needs to be able to get from her mother what she needs as she continues to mature.

JR

JR's simply stated goal is to "Get a job as a cook in a restaurant." This particular goal builds upon JR's strengths, his interest in cooking, his past work experience and attending culinary school and having had some prior work experience. The plan also lays out clearly the barriers JR will need to manage in his effort to reach his goal. It's easy to anticipate the objective(s) and interventions that will likely focus on rehabilitative strategies to help restore his previous level of functioning.

Keisha

Keisha's goal "I want to get back to my Baptist Church" should be no surprise based on our understanding of her from the assessment and the integrated summary. Overall Keisha's spiritual and church resources have been a tremendous source of stability and meaning in her life and a dependable source of helpful support. Losing that connection to her church has been a great loss in her life so it seems natural that returning to her church is of paramount importance to her.

Roberto

Roberto's goals are clear and could be anticipated from the integrated summary. He has declared "I want to be back with my family…eventually go back to school" for his life recovery goals, and for his immediate inpatient treatment goal he states, "I want to be less anxious so I can cope at home." This is to be expected. When an individual is in the hospital their immediate needs may well be more treatment focused and geared towards being discharged for continued outpatient services. Roberto and the treatment team are ready to focus on removing the barriers to his ability to be safe at home and in the community. At the same time it is also reasonable to note the person's more long-term goals—in some respects this will help with the planning for follow-on care once he is discharged and steps down to a lower level of care. It is easy to see Roberto's desired results as a conclusion to his integrated summary—it all flows and follows along nicely.

REFERENCES

1. Daniels A, Grant E, Filson B, Powell I, Fricks L, Goodale L, eds. *Pillars of peer support: transforming mental health systems of care through peer support services.* January 2010; www.pillarsofpeersupport.org.
2. Chinman M, Young AS, Hassell J, Davidson L. Toward the implementation of mental health consumer provider services. *J Behav Health Serv Res.* 2006;33(2):176-195.
3. http://www.magellanhealth.com/training/peersupport/magellanmodule1/graphics/job.pdf.
4. Maslow A. *Motivation and Personality.* 2nd ed. Harper & Row; 1970.
5. Tatarsky A. *Harm Reduction Psychotherapy: A New Treatment for Drug and Alcohol Problems.* 1st ed. Jason Aronson, Inc; 2002.
6. Tsemberis S, Gulcur L, Nakae M. Housing first, consumer choice, and harm reduction for homeless individuals with a dual diagnosis. *Am J Public Health.* 2004;94(4):651-656.
7. Sasson S. Beneficence versus respect for autonomy: an ethical dilemma in social work practice. *J Gerontol Soc Work.* 2000;33(1):5-16.
8. O'Brien J, Lyle O'Brien C. Responsive Systems Associates. www.soeweb.syr.edu/thechp/rsapub.htm.
9. Oades L. Collaborative recovery: an integrative model for working with individuals who experience chronic and recurring mental illness. *Austral Psych.* 2005;13(3):279-284.
10. Blackman L. Personal communication.
11. Daniels AS, Tunner TP, Bergeson S, Ashenden P, Fricks L, Powell I. Pillars of Peer Support Summit IV: Establishing Standards of Excellence. www.pillarsofpeersupport.org; January 2013.
12. http://www.yale.edu/prch/research/documents/toolkit.draft.7.24.09.pdf.
13. Copeland M. *Wellness Recovery Action Plan & Peer Support: Personal, Group and Program Development.* Peach Press; 2007.
14. Frese F, Davis W. The consumer–survivor movement, recovery, and consumer professionals. *Prof Psychol Res Pract.* 1997;28(3):243-245.
15. Tennant A. Goal attainment scaling: current methodological challenges. *Disabil Rehabil.* 2007;29(20–21):1583-1588.
16. Council on Quality and Leadership. *Personal Outcome Measures®.* Towson, MD; 2005.
17. Hargraves J, Hays R, Cleary D. Psychometric Properties of the Consumer Assessment of Health Plans Study (CAHPS®) 2.0 Adult Core Survey. *Health Serv Res.* December 2003;38[6 (pt 1)]:1509-1528.
18. http://www.hcp.med.harvard.edu/echo/.

CHAPTER 5

Focusing on Change: Identifying Barriers and Specifying Objectives

You Don't Just Luck into Things…You Build Step by Step, Whether it's Friendships or Opportunities.

Barbara Bush

I. STATING THE CASE

Moving along the path to recovery and wellness, there are barriers and challenges that get in the way of achieving the goal; somehow those barriers must be overcome if we are to make progress towards the destination. If it weren't for barriers, the journey en route to attaining the goal would be easy, and the need for assistance minimal. However, individuals and families seeking help do so because the impact or consequences of a health, mental health and/or substance use problems make realizing the goal seem difficult if not overwhelming to the point of seeming nearly impossible; if it weren't for these challenges, the trip would be relatively easy and manageable on one's own. It is not unusual to find that there are many barriers; some are interrelated while others stand alone.

These barriers can take different forms for each individual and can vary over time. Identifying them and understanding their source, and why they cannot be surmounted without assistance, is critical to good person-centered planning and effective support of the recovery journey. Sometimes barriers reflect a lack of resources—either medical, psychological, psychosocial and/or physical. Fear and anxiety, confused thinking, irritability and/or poor anger control may be symptoms of a diagnosed disorder and are but one example of psychological barriers. Discomfort around others, social isolation, difficulty with completing the "activities of daily living," stressful relationships or lack of support are among a host of possible psychosocial issues that need to be resolved. Poor nutrition, ill health, continued drug use, lack of housing, the need for warm clothes, inadequate access to transportation, and so on are representative of physical and medical obstacles to overcome.

Treatment Planning for Person-Centered Care
http://dx.doi.org/10.1016/B978-0-12-394448-1.00005-6

133

Sometimes these barriers and their impact can be attributed to the mental health and addiction problems that lead people to seek help, other times they are simply a consequence of life. As providers of recovery-oriented services, we are concerned about all of these, but oftentimes we only have the resources or payment authorizations to address those issues that can be directly attributable to the medical, mental health and substance abuse problems. In an environment where health insurance—be it public or private—or government funds are paying for services, this can become a particularly difficult but important concern for providers who need to be compensated for their work. This occurs most commonly in a fee for service environment where only "medically necessary" services are authorized. Ideally, money and resources for supporting an individual's recovery should be available on a "whatever it takes" basis, but in most service delivery settings, this is not the case.

Objectives can be thought of as the strategies and accomplishments that somehow ameliorate or resolve the barriers. They can include access to additional resources, re-learned skills, new behaviors, a reduction in the impact of symptoms or finding ways to access assistance, to name but a few. As such, they become the milestones and wayposts along the route toward reaching the goal or destination point. Sometimes objectives are called "short-term" goals. Building on the roadmap analogy, objectives are the directions and route plan to reach the destination, such as "drive 30 miles to the town of Success," "meet me at the Recovery Center Post Office" or "when you come to the circle, go halfway around and bear right and pull into the Wellness Lodge." The barriers no longer hamper or detour the individual and they are able to move closer to the final destination or goal each time one of these waypoints is reached or a change in his or her medical mental health and addictive disorders status and needs is achieved.

Recovery plans often require multiple objectives to reach the goal; they may be sequential or concurrent but should always describe the near-term changes necessary to help the individual and family succeed. Objectives become the immediate focus of treatment and services; they are the incremental changes and manageable tasks the individual and family will focus on, bit by bit, as they move towards realizing their recovery vision. These are often seen as the real engine of the individual plan that drives overall progress.

Objectives should help the individual and family address barriers and bring about changes in physical and psychological status, function, behavior, symptoms, potential or capabilities that empower them to resolve the needs and concerns that led them to seek help. Objectives are typically described in action words and should not involve changes in thinking, understanding, insight, and so on. Rather, changes in behavior or function that result from such understanding or knowledge should be identified in the objective. Achieving objectives usually requires the individual and family to master new skills and abilities that support them in developing more effective responses to their needs and challenges.

Objectives are about action and change; they are not passive or abstract. Objectives are of the moment and practical; they are not distant or remote. An objective should include a measure of success as well as a timeframe for its completion. Objectives should empower, engage and break a larger challenge into smaller more manageable steps; this alone can be motivating by making the larger goal seem attainable rather than overwhelming and impossible.

Attainment of an objective is supported by the activities, services and interventions of the entire team, including the individual and family, peers, as well as access to other natural supports and resources within the community. These efforts may include a range of services from traditional professional treatments such as psychotherapy, addictive disorders counseling, pharmacotherapy, case management, occupation or rehabilitation therapy, and so on, to psychoeducation classes, participation in self-help and wellness centers or even culturally appropriate folk remedies as but a few examples. Overall, the emphasis should be on teaching skills, enhancing the ability of the individual to manage his/her own life, utilizing the natural resources of the community and being less dependent on professional resources. These are the interventions/services/supports that are discussed in the next chapter.

Objectives should not be confused with services or interventions and *this is one of the most frequent errors made in developing individual plans.* Objectives should not be a description of what the provider or others will do to promote and facilitate the change—those activities are more accurately interventions and are examined in depth in the following chapter. While seemingly basic to the process, specifying objectives is often one of the most difficult tasks for providers in preparing person-centered plans. A properly written objective should typically begin with a description of a significant and meaningful change in behavior, status or function as a step towards reaching the larger goal that will occur *as a result of the services and interventions specified in the plan.* The description of the change should be included and prefaced by the term "as evidenced by…." Stating "Susie will attend the intensive outpatient program three hours a day three days a week" is not an objective—it is an intervention or action step; the only reasonable evidence

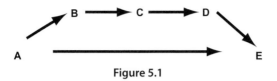

Figure 5.1

would be an attendance log and that makes little sense and is of little if any value in terms of helping Susie in her recovery. However, "Susie will improve her ADLs as evidenced by staff evaluation of her cleanliness and grooming during IOP attendance" is an appropriate objective and an observable measurable change in behavior and functioning that may be achieved by means of multiple interventions or activities—including IOP participation.

From Barriers to Success

The integrated summary (Chapter 3) should include at least some description of the identified barriers to attaining the stated goals. During the assessment process, some attention should be focused on understanding what stands between the individual and family today and their hopes, dreams and goals for the future. For example, in Figure 5.1, what hinders pursuit of the direct course between A and E? The simple but powerful question "What keeps you from doing [blank] tomorrow?" is often an effective entrée into a discussion of barriers—those that are a result of a mental health or addictive disorder as well as those that are brought about by physical health, social, economic and other challenges. Objectives in the individual service plan should reflect the removal, resolution or mediation of those barriers. If the barriers are not clearly identified or understood, then the creation of meaningful and effective objectives will be difficult if not impossible.

For example, a barrier to obtaining a goal related to employment might be a lack of personal transportation (resource barrier) and a fear of using public transportation (personal barrier). In such a case, at least one of the plan's objectives toward the goal of obtaining employment might be: "Within 30 days, Taisha will be able to take the bus from her home to downtown and return by herself." If the narrative summary has identified social phobia anxiety, withdrawal, learning problems and an overprotective mother as challenges for her to overcome in learning how to ride the bus, then the services provided should include a web of interventions and activities that address these challenges. With those supports and skill-building steps in place, Taisha should then be able to succeed in meeting her objectives and taking a first step towards employment.

A second objective might address the barriers and challenges she faces in either developing job skills or overcoming her fears and inexperience in submitting applications and enduring interviews. The sequential nature of the process becomes clear. It is the judgment of the individual and family as well as the provider as to whether or not objectives should be sequential or concurrent. A number of factors, including the complexity of the overall plan, the anticipated timeframes, the ability of the individual to multitask, and the viability of resources for both the individual as well as the service system all play a role in the selection and sequencing of objectives. Regardless, each objective should address or specify only one change at a time.

Key Features

Objectives should be:
- reasonable
- measurable
- appropriate to the treatment setting
- achievable
- understandable to the individual
- time specific
- written in behaviorally specific language
- responsive to the individual's disability/disorder/challenges and stage of recovery
- appropriate to the individual's age, development and culture

A popular mnemonic says that objectives should be SMART:
- **S**imple or **S**traightforward
- **M**easurable
- **A**ttainable
- **R**ealistic
- **T**imeframed

Objectives are about success, realizing that things can be different, and experiencing the power of change. As individuals and families struggle to overcome barriers and challenges and successfully address their needs, nothing succeeds like success.

Role of the Team

The elaboration of objectives, and the development of a strategy that works to remove barriers and help individuals reach their goals, should be done in active collaboration with the individual and family. Guiding the process and suggesting strategies to overcome barriers is one of the provider's essential contributions to the recovery journey. Individuals and families seek help because they have reached a point where they are unable to address their needs and challenges on their own. They may be able to identify their destination or goals, but they cannot envision the route or overcome the barriers that lie in the way.

By helping to remove the barriers, objectives effectively establish waypoints and set the journey's course. The provider becomes the guide who can lead the way. The important role of the provider in this task as counselor, advisor, recovery consultant, coach, expert partner and planner should not be underestimated or ignored. While the provider can and should offer experience and perspective to overcome barriers, it is important that the provider not unwittingly limit the individual's and family's choices or ability to take risks and try new things. The setting of objectives builds upon the strength of the individual and family as well as the collaboration and partnership between them and the other team members. The task should reflect the mutual experience of dignity and respect for all participants.

The intermediate steps or objectives that an individual and family pursue to achieve their goals should be substantial and significant, but at the same time manageable. They should reflect valuable and meaningful change. There are potential pitfalls in the process of creating objectives to include in the recovery plan. One is a tendency to trivialize objectives instead of making them meaningful and relevant; the other is to describe such a substantial change that it is difficult to distinguish the objective from the goal. Part of the "art" of good planning is knowing how to "right-size" the scope of an objective. Some of this varies by level of care, some by individual and stage of change, or the extent of the strengths and resources they have to draw upon. This is also linked to some degree to the question of timeframes discussed below. For example, the complexity of an objective in an acute inpatient setting will be different from that of a community-based rehabilitation program. Typically, when people seek help, whether for a problem that has emerged recently, or for a concern that is long-standing and persistent, they are eager to see change occur. Objectives should describe meaningful and substantive movement and headway in the direction of the goal that can be achieved within a timeframe that meets the individual's and family's perception of timely progress.

For instance, if the problem is "depression" and the goal is "I want to feel happier by being a better mom," merely stating "Susan will keep a mood journal" does not explain how that action or activity will help bring her happiness or improve her parenting. In fact, this is a good example of how the difference between objectives and interventions can blur—keeping a mood journal is much more of a self-directed task or intervention than a significant change in behavior or function. On the other hand, an objective that states "Susan will report being in a good mood most days" is an example of an objective that is too large and akin to a goal. Individuals seek help and receive services because they have reached an impasse and are unable to solve their own problems. The team assists in helping to establish realistic, responsive and attainable time-specific objectives that individuals can achieve as tangible steps towards meeting their goals. It is said that "nothing succeeds like success" and the value of accomplishment that brings them closer to their goal reflects significant progress cannot be overstated.

Timeframes

Specifying a timeframe for attainment of an objective is a critical component of the overall planning process. Goals are long term; objectives are near term. The specific timeframe established in an objective carries with it a message of hope, expectation and accountability for the provider as well as the individual and family: change is expected and appropriate progress will be monitored. In many settings, the time to accomplish an objective is automatically tied to the minimum administrative requirement for review and update of a plan. For example, if the plan needs to be reviewed every six months or every year, there is a tendency for all of the objectives to have a six- or 12-month timeframe for completion. This typically does not communicate a message of hope or expectation of change—in fact it can communicate just the opposite.

A person-centered, recovery-oriented approach to planning and services has timeframes that are relevant to the scope of the objective, the individual's and family's motivation, and the resources available to support and facilitate the change. More importantly, setting extended timeframes subtly communicates a message of low expectations and hopelessness. While each objective must be individual and relevant to each person's goals, as a general rule 90 days should be considered as an upper limit timeframe in crafting objectives. If nothing else, 90 days is a reasonable period for review and reassessment, and in many settings it is a standard of care.

It can be useful to think of yourself or a family member. If you were in distress and feeling stuck or overwhelmed with a problem, how quickly would you hope for some positive change and relief? Sometimes even tomorrow or next week seems too far away. How would you feel if you were told that it would take two months for even a very modest change to occur? The timeframes that are included in an objective are not just a detail; rather, they are an important element of the social contract between the person seeking help and the provider.

Strengths-Based Approach/Stage of Change

With much attention focused on the principles of a strengths-based approach, many providers struggle with how to actually employ strengths in an individual plan. Nowhere is the recognition and engagement of the individual's and family's abilities and resources more important than in specifying objectives. Objectives should not focus on deficits; rather, they should describe positive changes that can build on past accomplishments and engage existing resources. Once the strengths are identified in the assessment process and noted in the integrated summary they should be utilized in the plan, most likely in the objectives or perhaps the interventions.

For example, if the person has the identified strength of having natural supporters in his life, then perhaps an objective to help reduce Sam's long-standing difficulty in leaving his apartment due to his paranoia could be "Sam will participate in a minimum of one social activity outside of his apartment each week for the next 90 days with his cousin Tommy." Or if Joe is struggling with addiction issues, but he has had some sobriety in his life, even if it has been tenuous or short lived, and he has a goal of wanting to reconcile with his wife, then the objective of "Joe will maintain sobriety for two months, as evidenced by urine drug testing" would be a good objective based on his strength of having had some periods of sobriety in his life.

There are times when it can be difficult to recognize a person's strengths in the midst of their distress and need; their motivation for improvement and change is one that is often overlooked. This alone can be a powerful strength upon which to build a plan and mobilize success. Imagine trying to create an effective plan without this resource to build upon. In fact, a lack of motivation is often a factor when individuals and families seek services only to satisfy the requirements of the courts, school or other authorities. In these instances, providers could help individuals become motivated to change as a way of supporting and sustaining person-centered strengths. It could be appropriate to have a first objective statement which anticipates the individual's and family's ability to recognize and "own" the need for services and change. Such an objective might be: "Karen and her mother will be able to identify a self-defined goal and agree upon at least one objective that removes a barrier to that goal within 30 days." In this circumstance, interventions would focus on the issues of awareness, motivation and engagement.

Having identified the person's stage of change/stage of readiness/stage of recovery in the integrated summary helps us to craft and agree upon objectives to be achieved by the person. Objectives should be stage appropriate, such as: acknowledgment of a problem, exploring possible solutions, identifying coping strategies, demonstrating the behavior a portion of the time and full achievement of the desired outcome. This continues the "meet the person where they're at" principle. By identifying stage of change, you increase the likelihood of success. Objectives will then target the improvement that the individual is most likely ready to realize.

If someone is "pre-contemplative" about their illness/not aware of their illness, then asking that individual to make some behavior change to ameliorate symptoms is most likely not going to lead to meaningful engagement or a successful outcome. For these individuals, it is often helpful to employ motivational enhancement strategies for the interventions, and the use of "learning" objectives to increase awareness and acknowledgment. For example, "Joan will have a better awareness of how her behavior negatively impacts others as evidenced by her ability to identify two possible reasons for eviction from her apartment within four weeks" might be an appropriate objective and starting point for someone who has little insight into how her behavior impacts others. Or in another instance, Mai has a goal of "I want to have a full-time job" and says she's frustrated with the lack of progress. Yet, Mai has missed every appointment with her vocational counselor; her voices tell her that the mental health system is preventing her from getting jobs and so she avoids coming in for help and is unable to appreciate the connection between the two. One objective on her plan might be: "Within 30 days, Mai will better understand her self-defeating pattern of behavior as evidenced by her ability to identify three barriers that reduce her ability to get a job."

What if the person is in the contemplation stage of change? They recognize there is a problem that needs to be addressed, but they are uncertain of engaging in the process of seeking help and making changes. For example, Frank wants an intimate relationship with a woman and says his goal is: "I want to get married." He dated a long time ago, but never found the right person. Now, he would like to attend singles events, but doesn't go because he feels certain he'll fail. The last time he went to a church social for singles he only stayed for 15 minutes due to intense anxiety and his belief that people were talking badly about him. He would like to get some help with this problem but isn't sure he can really commit to making changes that would help his situation. An objective could be: "Within three weeks Frank will overcome his fears of failure as evidenced by his ability to identify one potentially attainable change/objective for himself to work on in therapy."

A person in the action or maintenance stage of change is by definition ready to change behaviors, do something different and attain a different level of functioning. An example is the goal of "I want to have friends." Alphonso is working full-time and enjoys his job. He struggles with fatigue due to medication side effects and has not been able to develop any co-worker relationships. He has a very negative self-image, experiences a constant litany of negative self-talk and isolates himself in his apartment. An objective on his plan might be "Alphonso will overcome his self-doubt as evidenced by his socializing with co-workers once per week for three consecutive weeks within two months."

In an inpatient setting, an objective for someone hospitalized for self-harm and aggressive behaviors could be "Within seven days Sarah will be able to effectively communicate her needs and feelings without resorting to aggression or self-harm as evidenced by three consecutive days of no cutting." A more positively stated objective could be "When Sarah is feeling that she wants to harm herself, instead she will draw a picture about her feelings and share it with staff, for 7 consecutive days." The intent is that Sarah will learn how to better use her verbal skills to communicate and her coping skills such as listening to music and drawing (*based on her assessed strengths*) to reduce the impact of strong negative emotions. For someone who is hospitalized due to being suicidal, one objective might be "Within five days, Dick will experience some relief of his feelings of hopelessness and despair as evidenced by his rejection of suicide as an option for two consecutive days."

For youth and families, consider this circumstance: Liza is a 14-year-old who has been using marijuana daily for the past year. She has a family history of alcoholism and amphetamine abuse and social services has considered placing her in foster care. The family's goal is "we want to stay together as a family" and they recognize that Liza's continued drug use can no longer be tolerated. Liza says she can't stop because "all my friends smoke." An objective might be "Within one month Liza will make a commitment to working on sobriety as evidenced by her making two new friends with schoolmates who do not use drugs or alcohol." For a child who has not been attending school regularly (i.e., been delinquent, going AWOL, etc.) because of conflict at home between his parents that he finds upsetting and makes him too anxious to go to school, an objective might be "Luke will be able to better cope with his problems at home as evidenced by regular school attendance for two consecutive weeks within two months." For a young child, age 9, who is experiencing behavioral difficulties at school due to his impulsiveness, poor boundaries and anger, he is able to say his goal is "being a happier family" and his father's stated goal is "I want the school to meet his needs." A potential objective could be "Joey will learn how to better deal with his feelings, frustrations and anger as evidenced by his ability to ask his teacher for help to listen to music at least once a day for a week. A second objective could be within two months Joey will ask his teacher to help him listen to some music whenever he is feeling angry/frustrated for a period of 3 months.

As much as possible, objectives should reflect an increase in functioning and ability, along with the attainment of new skills, rather than merely a decrease of symptoms. In the examples provided above, the objectives are all very specific and focused on changes in motivation, attitude or behavior and are measured by observable meaningful change that represents real progress towards resolution of the problem. In formulating an objective it is important to ask: What are the individual's strengths that can be utilized and enhanced to help bring about change? Objectives that build upon these existing resources and abilities are far more likely to succeed and sustain the journey. Objectives that merely ameliorate the current distress will inevitably lead to distractions and detours on the path to recovery and wellness.

Avoiding the "Dead-Man Standard" and Other Pitfalls

The creation of objectives that are simply the cessation of a particular behavior or symptom is another problem in developing an effective and meaningful plan. For example, consider the objective "John will stop having temper tantrums." The problem with this objective is that if John were to die, he would meet the objective by no longer losing control of his anger. This is sometimes referred to as the "dead-man standard"; instead, whenever possible objectives should as much as possible describe active, positive change if they are to be meaningful midpoints, as well as measures of progress and success. Admittedly, sometimes this is difficult to do. In this instance a rewording of the objective might be "Within 30 days John will have mastered anger management skills as evidenced by his self report of remaining calm when faced with frustration on five occasions" or "Within two months John will be able to express anger in a socially acceptable manner as evidenced by his self report of using a normal tone of voice when he is upset at least 80% of the time for seven consecutive days."

An objective is not the mere removal of the barrier—this runs the risk of reinforcing a deficit-focused approach. Rather, the objective should capture the positive alternative to the current needs and challenges. For example, if an individual is struggling with thoughts of suicide, the objective should not be that "Carla will report that she is free of suicidal thoughts within 30 days." Instead, the healthy alternative is that "Within 90 days, Carla will report enjoying at least two activities that help her to feel life is worth living." While some might dismiss the difference as a trivial matter of semantics, experience teaches that this type of reframing is empowering and leads to better outcomes.

Another pitfall is the use of activities that merely indicate attendance or participation in service activities as an objective. Statements such as "Bill will attend medication groups weekly," "Gayle's mother will participate in family psychoeducation groups every other weekend" or "Juan will keep 70% of his cognitive-behavioral therapy appointments" are all examples of such objectives. These statements should be considered a description of interventions. They demonstrate how services and objectives can become commingled and confused. Attendance may be necessary to begin the process of change; however, it is not a meaningful change in function or behavior that helps move the individual and family closer to their goals.

Mere participation in services in no way indicates that any learning, development or change has occurred. Understanding, insight and knowledge alone are not sufficient objectives. Instead, there must be some active and measurable demonstration that the input and benefit of services has been incorporated and helped to cause positive and desired change. The skill of developing an individual plan is to clearly articulate intermediate accomplishments in support of the larger goals. This requires an understanding of how services such as medication groups, family psychoeducation, case management, and so on, all contribute to meeting objectives and promoting change.

There is one exception when participation in some treatment-related activity could be a valuable and legitimate objective. For example, if the individual is persistently withdrawn and unable to join in because of intense social anxiety and avoidance, then participation in an activity or intervention can be a measure of change and progress. The objective is really "relief of the anxiety" or the "development of skills to reduce social avoidance," and the participation becomes a way to determine that the individual has been able to overcome the worries that previously made participation too difficult.

All too often, otherwise thoughtful and well-developed plans are undermined by the efforts to do too much at once. There are no hard and fast rules about how many active objectives are required at any one time, except for the expectation that there is at least one objective for every goal. There are circumstances when it may be perfectly appropriate to have only one active objective; there may also be times when having two or three simultaneous and concurrent objectives is necessary and beneficial.

However, as with goals, there may be value in strategic parsimony. Having fewer objectives that are more short term and targeted can help to make the overall plan more manageable. Sequencing one objective after another rather than trying to accomplish three things at once is another example of this strategy. This alone may help to make a plan more effective. In general, plans with more than two or three current active objectives are too complex for both the individual and the provider to manage successfully and should be carefully reconsidered.

However, there are important exceptions to this guidance—especially when the individual's needs are complex or urgent. For example, an Assertive Community Treatment (ACT) team or a multidisciplinary inpatient team may need to provide a broad array of different services, such as medication management, skills training group, care management to address the multiple needs of the individual with an intensity appropriate to the individual's circumstances. However, all the billable services need to be purposeful and connected to an objective that reflects a clinically relevant change in order for them to be medically necessary. In this instance, not all the required clinical activity can be reasonably justified by having only one objective; that may be too limiting for multiple providers to actually provide services and do their billing. In this instance, multiple concurrent objectives may be the most effective strategy.

But for the most part, objectives can be viewed as building blocks of successive learning in which one step builds on the other and there is a logical order and sequence to follow. For instance, an individual may first need to be able to recognize and acknowledge his or her addictive behaviors before being able to demonstrate two alternatives to drug and alcohol use as a way to relieve uncomfortable emotions. Figure 5.1 is a reminder of the relationship between assessment (point A), goals (point E), objectives (points B, C and D) and the services and interventions (small arrows). Although this diagram suggests that objectives are sequential, there are times when two or more concurrent objectives are warranted.

Review

Not all of the objectives need to be developed at the time the goal is established or the first objective is set. Sometimes it is possible to anticipate the entirety of the journey early on, while at other times it is only possible to see just a few feet ahead. The attainment or completion of an objective is a time for review of the individual plan; this success inevitably provides new information and may create new opportunities or possibly identify unanticipated needs and challenges. It is an opportunity to re-evaluate the goal, review barriers and check on the overall course. New objectives that are accurate and responsive to the goal can then be established. Not meeting an objective within the anticipated timeframe should also initiate a review of the plan.

Plan review help to inform priorities and maintain the stepwise progress towards attainment of the goal. The individual and family must be active partners with the provider in establishing objectives; they are often better able to participate as the entire process unfolds and they come closer to their goal. They must also collaborate in the process of review and re-evaluation and further planning. After all, the objectives and their successes should be empowering and should provide them with new skills and abilities to express their preferences as well as to meet their needs and challenges.

II. CREATING THE SOLUTION

A better understanding of the essential features of an objective often helps providers to write more appropriate and effective objectives on the plan. This is not trivial—language and construction can make a tremendous difference. Properly worded objectives empower both the provider and the individual, while poorly written plans can create confusion, unanticipated roadblocks and impede progress. This section carefully examines the criteria and descriptions for a well-crafted statement of the objective.

A statement of the objective should generally satisfy all of these criteria. An objective should be the following things:

- *Measurable*

  The intended change should be obvious and readily observed by the individual and family as well as the provider. It is important, however, to agree about how that change will be measured or noted. It is perfectly reasonable and acceptable to measure the change specified in the objective by observation, self-report, completion of an assignment, statements made in group/individual/family therapy, reports from other agencies, and so on. A simple and almost intuitive approach is to ask the individual to rate the current status of a problem on a scale of 1 to 10 (with 10 being the best or worst depending on the circumstances). Follow-up assessment and monitoring for attainment of the objective becomes a matter of re-rating using the same self-defined scale. Measurement is often thought to imply the use of elaborate research-based scales and other measures, but that is not necessarily the case. That said, there may be instances when the use of a standardized test of even laboratory studies, such as urine drug screens, may be useful and appropriate.

- *Appropriate to the treatment setting or level of care*
  Objectives need to be considered in the context of the level of care and discharge or transition criteria. In other words, if services are being provided in a 24-hour care facility or program, the objectives should focus on immediate treatment goals rather than more long-term life goals. Movement and progress towards safe treatment at a lower and less restrictive level of care should always be considered when the individual is away from their home and not receiving outpatient services.

  There may also be restrictions in such a setting that make some objectives less appropriate or relevant. For instance, many residential detoxification and rehabilitation programs do not allow contact or visitation in an effort to control the introduction of contraband. An objective that expects the individual to "strengthen their social network with friends" so that they can move toward their goal of "feeling included with peers" is not appropriate to that setting. Instead, an objective focused on developing relapse prevention skills that prepares the individual to face the challenges of returning to the community is very appropriate to the setting.

- *Achievable and reasonable*
  The individual should have the capacity to actually meet the objective— sometimes this is also about being reasonable. Expecting a child to never have any disciplinary problems at school is not reasonable. Instead, expecting that Jorge will reduce the number of aggressive outbursts at school from three to one per week may be attainable. Achievable should also include some consideration of the number of objectives. Having too many simultaneous active objectives for each goal is not realistic and probably not attainable!

- *Understandable*
  Writing objectives in a language and style that is understandable to the individual and family is essential. The objective should be practical, simple and easy to recall—after all, it is the individual's plan! Writing in an excessively professional style does not meet the intent of a person-centered plan. An objective that seeks to "restore euthymia" for a depressed mother with a history of mood swings may not be particularly meaningful or useful. Instead, an objective that states "Sheila and her husband

will report seven consecutive days of emotional stability and well-being within two months" meets the criteria for a well-written objective.

- *Time specific*
  Timeframes are specific to each objective and predict how long it will take the individual to achieve the change. Timeframes are not necessarily all the same, nor are they based on a program's established review dates for plans (i.e., quarterly, annually, and so on). Rather, they should be specific to the individual's and family's needs, strengths and desires for change. Most people are responsive to deadlines and due dates; they often motivate our actions and organize our energies. While setting realistic expectations is important, it is possible to create hope and momentum by establishing relatively short-term expectations for success.

- *Written in action-oriented and behavioral language*
  Given the historic emphasis in the mental health field on process over outcomes, it is not uncommon to find objectives written anticipating that the individual will "gain insight," "have understanding" or "be able to accept." These are not action-oriented changes that meet the criteria for an objective. Instead, the focus needs to be on what the individual and family will do differently with the insight, understanding, knowledge and acceptance that they gain through services. Oftentimes these cognitive processes are components of behavioral change, but the focus of the objective should be the actual demonstration of new skills and abilities.

- *Responsive to the individual's unique needs, challenges and recovery goals*
  The development of objectives needs to be informed by the assessment and the understanding reflected in the integrated summary. For example, if an individual is in the pre-contemplative stage about their use of alcohol and other drugs, then an objective that expects that "Jordan will meet with his narcotics anonymous sponsor weekly for the next 10 weeks" does not reflect an understanding of the individual's stage of recovery. However, if the individual has been in multiple treatment experiences, has had several relapses, has a sense of awareness of his or her addiction and is motivated to maintain sobriety, then an objective which states "Within two weeks Leroy will have an actionable plan to avoid his triggers (e.g., people, places and things) for heroin use" may be quite reasonable and meaningful.

- *Appropriate to the age, development and culture of the individual and family*
  Objectives must be tailored specifically to the individual as well as consider and include the family as appropriate. Not only should they build on strengths and resources but objectives also need to account for the unique

qualities and attributes of each person and family. These characteristics are often determined by factors such as age, development, race, ethnicity and culture. Expecting a young single woman from a family-centric culture to establish an independent residence may be an example of an inappropriate objective. Instead, an objective that focuses on resolution of cross-generational differences and expectations of autonomy and self-determination is consistent with a person-centered approach sensitive to issues of acculturation. Similarly, an objective seeking full-time employment for a 16-year-old boy may not be consistent with his age and development. An objective that focuses on his need to succeed in pre-vocational education is more likely to be acceptable to both he and his parents.

Risk and Choice

One of the more difficult challenges in setting objectives involves the questions of choice, preference, risk and the potential for failure. However the final selection of an objective must be a shared decision between the individual, family and provider team. Achieving true and meaningful shared decisions requires a complete as possible consideration of potential risks and benefits; inevitably each choice or option carries both. This is where the "productive interactions" between the provider team and the individual and family described in Wagner's Care Model (Chapter 1) occur. There is a tendency to focus only on the risks associated with action or treatment; too often the risks of not acting are overlooked and not fully considered. A transparent process that considers a range of options is often the best way to achieve common ground and shared decisions.

Providers have an inclination to be risk aversive advocates for vulnerable individuals and families—they often try to steer individuals and families towards choices and options that the provider feels are safe consistent with a duty of beneficence. With the best of intentions, providers often assume a somewhat paternalistic role and act in a controlling and restrictive fashion, even to the point of becoming somewhat dictatorial and offering a limited menu of "choices" for action that appears to be reasonable and protective. This can lead to conflict between the individual, family and provider, especially when the individual has other preferences and priorities, is less risk adverse, and feels constrained by the choices offered. Providers therefore must strive to lay out all the possible options and possible actions—including no intervention or treatment or "watchful waiting." A provider can suggest and encourage based upon their knowledge, experience and commitment to help, but ultimately the individual and other members of the team must reach agreement and find true common ground in developing objectives. This is what shared decision making is all about.

On the other hand, providers are vulnerable to becoming slavish adherents to the notion of individual choice and stand by passively while individuals make poor decisions that put them in harm's way. At some point leaving individuals and families to bear the "natural consequences" of their choices becomes a form of abandonment or neglect. What is a provider to do in the face of disagreement over individual preference and choice? Work towards finding common ground and a shared decision. The risk assessment identifies things like unsafe sex, suicidality, aggression, etc. These factors necessitate objectives that directly address these issues, especially in a hospital setting.

As mentioned in Chapter 2, Patricia Deegan and her associates have developed Intentional Care Performance Standards (Common Ground) to help bridge the gap between the principles of recovery and empowerment and the real-world application of these principles in the everyday work of direct service staff and their supervisors[1]. These standards attempt to provide a framework to reconcile some of the differences and tensions that can occur. Some of the principles of Intentional Care include the ideas that:

- individuals and families deserve to have the dignity of risk and right of failure
- providers should always be advocates of individual choice over a wide range of options
- individuals should not be abandoned to suffer "the natural consequences" of their choices
- neither providers nor individuals and families are failures if a choice results in failure

Figure 5.2 depicts some of these ideas in a simple graphic. The suggestion is that providers need to learn to find common ground somewhere between unacceptable provider control and unacceptable risk by the individual and family. Objectives need to be selected with awareness of and sensitivity to this underlying dynamic. Most individuals learn and grow from taking risk

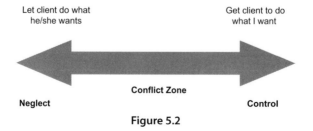

Let client do what he/she wants   Get client to do what I want

Conflict Zone

Neglect   Control

Figure 5.2

and learning from both their successes and failures. In a person-centered approach, individuals and families on the road to recovery should not be unreasonably denied the same opportunities.

III. MAKING IT HAPPEN

As stated in the quotation at the beginning of this chapter, opportunities are not created by luck; rather, they are built step by step. Attaining goals is not a matter of mere fortune. Goals are reached by establishing a shared understanding of priorities and barriers and pursuing objectives that are derived from a process of shared decision making and built on each increment of success over time.

Objectives must be created in the context of each individual's assessment, reflect an understanding of their unique strengths, needs and challenges, and respond to their specific individual goals. Yet there are many resources—ranging from books and manuals to various software programs and service planning tools—designed to help providers create service plans that do not follow these basic principles. Instead, these training and practice guides are often organized and driven by a predetermined inventory of problems largely driven by diagnosis.

In such approaches, if the diagnosis is depression, then the problem is predictably described as low mood, the goal is to feel better and the objective is to reduce symptoms on an established mood rating scale. There is nothing in this method that recognizes the unique needs, circumstances, concerns, desires and qualities of the individual nor does it account for differences driven by culture. This is the antithesis of a person-centered approach. Many providers believe that using these tools will assure that they meet regulatory and administrative requirements for planning, but they are unresponsive to the unique needs and abilities of each individual. In some instances, providers run the risk of sanctions for having cloned plans that are not individualized and not person-centered. Objectives cannot merely be chosen from a predetermined menu of diagnoses, problems and goals. Rather, they must always be responsive to the unique attributes and challenges of each person.

Examples

The study examples provide an opportunity to examine how the ideas and values of a person-centered approach can be applied to developing objectives for an individual plan.

Diana

Diana's objective is focused on her need to do better at school. It states: "Diana will have improved academic performance within two months as measured by having at least one week with 100% homework completion with a grade of C or better, as reported by her classroom teacher and parents." This is a good example of making the objective and what she needs to accomplish understandable to a young person as compared to using jargon like "improved academic performance." The objective is very meaningful, relates to her goal, is concrete, realistic and potentially achievable, for her. When attained, it will go a long way to helping reduce her conflict with her parents which is her goal, as well as begin to address some of her behavior problems at school, which is one of the other identified barriers.

JR

JR has many mental health barriers getting in the way of his becoming a cook in a restaurant. The plan's objective focuses on helping him to overcome several of his symptoms (lack of energy, depressed mood, anxiety around people) and move him closer towards his goal. It states "As a result of treatment services, JR will be able to manage his symptoms so that they do not interfere with his ability to look for work, as evidenced by his completion of at least two job applications for two consecutive weeks within three months." This objective also builds upon his previous work experience as one of his strengths.

Keisha

The objective "Keisha will be better able to manage her anxiety and fear of social interactions as evidenced by her participation in at least one service at her church within 90 days" is very responsive to the barriers that keep her from her goal. This objective provides Keisha and her provider team with a clear direction toward her goal of returning to her church. The objective would appear to be realistic and attainable considering that Keisha is in the active stage of change concerning her mental health issues.

Roberto

One of the principal barriers to Roberto's goal of being less anxious and able to return home is the lack of quality restorative sleep. Therefore, a focus on improving his sleep is quite appropriate. The objective "Roberto will sleep seven hours a night without interruption for five consecutive nights as evidenced by a nursing staff report" is a good starting point to help him reduce his anxiety. The objective also makes things clear to Roberto and to the staff who will be monitoring his progress. This plan contains a second objective that begins to address his problems with substance misuse and the way this complicates his stated long-term goal.

REFERENCE

1. www.intentionalcare.org.

CHAPTER 6

Interventions

Never Confuse Movement with Action.

Ernest Hemingway

I. STATING THE CASE

Interventions are the activities and services provided by the members of the team—including professional and/or peer providers, the individual and family themselves, or perhaps other sources of support within the community—that help the individual achieve their goals and objectives. Interventions may be synonymous with treatment, care, services, therapy, support, medications, programs, and so on. They are different than objectives but are also closely linked. While an objective describes desired changes in status, abilities, skills or behavior for the individual, the interventions detail the various steps taken by the team, or self-directed actions and/or the natural supports in the person's life to help bring about the changes described in the objective.

The elaboration of the interventions is simply a description of the methods of the plan. If the individual plan is a contract between the provider, individual and family, the goals are the ultimate deliverable, the objectives are the intermediate products and the interventions are the methods used to fulfill the agreement. The individual and family, as well as the provider, should view this contract as a mutual commitment to a series of actions designed to bring positive desired change.

In the roadmap analogy, interventions can be thought of as resources and equipment to support completion of the journey. Interventions can be compared to having the tires changed, adding fuel, stopping to get directions along the route or any sort of other assistance and guidance the individual and family needs to keep moving towards the destination. Interventions as described in an individual plan are the proposed resources and services to be delivered, accessed and engaged; they should specify who will do what, when, where and how often. Interventions are not entirely about "doing for" or "doing to" the individual and family. Instead, they

Treatment Planning for Person-Centered Care
http://dx.doi.org/10.1016/B978-0-12-394448-1.00006-8

describe how assistance can be provided to individuals so that they can achieve their desired outcomes. In a person-centered planning approach, natural supports (those people/agencies/organizations in the community who can become part of the recovery support system for the individual) should be considered and included as interventions, along with any self-directed action steps the individual himself/herself may take to achieve the objective. Of course, these natural support and self-directed interventions are non-billable as provider-delivered services.

Many providers are anxious about documenting the medical necessity of the services they provide and worry about their vulnerability to audits, recoupments and the like. But how and where medical necessity is demonstrated and documented is often poorly understood. The entire individual plan, including the assessment and the integrated summary, documents the medical necessity of services and supports billing along with other utilization review functions. However, possibly nowhere is the statement of medical necessity made more clear or succinct than in the section on interventions. If the objective is properly conceived and constructed, then the description of the intervention and its intended impact or purpose related to the objective makes the indication, appropriateness and efficacy of the service clear. This is at the heart of an operational definition of medical necessity and provides an unassailable justification for the services provide and billed.

Key Elements

There are five key elements to the specification of an intervention in the individual plan. It is not unlike the proverbial 5 Ws of journalism: *What, Who, When, Where and Why*. For purposes of developing an individual plan, the elements include:
- describing the modality or type of service or activity
- identifying who is responsible for the activity by name, role, function or discipline
- specifying the frequency, intensity and duration of the interventions
- specifying the location, as appropriate
- stating the purpose, intent or impact of the intervention in support of the objective

What

Specificity about exactly what is the proposed activity or service is extremely important, and the more specific the better. It is not sufficient merely to write "individual therapy." The interventions should specify as much as possible the type of therapy. Is it individual, family or group therapy? Is it psychodynamic or cognitive-behavioral? In some settings these service descriptions may be tied to billing codes and other documentation of provider activity.

Sometimes it is challenging to be this specific, but it is an important component of a person-centered recovery-oriented approach. To a degree, this attention to detail distinguishes this model from other methods for creating plans. There is real concern, especially in the mental health and addictive disorders fields, that individuals and families seeking services do not necessarily get what they need, but rather what the provider is able and willing to deliver. From the perspective of the individual, it can be compared to the old joke about Ford's Model T—you could get any color you wanted, as long as it was black. From the provider perspective, it is the risk that if all one has is a hammer, everything begins to look like a nail. Being able to be clear and specific in the description of the service makes elaboration of the other details much easier, more accurate, far more effective and person-centered.

Who

There is some latitude in specifying who is responsible for providing or assuring the provision of a particular service; it may require adaptation from setting to setting—for example, in a traditional outpatient private-practice treatment setting, specifying who may seem superfluous. However, in a multidisciplinary team, specifying who, not only by professional discipline but also by name, may be critically important in ensuring that every member of the team knows exactly who is responsible for what activity. In some settings, this specificity also helps to assure that providers are working within their scope of practice and are not being expected to do things beyond their capability, role or credentialing.

When the activity or service is the responsibility of the individual, family or other supports within the community, specifying who is responsible may take on another level of significance or importance. Being explicit and ensuring that everyone on the team knows their role helps to ensure follow-through and completion. For the purposes of record audits (either conducted internally by the organization or externally by utilization reviewers, accreditation and licensing entities, funding sources, and so on), it is helpful for these auditors to have an understanding of who the team members are (by either credential, title, discipline, organization or association). Merely identifying a name does not inform the reviewer. In some settings, it may be useful to divide those activities for which the individual, family or other natural supports have direct responsibility from those of the provider. When review of the individual plan for documentation of medical necessity and billing is a consideration, making this distinction may reduce confusion.

When
There are three components to describing the time elements of an intervention. These include the following:
- *Frequency*: This should include a description of how often the service is to be provided within the timeframe of the objective. For example, is it a one-time event, twice a week, weekly, once a month or quarterly.
- *Intensity*: Is the service provided for 30 minutes or one hour?
- *Duration*: Is the service provided over one month or two months, or for a more extended time?

There are some services or interventions for which this level of specificity is difficult to achieve, particularly activities such as case management/coordination and others that are often provided on an as needed basis. For the purposes of medical necessity documentation, specifying either upper or lower limits of service frequency, intensity and duration can satisfy this requirement as well as clarify expectations and help to organize team resources.

Where
In some situations, this item may be unnecessary to specify and may well be assumed to be at one location or in one setting. However, in a rehabilitation model, the provision of field-based *in situ* or on-site services in a number of different locations in the community, such as at home, school or work, is increasingly becoming the norm. In such circumstances, there may be value in specifying the location of the intervention. Providing services in sites away from a clinic or facility often enhances the efficacy of the interventions.

Why
While all five elements specifying an intervention are important, the description of the intended purpose, impact or outcome of the service is perhaps the most critical. This description should closely relate to the *what* of the intervention and describe the role of this service or activity in support of the desired change specified in the objective. It is in essence a statement

about the efficacy of the service and speaks to the likelihood of it being effective. A clear statement of the intended purpose or impact of each intervention is probably the most explicit statement of medical necessity for each service provided. When there is a close linkage between what is expected to occur as a result of the service and the outcome or objective, the medical necessity of the service is beyond question. In contrast, when the intended purpose or impact of the service is not made explicit, it can be difficult to justify the service as part of a change strategy. This clarity helps the provider as well as the individual and family to understand the expectations and values of each intervention and service. In turn, this understanding promotes engagement and change.

For example, it is not sufficient to simply specify group psychotherapy as the intervention. Rather, a brief phrase that describes how group therapy will help that individual or family meet their objective should also be included. In other words, it is conceivable that everyone in the group therapy session may be working on a different issue and objective, each of them gaining from the experience of group therapy unique and relevant information for their own plan and stated objective. In addition, there are many different types of groups, so stating the type/name of the group can also help enhance the individual's understanding of the purpose of the group, such as anger management, cognitive behavioral therapy, family therapy, medication education, etc.

The link between the objective and the intent of the intervention should have "face validity" efficacy. Services noted in the plan should be linked (i.e., have a logical relationship) to the objective they are intended to achieve, e.g., Coping with Anger group for reducing aggression or Dialectical Behavioral Therapy (DBT) for improving emotional regulation and reducing self-injury. Frequently, this logical link breaks down, and it is not unusual to see a large number of services listed under an objective that do not appear to be directly related.

At the time of initiation of a new plan or objective, the interventions selected and included should be efficacious, i.e., there is a reasonable likelihood that they will be effective; over time the actual outcome will determine whether or not it was in fact effective. There should be a reasonable link between the desired changes and the service. The statement of purpose or impact that is part of specifying an intervention should make the efficacy—the likely effectiveness of the intervention—clear to the individual as well as the provider.

Whenever possible, evidence-based practices/interventions (EBPs) should be used as they are by definition the most efficacious approach when they are appropriately linked to a diagnosis and/or the specific change described in the objective. That said it is not required, *per se*, that there be strong evidence linking the intervention to the desired change—in many cases such evidence does not exist. However, when there are relevant and applicable EBPs they should be included in the interventions; if not, there should be a very clear explanation as to why another service strategy has been selected.

The Number of Services

Although not included in the 5 Ws, the question of how many services or interventions should be provided is a closely linked issue to also consider. Unfortunately, there is no magic number or easy guideline. It is similar to the story of the Three Bears and their porridge—not too many and not too few is just right. Neither the individual and family nor the provider members of the team should feel overwhelmed with too much to do. By the same token, neither should there be so little activity that change is not likely to occur in the specified timeframe.

Determining the optimal array of services and interventions is highly dependent on a number of factors beyond the needs of the individual and family, including the objective itself, the extent or complexity of their challenges and their strengths. This said, the risk of having either too few or too many interventions needs to be considered. In general, every member of the team is likely to contribute to helping the individual and family achieve their objective. Accordingly, over time, the interventions and services should include and reflect the rich resources of the team and the natural supports of the community. The more complex and challenging the objective, the greater the number and range of services that are likely to be necessary to achieve the objective.

Choice and Shared Decision Making

Possibly nowhere is the issue of choice by the individual and the family more critical or essential than in the decisions made about interventions. There may be indicated services or treatments that are simply not acceptable to the individual and family, based upon their past experiences, preferences, culture and a wealth of other factors. The choice and preference of the individual must reign supreme in making decisions about what can be provided to help them attain their objectives and goals. Choice is one of the central features of a person-centered, recovery-oriented approach to providing mental health and addictive disorders services.

But what to choose and how to choose it? It has been said that shared decision making is all about making recovery real[1]. Although the values and principles of shared decision making are threaded throughout person-centered and recovery-oriented planning, it is in the selection of interventions and treatments that the collaboration and partnership in making shared decisions is at the center of the task. Ideally, no intervention is included in a person-centered plan without the informed and consensual decision of the person seeking help and the provider team.

There is growing understanding and interest in how approaches to shared decision making emerging in the physical health arena may be adapted to the mental health field. However, currently there is limited research and few decision aids or other material on shared decision making specific to the mental health context[2]. What is known is that emotional reactions to risky situations often diverge from cognitive assessments of those risks[3].

According to Deegan, decisional conflict is often related to the level of certainty that is available regarding treatment options[1]. Treatment options that have a strong evidence base and have risen to the level of a standard of care—such as antibiotics in the case of bacterial infection—rarely cause decisional conflict. However, when the benefits of treatment are not so well known, or when treatment carries a risk of significant side effects— such as the risk of metabolic dysregulation following the use of psychiatric medication—decisional conflict is more common. In the process of developing a person-centered recovery plan and choosing interventions to help attaining goals and objectives, the individual and the family as well as the provider are challenged by decisional uncertainty and as a result decisional conflict. This pertains in many instances to the entire spectrum of interventions be they biological or psychosocial.

In an effort to help resolve decisional uncertainty, decision aids are tools used to help individuals understand and clarify their choices and preferences in regard to a discrete decision. Decision aids attempt to help the individual understand the potential risks and benefits associated with any intervention—as well as the risk of inaction. Decision aids are offered in a variety of forms, from printed brochures to interactive electronic tools. Some are designed to be completed by the individual in advance of developing the person-centered plan; others are designed for completion in the course of the planning meeting. However, there are relatively few decision aids available regarding interventions commonly considered in a wellness and recovery plan for mental health and addictive disorders services. In the face of this, many individuals will defer to the provider's expertise and ask them to simply make a decision because they feel overwhelmed or unsettled by the choice and the uncertainty.

What then is the role of the provider in trying to help the individual make decisions about interventions to be included in the plan? The provider's role is to draw upon his or her expertise and bring forward ideas, possibilities and suggestions about action steps that might be effective in helping the individual to bring about the changes described in the objective. It's important to remember that interventions and their intended impact or purpose are specific to an object and should be presented in that context. It is also the provider's responsibility to be open, honest and transparent and to acknowledge their own lack of certainty or lack of knowledge regarding solutions and strategies. Perhaps most important of all it is the provider's responsibility to listen, question, elicit and carefully consider the individual's and family's idea about what might be most effective or helpful.

Mental Health America has done an excellent job of providing guidance to individuals and families seeking services about how to participate effectively in a shared decision-making process. Providers can learn a lot about their own role by better understanding the experience and perspective of the person served. Here are some suggestions for persons served about how best to engage with their provider[4]:

If you think you are not being heard:
> Tell your provider that your concern is important to you and that you want to talk it over. Explain why it matters to you and ask what can be done.

If you have doubts about an intervention that your provider recommends:
> Explain your doubts and ask for more information.

If your doctor suggests a treatment you object to:
> Explain why you object and ask if there are other options to try.

If you feel the doctor is deciding for you:
> Tell the provider you want to take part in deciding about the interventions on your plan and you would like to use shared decision making. Shared decision making is a new concept, so your provider may not be comfortable or familiar with it

If you feel the doctor is rushing past your concern because of time:
> You can save time by preparing for your appointment. By writing down your questions and concerns beforehand, you can quickly inform the provider about how you are doing and what you need.

If you feel like you and your provider are not understanding each other:

> Ask to bring a person you trust to your appointment. It could be a trusted friend, an advocate, a peer specialist or a family member. The presence of another person can help you and your doctor listen carefully to each other.

In the midst of an effort to engage the individual and family in shared decision making, there may at times be requests for services from the individual and family that the provider is unable to address. This may be due to a lack of resources or access, but may also result from a request that the provider feels is likely to be ineffective or perhaps even harmful. While a commitment to individual and family preference is the driving force in creating the individual plan, providers should be careful about agreeing to activities that they believe will result in the wasteful use of limited resources or negative outcomes. At the same time, caution must be taken to ensure that providers do not inappropriately use these concerns as an excuse to avoid going beyond usual practice and failing to respect the preferences and choice of individuals.

In some settings and for some groups, there have been recent service innovations that have placed an emphasis on a "whatever it takes" approach to providing services—albeit within some boundaries of reasonableness and legality. The success of programs such as California's AB 2034 initiative to help homeless mentally ill people, a host of supported housing programs by the Corporation for Supported Housing, and New York State's Medicaid funded "PROS" program (Personalized Recovery Oriented Services) are only a few examples of flexible, humanistic and compassionate approaches to providing services driven by individual needs rather than proscribed program menus[5,6]. This is the essence of person-centeredness and requires a significant rethinking of service provision to succeed—on the part of direct-service providers as well as administrators and policy makers. Flexibility can promote recovery and foster significant creativity in person-centered problem solving and innovative approaches to meeting the needs of individuals and families. Hopefully there will be further opportunities for such flexibility and changes in service-delivery systems. Unfortunately, most providers still work within systems that are far more constrained and limited in terms of what is acceptable and what is reimbursable.

The commitment to culturally competent care should always be a consideration in deciding upon and selecting interventions. There may be instances when individuals and families desire services consistent with their cultural beliefs and experience. Sometimes these preferences extend beyond what the traditional service-delivery system can readily provide. Acknowledgment, support and creative problem solving can help individuals and families obtain services consistent with their expressed preferences and values. As much as possible, services should be sensitive to culturally determined choice. Providing services that are culturally alien or dystonic will not likely be effective and may result in driving the individual and family away. Interventions that are consistent with cultural values and experience will foster engagement and success.

While making every effort to respect and honor choice and preference, providers cannot reasonably be expected to deliver a substantial amount of services for which they cannot be reimbursed, particularly if those interventions are of questionable value from the provider's perspective. In these circumstances, a respectful acknowledgment of the differences must be made. In many instances, a workable resolution is for the provider to help the individual and family find access to those desired services and activities that the provider is unable to deliver. Again, the caveat must be clear: providers cannot facilitate activities that they believe present a significant risk of harm to the individual. Rather, they have an important obligation to make their concerns clear to all.

Decisions by individuals and families to refuse a particular intervention or to decline services entirely can be equally problematic. If the individual and family have been able to successfully identify a goal, then motivational interviewing and enhancement techniques might be helpful in fostering engagement and promoting participation. Regardless, mindfulness of the process as well as the willingness by the provider to discuss and negotiate as differences emerge can help to ensure that services and plans are effective while at the same time preserving individual rights, dignity and respect.

Shared Care Planning

Both providers and persons seeking services seem to find advantages in providing services that address the individual's general health, mental health and addiction issues in a coordinated and integrated fashion[7]. Studies report high levels of provider satisfaction with the ability to coordinate and manage care and decrease access barriers. The benefits can be seen in reduction of hospital admission and access to appropriate medical care and assuring that the individual is receiving the appropriate care at the right time, in the right place[8].

There is substantial data from the medical and behavioral literature that integration of care and collaboration is an optimal model that yields better outcomes, and "shared care plans" are frequently referenced as a strategy for promoting integration. According to a seminal report from the Milbank Memorial Fund, "Shared plans of care can also significantly enhance the quality of care, prevent duplication of services, and reduce risk of adverse events"[9]. Ideally shared care plans are bi-directional and regardless of the configuration of the service delivery system, general health, mental health and addiction services providers should all know about the active objectives that are the current focus of the recovery plan and the totality of the interventions provided to promote health and wellness outcomes. There is some hope that electronic health records (EHRs) will provide a solution to this problem, but experience from the field is that information management solutions in the general medical field and behavioral health for the most part have limited interoperability. As a result, there are few if any models available for shared care planning.

This is a point in the planning process where referring back to the integrated summary can be of tremendous value—especially when the individual has co-occurring needs that impact any combination of their physical health, mental health and challenges with addiction. In these instances, the integrated summary should offer some insight and understanding about the interrelationships between these three facets of a person's life, and that understanding should inform not only the objectives that are developed but also the interventions. In other words, the person-centered plan to support the individual's wellness and recovery journey should include all interventions and treatments that are being offered or provided in an effort to help the individual—and this includes medical treatments offered by a primary care provider or medical specialist.

The totality of all of the action steps taken to help the individual meet an objective plan, and the ways in which multidisciplinary and transdisciplinary interventions should all be noted and included in the interventions section—even when another provider may be responsible for the service. In situations where services are not co-located in the same physical plant and there is no actual physical or electronic person-centered shared care plan, other means to establish and maintain active bi-directional—or even tri-directional—communication to promote collaboration and integration of services among all the involved providers should be made. In this way the plan is not just a behavioral health recovery plan but also a holistic and integrated plan to support the individual's overall health and wellness.

It is said that all health care is local and varies substantially from community to community. The strategies to increase care collaboration and integration of behavioral health and primary care inevitably must build on the configuration and local organization of resources. Efforts to create shared care plans can be a catalyst for efforts at improved bi-directional integration. Implementation of the Affordable Care Act and its focus on the creation of person-centered health care homes may help to advance this practice[10].

The Use of Natural Supports

A person-centered approach to planning should include and involve resources beyond the professionals and paid providers working with the individual and family. The professional provider does not always have all the answers or resources that are needed to help individuals and families meet their goals. Yet, at the same time, there are many people in the person's life or other resources within the community that may be a source of help and assistance. One component of identifying strengths for each individual should be identifying these natural supports and resources. This is, in part, why strengths are specified and tied to each objective—they are part of the building blocks and resources available to help create a menu of services and activities in support of the objective.

Natural supports include those individuals, organizations, institutions and resources available to the individual and family, which are not part of the formal mental health and addictive disorders service-delivery system. Natural supports in the community can include extended family, neighbors, friends, volunteers, other individuals in recovery, clergy and traditional healers (e.g., tribal elders, curanderos, and so on), as well as representatives of community agencies or any other resources acceptable to the individual and family. The individual and family themselves are often aware of and highly knowledgeable about resources in their own community, and should be encouraged to identify and consider these supports and assistance.

The value and attraction of natural supports is that, over time, they can become a part of the individual's and family's strengths and resources and help to lessen their dependence on professional services. The connections with these individuals and organizations can help promote recovery and wellness; they further support community integration, reduce isolation, expand interests, help to overcome stigma, increase motivation for recovery and promote friendship and social networking. In considering a possible transition away from a dependence on the provider, access to these supports and non-specialized services can be critical to success and long-term community stability. The use of natural supports is not intended to replace the provider, but rather to augment and enhance the team and success of the individual plan. The individual and family are still in need of the provider's assistance, skills, knowledge and expertise, but may need less professional time if they have access to community resources and supports. Joan King, Integrated Health Senior Consultant at the National Council, notes that improved health for people can be encouraged by the use of "a support system comprised of people who believed in you and your capacity for change even before you did"[11]. That person may be a provider, a peer or perhaps someone else in the person's natural support system who can be identified in the plan as a supporter.

There is ever-increasing evidence of the value and effectiveness of peer-based services, both in a traditional treatment setting and in consumer-operated services, for individuals seeking mental health as well as addictive disorders services[12]. This growth in peer support has been so robust that a recent US national survey identified a total of 7467 such mental health mutual support groups and consumer-operated services—a figure exceeding the number of traditional mental health organizations[13]. Peer supporters are those staff members with a lived experience who can engage in a meaningful and reciprocal dialog with people receiving services, both in an informal and formal manner. "There are many tasks performed by peer support specialists that may include assisting their peers in articulating their goals for recovery, learning and practicing new skills, helping them monitor their progress, assisting them in their treatment, modeling effective coping techniques and self-help strategies based on the specialist's own recovery experience, and supporting them in advocating for themselves to obtain effective services"[14]. A well-developed plan should appropriately include access to such services as part of an overall strategy to meet the individual's goals and objectives.

Stages of Change and Phases of Recovery

Interventions need to be person specific, not diagnosis specific. One aspect of being person-centered is the recognition of each individual's and family's stage of recovery and their current status in a stage-wise approach to under-standing change. Matching interventions to the phase of recovery requires assessment of the stage and the individual. For example, individuals who have co-occurring substance abuse and psychiatric issues might benefit most from interventions that are small, incremental and concrete. For an individual who is in a pre-contemplative stage of recovery, the most appro-priate interventions might include basic help and support to assure safety and well-being along with motivational enhancement strategies and educational opportunities, which together can help them progress to the contemplation stage. On the other hand, if the person is actively seeking treatment for substance dependence, then interventions could be appropriately geared towards learning new skills and supports in order to achieve abstinence and to improve stability and sobriety.

Evidence-Based Practices

A person-centered approach should strike an appropriate balance between the use of evidence-based practices (EBPs) at all stages of the recovery process and the unique needs, preferences and values of the individual and family. Typically, "evidence" includes scientific studies as well as professional consensus regarding promising approaches and efficacious services. However, the ultimate demonstration of evidence is the fit between the intervention and the individual at a particular point in time as judged by the participation and response of the individual (i.e., the difference between efficacy and actual effectiveness). There are also concerns about the appropriateness of EBPs for multicultural populations. This has led to a growing interest in community defined practices which should also be considered in crafting a plan and identifying efficacious interventions[15].

There is an inherent tension in the commitment to person-centered care and the increasing emphasis placed on providing evidence-based services. There is little in the literature that speaks to reconciling the differences and discrepancies that can exist between what science predicts as being most efficacious and the variability of personal choice and preference. While most individuals and families want the very best care and service, this does not always mean they are prepared to accept, without question, the recommendations of providers.

Brent James, MD, of Intermountain Health Systems, has attempted to resolve this problem in an approach that he describes as "mass customization"[16]. Using the proverbial 80/20 split, he posits that all humans share about 80% of their genetics and characteristics with everyone else—we are all part of the *mass*. But the other 20% is what makes each person truly unique and individual. This idea can be applied to *customize* evidence-based practices to meet individual preference and honor a commitment to person-centered services. The 80% core should help to organize the bulk of the practice; it contains what is probably most effective most of the time. In the remaining 20%, the provider and individual need to consider how to make changes and accommodations so that personal preference is respected without unduly compromising the value of services with demonstrable benefit.

Ideally, the mental health and addictive disorders fields will evolve to a point where matching individuals' needs and objectives to the most effective interventions is a standard and routine procedure. There is some data now to suggest the merit of using evidence-based research to specify interventions in the plan. *The Journal of Studies on Alcohol* notes that persons who are appropriately matched to treatment will show better outcomes than those who are unmatched or mismatched[17].

Despite the intense interest in evidence-based practices, there has been little research done on how to best include them in individual person-centered plans. This is partly due to the very nature of the practices themselves. Evidence-based practices, such as assertive community treatment (ACT), supported employment or integrated dual diagnosis treatment, are not discrete interventions that can readily be identified in a service plan. For the most part there is no billing code attached to any of these practices or services. Rather, they reflect a set of values and principles, the availability of an array of services, an approach to understanding individual needs and the organization of service-delivery systems. Much of the effort to implement these practices is required at a systems and organizational level.

For example, supported employment appears to be a very effective approach to helping individuals with severe mental illness who are motivated to return to work succeed in attaining and maintaining employment[18]. It involves a complex mix of case management, supports and rehabilitative skill development in coordination with other services as each person's individual barriers to successful employment are addressed and resolved. The real success in the implementation of supported employment at an individual level lies in the ability of providers to develop objectives and organize interventions both consistent with the model and responsive to the unique needs of each person. The clear articulation of interventions and services is where the real implementation of evidence-based practices occurs.

Level of Care

Although it may seem perfectly obvious, interventions also need to match the level of care needed and chosen by the individual. For example, if the assessment process, including the use of tools such as the American Society of Addiction Medicine's (ASAM) level of care tool, the *Treatment Criteria for*

Substance-Related, Addictive, and Co-Occurring Conditions and the Level Of Care and Utilization Scale (LOCUS) (described in detail in Chapter 2), determines that the individual needs outpatient care, then developing interventions that are unattainable or unavailable within that setting is unrealistic.

It is surprising how often there is a mismatch between the individual's needs, the level of care assigned and the services provided. This is another example of the problem of providing services simply because they are what is available and offered by the provider rather than what is needed by the individual and family. The LOCUS and ASAM level-of-care tools, as well as others, can be helpful in describing the range of services and interventions that should be available at each level of care. These systematic approaches to matching need with level of care can be a useful resource in designing systems of care as well as individual plans. Although frequently a challenging task for providers, the specification of interventions should not be that difficult. If the objective is clearly stated and the individual's and family's strengths are identified, then deciding upon the activities to help promote the desired change should be rather straightforward. There are a few simple guidelines that can help all of the members of the team properly complete this important part of the planning process.

II. CREATING THE SOLUTION

Following an assessment and integrated summary, the essential components of the person-centered plan are:
- *Goals: what the individual wants to change or accomplish*
- *Objectives: how the individual will accomplish the goals*
- *Interventions: what the individual needs in terms of services and community resources to meet the objectives*

These three elements should always be found in some fashion on individual plan forms and documents. Some care systems have developed individual service plan forms that are structured with the italicized phrases as headings, instead of the traditional goals, objectives and interventions[19]. The challenge to successful individual person-centered planning goes well beyond forms, but for many providers having such prompts can help to structure the task and support the development of a plan that is more responsive to individual needs and concerns.

There are four basic strategies for providers to consider in developing interventions for individual person-centered, recovery-oriented plans.

Providers should approach the task of identifying interventions and services to meet specific objectives with:

1. an understanding of the individual from a strengths-based, cultural, recovery stage and other perspectives as identified in the integrated summary
2. complete knowledge and understanding of the full scope of services available within the organization that can be provided directly
3. extensive knowledge of the resources available in the community that extend beyond the formal care system and scope of practice
4. an accurate understanding of the preferences of the individual and family for the types of services and levels of care that they find acceptable

Matching Interventions to Stages

Table 6.1, developed for the California State Hospitals by Nirbhay Singh, PhD, can be a useful tool for providers in trying to match interventions with the individual's and family's stage of change. Knowing the stage is important because when interventions are not matched, they are likely to be inappropriate and ineffective. Engagement and participation in the intervention is critical for its success, and not all interventions are appropriate at a particular stage. Individuals who are in the pre-contemplative stage, or overwhelmed by their illness, need a very different approach than those that are actively involved in their own recovery. More than prescribing specific services, as these must be determined by the objective, Table 6.1 provides recommendations and suggestions for how best to approach the individual and family and how to frame or structure an intervention or service.

Throughout the entire process of developing a plan, dialog, participation and meaningful involvement are all essential—and this is particularly true in making decisions about action steps to promote change. As with most things, it is not just about what is done but also about *how* it is done. The conversation and engagement with an individual and family in pre-contemplation are necessary and can be different from the discussions at later stages. Recognition of this continuum, and the proper adjustment of strategies to promote involvement and participation, can be the keys to success in helping the individual and family move from one stage to the next.

Service Array

Individuals' and families' needs and challenges should be understood from a broad bio-psycho-social perspective. *Bio* should include concerns related to physical status and well-being, *psycho* is related to the individual's internal

Table 6.1 Stages of Change Continuum and Matching of Interventions

Stages of Change Continuum	Approaches to Person-Centered Planning
Stage 1: Pre-Contemplation	
Denial	Consciousness-raising interventions, e.g., sharing observations, confronting the individual with specific consequences of their behavior
Unwillingness to change	Therapeutic alliance or relationship building with the provider; understanding and emotional relationship
Unaware of having a disease, disorder, disability or deficit	Nonpossessive warmth—the provider relates to the person as a worthwhile human being; shows unconditional acceptance of the person (as opposed to the behavior, e.g., addiction, offense)
Unaware of the causes and consequences of the disease, disorder, disability or deficit	Empathic understanding—extent to which the provider understands what the individual is experiencing from the individual's frame of reference
Unaware of the need for treatment and rehabilitation	Catharsis—expression of emotion; provider engages in active listening skills, empathic observations and gentle confrontation (reality checks)
Lack of motivation to engage in treatment and rehabilitation	Motivational interviewing—a person-centered, directive method for enhancing intrinsic motivation to change by helping the individual to explore and resolve his or her "issues"; provider facilitates the individual to resolve his or her ambivalence with regard to change. Based on four general principles for providers: express empathy, develop discrepancy, roll with resistance, and support self-efficacy
	The intervention—confronting the individual in a nonjudgmental, caring and loving manner
	Provider approaches—authoritarian approaches to behavior change lead to greater resistance to engage in change
	Promote emotional well-being—poor emotional well-being inhibits an individual's progress, positive well-being facilitates positive intervention outcomes
	Continue with pre-contemplative stage consciousness-raising interventions and slowly introduce new interventions

Table 6.1 Stages of Change Continuum and Matching of Interventions—*cont'd*

Stages of Change Continuum	Approaches to Person-Centered Planning
Stage 2: Contemplation	
Aware of their issues ("problems")	Receptive to bibliotherapy interventions
Know the need for change	Receptive to educational interventions
Not yet committed to change	Pre-suppositional questions—used to encourage individuals to examine and evaluate their issues, situation or predicament. Providers can use pre-suppositional questions to think about change in a non-threatening context. As an example, consider an individual who thinks he does not have a problem. The provider's pre-suppositional question could be, "Let's agree that what you are saying is true…How would you know when you are ready to be discharged?" Circular questions—used in a nonthreatening manner to ask a question about the individual's issues, situation or predicament from the perspective of an outsider
	Miracle questions—used as a method to assist an individual in imaging change and with goal setting. Classic example: "Suppose you go to bed tonight, and while you are asleep a miracle happens and all your issues, situations or predicaments disappear. Everything is resolved to your liking. When you wake up in the morning, how will you know that the miracle happened? What would be the first thing you would notice that is different?"
Stage 3: Preparation	
Ready to change	Continue with contemplative stage awareness enhancing interventions and slowly introduce new interventions
Need to set goals and priorities for future change	Providers encourage the individual's sense of "self-liberation" and foster a sense of personal recovery by taking control of his or her life
Receptive to treatment plans that include specific focus of interventions, objectives and intervention plans	Discrimination training and stimulus control interventions can be introduced at this stage. The provider enhances the individual's awareness of the conditions that give rise to his issues, situations or predicaments. Focus is on the presence or absence of antecedents, setting events and establishing operations.

Continued

Table 6.1 Stages of Change Continuum and Matching of Interventions—*cont'd*

Stages of Change Continuum	Approaches to Person-Centered Planning
	Scaling question—used as a tool by the individual to "buy into" the treatment planning process. Providers can use it to obtain a quantitative measure of the individual's issues, situation or predicament, as perceived and rated by the individual and then assist the individual to think about the next step in the change process. Example: "On a scale of 1 to 10, with 1 being totally not ready and 10 being totally ready, how would you rate your current readiness to be discharged?" If the individual self-rates as a 4, the provider can follow this up with, "During the next month, what steps can you take or what can you work on to get from 4 to 5?" Scaling questions can be used to (a) obtain a quantitative baseline, (b) assist the individual to take the next step in the process of recovery, and (c) encourage the individual to achieve recovery by successive approximations (i.e., in incremental steps—one point at a time, one month at a time).

Stage 4: Action

Make successful efforts to change	Cognitive-behavioral approaches
Develop and implement strategies to overcome barriers	Explore and correct faulty cognitions—catastrophizing, overgeneralizing, magnification, excessive responsibility, dichotomous thinking, selective abstraction
Requires considerable self-effort	Learning-based approaches
Noticeable behavioral change takes place	Action-oriented approaches
Target behaviors are under self-control, ranging from a day to six months	Skills that support rehabilitation
Meet discharge criteria	Adapt and adjust to situations to facilitate maintenance
Be discharged	Develop personal wellness recovery plans
Maintain wellness and enhance functional status with minimum professional involvement	Utilize coping skills in the rhythm of life, without spiraling down (i.e., if substance use is a problem, cope with distressing or faulty cognitions without using drugs)

Table 6.1 Stages of Change Continuum and Matching of Interventions—*cont'd*

Stages of Change Continuum	Approaches to Person-Centered Planning
Live in environments of choice	Learn about mindfulness, especially unconditional acceptance, loving kindness, compassion for self and others, and letting go
Be empowered and hopeful Engage in self-determination through appropriate choice-making	
Stage 6: Evaluation	
Assess personal outcomes Obtain social validation and feedback from significant others	Continue with dynamic change process Preempt relapse by engaging in personal wellness recovery plan
	Accept that change is a spiral rather than a linear process Practice and use mindfulness strategies

emotional and cognitive functioning, and *social* is associated with the surrounding external milieu. Services and interventions should ultimately reflect the same broad and holistic approach to supporting change. Although not every individual and family will have needs and challenges in each of these three domains, thinking about biological, psychological and social interventions can be a useful construct for contemplating the task of specifying an intervention.

- *Biological interventions*
  In general, biological interventions will involve providers such as physicians, dentists, chiropractors, nurses, nutritionists, laboratory personnel, and so on. In some cases, alternative approaches such as biofeedback, physical therapy and acupuncture may also be included.
- *Psychological interventions*
  This includes the variety of psychotherapies that range from traditional psychodynamic individual therapy to multi-family psychotherapy; psychologists, social workers, marriage and family therapists, counselors, pastors and peers, among others, typically provide therapy. The focus on such interventions is generally on the affective and cognitive functioning of the individual but may also address other needs such as behavior and impulse control, interpersonal relationships and family dynamics.

- *Social interventions*

  This range of services and activities often involves case managers and others related to care coordination at the interface of the individual and family, the community and the formal care system. Facilitation, linkage, brokerage and monitoring are all within the scope of these activities. These services are often provided in the community or in the home as compared to an office or facility setting. Many times these services will focus on helping the individual and family develop and apply skills that help to promote their recovery and sustain them in the community. Occupational therapy and other rehabilitation providers can also play an important role.

The aforementioned list is by no means intended to be exhaustive or complete. Rather, it is intended to provide some prompts for considering a broad array of services, interventions and activities as well as provider types. This multidimensional approach should be considered in specifying interventions, and developing an effective array of services to help the individual and family achieve their objectives and goals.

Trauma-Informed Interventions

Trauma-informed organizations, programs and services are based on an understanding of the vulnerabilities or triggers of trauma survivors that traditional service delivery approaches may exacerbate, so that these services and programs can be more supportive and avoid re-traumatization. Trauma-specific interventions are designed specifically to address the consequences of trauma in the individual and to facilitate healing[20]. The following are some well-known trauma-specific interventions based upon psychosocial educational empowerment principles that have been used extensively in public system settings.

- *Addiction and Trauma Recovery Integration Model (ATRIUM)*

  Twelve-session recovery model designed for groups as well as for individuals and their therapists and counselors. The acronym ATRIUM is meant to suggest that the recovery groups are a starting point for healing and recovery. This model has been used in local prisons, jail diversion projects, AIDS programs and drop-in centers for survivors. ATRIUM is a model intended to bring together peer support, psycho-education, interpersonal skills training, meditation, creative expression, spirituality and community action to support survivors in addressing and healing from trauma.

- *Essence of Being Real*

  A peer-to-peer structure intended to address the effects of trauma. This model is particularly helpful for survivor groups (including abuse, disaster, crime, shelter populations and others), first responders and frontline service providers and agency staff. The model is appropriate for all populations and is geared to promoting relationships rather than focusing on the "bad stuff that happened."

- *Risking Connection*
Risking Connection is intended to be a trauma-informed model aimed at mental health, public health and substance abuse staff at various levels of education and training. There are several audience-specific adaptations of the model, including clergy, domestic violence advocates and agencies serving children. Risking Connection emphasizes concepts of empowerment, connection and collaboration. The model addresses issues like understanding how trauma hurts, using the relationship and connection as a treatment tool, keeping a trauma framework when responding to crises such as self-injury and suicidal depression, working with dissociation and self-awareness, and transforming vicarious traumatization.

- *Sanctuary Mode*
The goal of the Sanctuary Model is to help children who have experienced the damaging effects of interpersonal violence, abuse and trauma. The model is intended for use by residential treatment settings for children, public schools, domestic violence shelters, homeless shelters, group homes, outpatient and community-based settings, juvenile justice programs, substance abuse programs, parenting support programs, acute care settings and other programs aimed at assisting children. The Sanctuary Model's approach helps organizations to create a truly collaborative and healing environment that improves efficacy in the treatment of traumatized individuals, reduces restraints and other coercive practices, builds cross-functional teams and improves staff morale and retention.

- *Seeking Safety*
Designed to be a therapy for trauma, post-traumatic stress disorder (PTSD) and substance abuse, this model works for individuals or with groups, with men, women or with mixed-gender groups, and can be used in a variety of settings (e.g., outpatient, inpatient, residential). The key principles of Seeking Safety are safety as the overarching goal, integrated treatment, a focus on ideals to counteract the loss of ideals in both PTSD and substance abuse, knowledge of four content areas (cognitive, behavioral, interpersonal and case management) and attention to clinician processes.

- *Trauma, Addictions, Mental Health, and Recovery (TAMAR) Model*
  TAMAR Trauma Treatment Group Model is a structured, manualized, 15-week intervention combining psycho-educational approaches with expressive therapies. It is designed for women and men with histories of trauma in correctional systems. Groups are run inside detention centers, in state psychiatric hospitals and in the community. The Trauma Addictions Mental Health and Recovery Treatment Manual provides basic education on trauma, its developmental effects on symptoms and current functioning, symptom appraisal and management, the impact of early chaotic relationships on health care needs, the development of coping skills, preventive education concerning pregnancy and sexually transmitted diseases, sexuality, and help in dealing with role loss and parenting issues.
- *Trauma Affect Regulation: Guide for Education and Therapy (TARGET)*
  TARGET is a model designed for use by organizations and professionals with a broad range of experience with and understanding of trauma. TARGET works with all disciplines and can be used in all levels of care for adults and children and is an educational and therapeutic approach for the prevention and treatment of complex PTSD. This model provides practical skills that can be used by trauma survivors and family members to de-escalate and regulate extreme emotions, manage intrusive trauma memories experienced in daily life and restore the capacity for information processing and memory.
- *Trauma Recovery and Empowerment Model (TREM and M-TREM)*
  The Trauma Recovery and Empowerment Model is intended for trauma survivors, particularly those with exposure to physical or sexual violence. This model is gender specific: TREM for women and M-TREM for men. This model has been implemented in mental health, substance abuse, co-occurring disorders and criminal justice settings, and is appropriate for a full range of disciplines.

Peer Support

Probably the most movement forward in recovery and wellness systems transformation and practice over the past 10 years has been the recognition of the value and inclusion of peer support systems by provider organizations—including hospitals—to assist the person seeking help at multiple stages of their recovery journey. Peer supporters (typically referred to as peer support specialists, peer recovery coaches, peer bridgers, whole health peer coaches, addiction recovery coaches, and so on) in many instances are certified by various organizations and states throughout the USA and internationally and can provide a wide range of services to the individual, whether a youth or an adult.

Peers may be employed staff and key members of the treatment team in some settings and therefore may provide billable services. In other instances, they may work with a variety of community-based organizations that provide services and supports and can be considered a part of the natural supports in the community available to the individual. There are many tasks performed by peer support specialists that may include assisting their peers in articulating their goals for recovery, learning and practicing new skills, helping them monitor their progress, assisting them in their treatment, modeling effective coping techniques and self-help strategies based on the specialist's own recovery experience, and supporting them in advocating for themselves to obtain effective services. Examples of the activities and services provided by a peer can include[21]:

- lead as well as teach consumers how to facilitate Recovery Dialogs
- support consumers in creating a Wellness Recovery Action Plan (WRAP)
- utilize and teach problem-solving techniques with individuals and groups
- teach consumers techniques for identifying and combating negative self-talk
- teach consumers techniques for identifying and overcoming fears
- support the vocational choices consumers make and support them in overcoming job-related anxiety
- support consumers in building social skills in the community that will enhance job acquisition and tenure
- support non-consumer staff in identifying program environments that are conducive to recovery
- lend their unique insight into mental illness and what makes recovery possible
- attend treatment team meetings to promote consumers' use of self-directed recovery tools

In considering possible interventions to include in the plan, providers should make certain that individuals and their families are fully aware of the availability and value of peer-based services. Based on this understanding, peer services and supports should be considered as appropriate for inclusion with the other interventions detailed in the plan. Especially for billable services where there is potentially a question about medical necessity documentation, the inclusion of peer services should meet all the specific criteria, i.e., the 5 Ws, for a properly written and described intervention.

Examples of peer support interventions on a plan might be:

- "Peer support specialist will conduct the peer support and wellness group weekly for the next three months so that Kathleen can work on improving her socialization skills."
- "Recovery coach to facilitate weekly WRAP group for three months to help Ken to better manage his feelings of hopelessness and worthlessness."
- "Peer wellness coach to lead whole health and resiliency group every other week for six months to help Dennis develop coping skills and strategies to better manage his isolation."
- In a hospital setting a sample intervention might be something like "Peer supporter will encourage Rebecca to walk around the halls, go to workout class, and attend yoga group, as a means of reducing her stress and aggressive behaviors." This intervention also builds on her strengths of liking to do physical exercise.

Community Resources/Natural Supports

Providers do not have to do everything! If services are not directly available within the provider organization, then referrals should be made to appropriate resources. The scope of available services may or may not encompass all of the needs of any one individual and may not be culturally appropriate for all individuals and families. In such instances it is critical that providers be creative, open-minded, able to utilize natural and peer supports, etc. The person-centered planning process also opens doors to a new life beyond the service system. Plans may be developed to help individuals re-engage in their natural communities that they have felt most excluded from as a result of past experiences. Believing that these communities can be re-engaged, or that new communities can be discovered, is a valued outcome and a critical motivator for involvement in person-centered planning activities.

Community resources for potential natural supports for adults and children may include the following:

- family members
- church and affiliated religious programs
- indigenous healers and alternative providers
- neighbors/friends
- community colleges
- YMCA, youth groups, sports leagues, and so on

- health departments
- local hospitals
- mentorship programs, self-help groups, peer support
- volunteer agencies
- library reading programs
- day camps
- social clubs
- teachers/guidance counselors
- governmental services, e.g., Department of Labor, Aid to Families, etc.

Natural supports available to those in a hospital setting include taking advantage of the chaplain services, peer support services, accessing family members for help, along with community providers whom the individual has already engaged for support.

Self-Directed Activities

In addition to professional, billable interventions and natural supports available to the individual, the intervention section of the plan should also include action steps individuals can take to help achieve their objectives when appropriate. The recovery and resiliency model emphasizes empowerment, accountability and responsibility for one's own wellness. At Bluebonnet Community Services in Texas the recovery plan in their electronic health record calls this *Personal Responsibility Steps*. On an inpatient treatment/recovery plan form/screen it might be titled *Patient Actions*. These interventions help to activate individuals in terms of their own recovery. The actual recoding of these self-directed activities in the intervention portion of the plan does not need to rise to the level of specificity as the billable interventions.

These self-directed activities can range from taking a walk with the dog (when trying to lose weight, reduce anxiety/isolation), to calling a friend/ sponsor when triggered to use alcohol/drugs, to practicing yoga, etc. In fact, yoga has been proven now to have positive effects on mild depression and sleep complaints, ADHD symptoms and symptoms associated with schizophrenia. A recent review of more than 100 studies focusing on 16 high-quality controlled studies looked at the effects of yoga on depression, schizophrenia, ADHD, sleep complaints, eating disorders and cognition problems and found them to be promising[22].

Another self-directed activity might include the use of web-based resources designed to support and promote individual health, well-being and recovery. But one example is DBSA's (Depression Bipolar Support

Alliance) Wellness Tracker, a free online tool for people to chart their symptoms, lifestyle choices and physical health as well as create a personal wellness plan[23].

There is a tendency when writing plans to include only those services and activities for which the provider is responsible and which will generate billing and document medical necessity. In some settings, these natural supports and self-directed activities that the individual or family has identified or taken are not included in the plan. Both types of interventions are important and contribute to the plan's success in an integrated and holistic manner and should be included. Sometimes there are concerns about the potential for confusion by commingling billable and non-billable services in one list of interventions. A practical solution is to break out and document non-billable individual and family activities in a separate list. This sometimes has the advantage of making even clearer the responsibilities and obligations of the individual and family in their own recovery journey.

III. MAKING IT HAPPEN

As in the preceding chapters, the following section discusses the move from the theoretical and didactic to the practical. The concepts, values and principles are all well and good, but what it actually looks like and how it is done need to be demonstrated and explained. For each of the individuals, Diana, JR, Keisha and Roberto, examples of services and interventions are provided that are linked tightly to the identified objectives.

Previous caveats about the limitations of examples need to be reiterated. In specifying interventions, questions about the clinical appropriateness and correctness of the services will inevitably arise. There is no claim or assertion intended in these examples that they are the only or even optimal response. Rather, the criterion for their inclusion is that they are reasonable. Regardless, the focus should be on considering the key elements of a properly constructed and documented intervention:

- Is the service or activity clearly described?
- Does the intervention build on the strengths of the resources of the individual and family?
- Is the provider or role of the individual included?
- Is there an array of service interventions and types of activity?
- Are self-directed and natural supports utilized when appropriate?
- Are the frequency, intensity and duration of the intervention specified?
- Does each intervention include a description of the intended purpose, impact or outcome related to the objective?

Examples

Diana

Diana's plan includes seven interventions—only three of which identify billable services. This is a prime example of engaging the individual's and family's strengths and demonstrating how the family can be instrumental in helping to attain the plan's objectives. The plan also engages natural supports within Diana's community such as her church and provides a healthy alternative to more case management services. In addition, an evidence-based practice, Incredible Years Parenting class, for Diana's parents is incorporated into the plan. Also, a pediatric consult is there to address the possibility of physical health issues that may be affecting her irritability, inability to get along with her mother and/or school performance

JR

JR's many interventions might be needed to best serve this young man with a complicated and multifaceted set of circumstances that may prevent him from achieving an ambitious objective of completing two job applications for two consecutive weeks. There is a role for specialists addressing substance abuse issues, physical health and mental health. It is a good example of the role that peer specialists can play in helping individuals achieve their goals/objectives, in this instance by coordinating/supporting his involvement in cognitive enhancement therapy (an evidence-based practice for people with a diagnosis of schizophrenia). In addition, there are three self-directed (personal responsibility) strategies that JR is set to employ; these build on his strengths of faith and his past enjoyment of sports. Finally, there is an action step for his parents, if they are willing to follow through. This is a good example of a comprehensive multidimensional and truly integrated and person-centered plan.

Keisha

The list of interventions in Keisha's plan include an array of supports and services that provide a multi-pronged approach to helping her succeed in overcoming her anxiety so that she can return to at least one church service within 90 days. The multidisciplinary and integrative approach to mental health, substance use and physical health concerns is also evident in this plan's interventions. Since she is pre-contemplative about her alcohol use, a stage-matched intervention of providing her education on the relationship between alcohol use and depression and anxiety is a good fit. Cognitive behavioral therapy (CBT) for acquiring coping skills to better manage her anxiety and stress, along with medications to reduce the impact of anxiety/depression, are just a few of the professional services to assist with helping her return to her church.

Since Keisha is in the active stage it seems reasonable that she can engage in several action steps for herself to help reduce her anxiety about returning to church: practice singing on her own (she used to sing in the church choir) and develop a WRAP (Wellness Action and Recovery Plan). This might be a self-directed intervention, or in some states it is recognized as a professional, billable service, as part of the state's Medicaid Rehabilitation Plan. Meanwhile her sister, who is a wonderful source of support, can provide additional help (with her permission of course!), by reconnecting her with their pastor and practicing forgiveness.

Roberto

Roberto has four interventions for the objective related to helping him to sleep better and with that hopefully be less anxious. There are four separate and additional interventions attached to the second objective of writing a harm reduction plan. This is consistent with an individual who is hospitalized requiring active treatment. The benefits from a combination of sleep hygiene skills, medications, trauma resolution therapy to reduce nightmares and the use of the hospital chaplain as a natural support, which builds on his strength of being a spiritual person, all together should result in improved sleep patterns for him while he is in the hospital, and hopefully upon discharge as well.

Due to his stage of change regarding his self-medicating with alcohol and other drugs, the second objective is about him attempting to control his drug use after discharge from the hospital. By utilizing hospital AA/NA meetings, along with peer support counseling, in addition to the professional services of group or family therapy (building another strength of his family support), it is hoped he can develop a meaningful harm reduction plan for himself.

In other words, the interventions are efficacious and give the sense that they are likely to help Roberto achieve his objective.

REFERENCES

1. HHS Publication No. SMA-09-4371. *Shared Decision-Making in Mental Health Care: Practice, Research, and Future Directions.* Rockville, MD: Center for Mental Health Services, Substance Abuse and Mental Health Services Administration; 2010.
2. http://kauaicounty.hi.networkofcare.org/mh/library/article.aspx?id=2482.
3. Lowenstein G. Risk as feelings. *Psychol Bull.* 2001;127(2):267–286.
4. http://www.mentalhealthamerica.net/go/youreontheteam/listen.

5. Scheffler R, et al. *Evidence on the Effectiveness of Full Service Partnership Programs in California's Public Mental Health System.* Berkeley: Nicholas C. Petris Center on Health Care Markets and Consumer Welfare School of Public Health, University of California; May 2010.
6. http://www.omh.ny.gov/omhweb/pros/.
7. Partners in Health. *Mental Health, Primary Care and Substance Abuse Interagency Collaboration Toolkit.* 2013; www.ibhp.org.
8. Greenberg L. *Best Practices Compendium for Serious Mental Illness.* Washington DC: MHPA Center for Best Practices; 2013.
9. Collins C, et al. *Evolving Models of Behavioral Health Integration in Primary Care.* New York, NY: Milbank Memorial Fund; 2010.
10. American Medical Association. *All Health Care Quality is Local.* CPPD Report #27, Winter 2009.
11. HRSA Center for Integrated Health Solutions, Joan King, Inciting Health Behavior Change through Consumer Engagement, 9/6/12.
12. Rogers ES, Kash-MacDonald M, Brucker D. *Systematic Review of Peer Delivered Services Literature 1989–2009.* Boston: Boston University, Sargent College, Center for Psychiatric Rehabilitation; 2009.
13. Goldstrom ID, Campbell J, Rogers JA, Lambert DB, Blacklow B, Henderson MJ, et al. National estimates for mental health mutual support groups, self-help organizations, and consumer-operated services. *Adm Policy Ment Health and Ment Health Serv Res.* 2006;33(1):92-103.
14. James B. *American College of Mental Health Administration Summit.* Santa Fe, NM; 2002.
15. Swesey M. *Evidence Based Practices and Multicultural Mental Health* [White paper] ; 2008. Retrieved from http://www.nami.org.
16. http://healthcareconnects.com/pdf/brentJames.pdf.
17. Matching alcoholism to patient heterogeneity. *J Stud Alcohol.* 1997;58(1):7-29.
18. Burns T. The effectiveness of supported employment for people with severe mental illness: a randomised controlled trial. *Lancet.* 2007;370(9593):1146-1152.
19. *ISP Training Manual.* State of Maine: The Department of Behavioral & Developmental Services (BDS); October 2002.
20. http://www.samhsa.gov/nctic/trauma.asp.
21. http://www.gacps.org/JobDescription.html.
22. http://www.frontiersin.org/Affective_Disorders_and_Psychosomatic_Research/10.3389/fpsyt.2012.00117/abstract.
23. www.facingus.org/tour/tracker.

Journey's End: The Destination

The odd thing about traveling is that sometimes you end up in places that you never intended—for better or for worse. It is a mystery how it happens despite following the map.

Sometimes the destination is exactly as planned—it is just not what was envisioned or expected—or perhaps you arrived at the wrong time of year expecting warmth and sun only to find cold and rain instead. But the inevitable question is: what is next? Do we keep on moving? Is this really just another spot on the road to take a rest, or is it more of a final destination, a new place to put down roots and stay settled for a while?

Arrival is a time for reflection and reconsideration—a chance to look back and reminisce about the trip, experiences enjoyed and lessons learned along the way, and to dream about what opportunities and distant lands might lie ahead.

Chapter 7 focuses on review and reconsideration—reflection is as much a part of the journey as the preparation and travel itself.

CHAPTER 7

Evaluating the Process

It is Good to Have an End to Journey Towards; but it's the Journey That Matters in the end.

Ursula K. LeGuin

I. STATING THE CASE

Chapter 2 asserted that "assessment is initial and ongoing," but what does this really mean? Evaluation should be a continual activity rather than an event that marks the beginning and conclusion of a service episode. The work of supporting an individual and family in their journey towards health, wellness and recovery involves a process of assessment and reassessment; but when and how should that occur? Ongoing review is needed so that goals, objectives and interventions are matched not only to the unique needs of each individual but also to the stage-specific needs of each person as they evolve through the process of recovery. And there is the proverbial $64,000 question: Did the individual reach the destination? Was the goal achieved? Was it where they really wanted to go? Do they want to stay? Where do they want to go next? The answers to these questions essentially lie in revisiting the individual plan with a fresh look and focus. The task is to review and evaluate the team's progress towards achieving the individual's and family's identified recovery goals.

Update and Review

Assessment and reassessment should, at minimum, occur at several key points in the overall service-delivery process or recovery journey. The information gathered can help to evaluate the trip, monitor progress and direct mid-course corrections or even possible detours to points of interest. In other words, based upon the information gathered in reassessment, there may be an update of the plan including modifications of the integrated summary, goals, objectives and/or services. This helps to ensure that at all times the plan is:

- a dynamic, current, accurate, relevant, working, person-centered document
- an up-to-date reflection of the individual's and family's challenges and needs

Treatment Planning for Person-Centered Care
http://dx.doi.org/10.1016/B978-0-12-394448-1.00007-X

189

- actually used by the treatment team to direct services, guide outcomes and support medical necessity

In a person-centered approach, if the belief is that the plan is a useful, meaningful, clinical tool, then it might be changed more frequently as the person moves along their recovery path. This does not mean the entire plan always has to be changed, but that a new intervention might be added, or a short-term goal/objective achieved. The plan is truly fluid and the revisions tell us if the short-term goals/objectives and interventions that were written are working or not. The initial plan was just a plan based on limited information if this is a new admission to the hospital or community program. It was based on what might be possible. As circumstances change, and as experience teaches us about the viability of those initial "best guesses," sometimes based on very limited information, the plan needs to change accordingly. If an old short-term goal/objective is not being achieved as originally anticipated, that does not mean it should be abandoned. It often means that we failed to anticipate all of the time and steps needed to accomplish that short-term goal/objective. When that happens, it's good practice to rewrite the short-term goal/objective as a more specific, more achievable step that will help the client to move in the same direction.

There are key points in the service-delivery process when some level of update, review and reassessment of the individual's and family's needs, status and plan is indicated. These include

- the time each service is provided
- the target date specified in the objective
- at intervals specified by licensure, certification, accreditation, policy, payer or other requirements
- at transition or discharge
- at some period following transition or discharge to evaluate the extended benefit and outcome of services

The last item in this list clearly goes beyond the scope of this book. While studies of the extended impact of service outcomes are important, they require system-level responses, are resource intensive and difficult to conduct, and are not the focus of the individual plan. This chapter will focus on the first four items in the list, although some discussion about the issue of monitoring and system re-entry is provided later in this section.

Reassessment should not be assumed to mean a start-from-scratch repeat of an original assessment. Instead it is meant to be a targeted, strategic and more specific update focused on details that are relevant and meaningful for that individual and family. In reassessment, the focus is on these questions, as appropriate to the individual and family, and their circumstances:

- Is there new information to inform *any* of the plan's elements?
- Has anything of significance changed in the individual's and family's life, within key domains such as: health, mental health, substance use, employment, relationships, living environment and other psychosocial factors?
- Have goals or transition/discharge criteria changed in any way?
- Have new strengths or resources emerged?
- Are there new or different barriers? Are there new concerns or needs?
- What has been the impact of the services provided? Have they helped? Are there other things that should be done? Should target dates be changed? Is the intensity and frequency of services appropriate?
- Are there new or different objectives?

In a properly written and prepared plan, there will always be an update and something to document: without exception, there must be at least a transition or discharge criterion, a goal and objective with a timeframe or target date. When that date is reached, there must be a determination of the status of that objective—either it has been met or it has not. If it has not, there should be some consideration as to why and that should inform the following steps. If the objective has been met, what is the next stop in the individual's and family's journey?

What is the process for obtaining input concerning progress toward goal achievement? There is not one uniform approach that necessarily works well across all settings, providers or individuals. What is important is that the process is a conscious and transparent activity. At the very least, the provider members of the team are accountable to the individual and family for monitoring the timeframes specified in the objectives. At those key dates, the individual and family should be involved in some meaningful determination of whether or not the objectives have been met and what should be the next steps in the plan.

Quality of Care

The following vignette, extracted from a community mental health center record, emphasizes how critically important a proper plan and ongoing review is to the lives of individuals and families receiving services.

An adolescent girl, living with her grandmother after both her parents have died, has recently been suspended from school. She is using drugs, has been charged with auto theft, and has been diagnosed with attention deficit disorder (ADD). Because of her multiple problems, she has been assigned a social worker through the local child welfare agency and has been referred for mental health services. Her treatment plan goals are that "she will express her anger in an appropriate manner" and "she will become skilled in DBT [Dialectical Behavioral Therapy]". The progress notes indicate she is deteriorating rapidly, violating probation, smoking marijuana, and exhibiting hypersexual and defiant behaviors. Her individual plan review documentation indicates "she will continue working on anger management skills, attend the intensive outpatient program and continue with the individual plan."

Unfortunately, this example is not uncommon. At minimum it represents a failure of assessment, planning and review at multiple levels. Without conducting a detailed analysis, it is immediately clear that these are not the individual's and family's goals and that they are written more like objectives—and quite poorly at that. Perhaps most importantly, there is a disturbing disconnect between the individual's deterioration and the interventions specified in the plan update. It is shocking to see how often plans perpetuate ineffective treatments! There is no better argument to be made for the value and importance of time well spent in assessment, planning, review and update of the plan than the need to ensure effective services and progress.

In addition to a person-centered focus on reviewing the process of services and the recovery/wellness journey, it is also important for providers to look inward from time to time and evaluate their own performance in serving individuals and families. While one could legitimately argue "it's all about outcomes," the preceding chapters have made a strong case that the process of how assessments are conducted, how plans are developed and implemented, the quality of services provided and how outcomes are achieved are also critically important. In other words, an important part of any review and evaluation of the individual plan is some consideration of the team's performance, ranging from the individual's and family's experience to the team's self-evaluation of their work process to the documentation of the plan and services in the clinical record. Is there general agreement that the process was person-centered and that the individual and family felt appropriately supported, respected and included? This type of review should be part of the ongoing quality improvement and peer review activities of any provider organization, ranging from the solo practitioner to highly complex and organized systems of care.

Documentation is inevitably an important aspect of the evaluation, review and update portion of the individual plan and service-delivery process. Essential elements of the review and reassessment process are tied to actual service provision that for a variety of reasons, ranging from billing to legal liability and continuity of care, must be recorded. However, it is often problems in documentation that make it difficult for providers to demonstrate their work in service planning and service delivery. Once again the old adage "if it isn't written down, it didn't happen" applies. Recognizing that providers frequently complain about the burden of paperwork and how it keeps them from performing their "real job," the following section will examine, in part, how documentation issues are closely linked to clinical processes and can actually support a person-centered, recovery-oriented individual plan and service system.

II. CREATING THE SOLUTION

In *Stating the Case,* four key points in the planning and service-delivery process necessitating a review and update of the plan were identified. These included service provision, target dates, mandated intervals, and transition or discharge. Each of these points or phases carries with it special considerations in terms of provider responsibilities, involvement with the individual and family, impact on the plan and service delivery and documentation. Accordingly, each point is a subsection of *Creating the Solution.* The last subsection addresses strategies for assessing provider performance in individual planning.

Documenting Services

Progress notes record an adult's or child and family's journey toward the achievement of their goals. They are a way to facilitate communication and coordination of services. The notes outline the work being done: what has been useful, what has not been useful and ideas to try, among other things. Progress notes keep all the members of the team working with the person and family informed so that ongoing coordination is possible. Progress notes also inform payers about the content and value of the services that are being provided and billed.

General requirements for progress notes include: information about how a child or adult is doing, the goal or objective that is the focus of a particular intervention, the actual service provided, the rationale and the impact of the intervention, and lastly the plan for future steps or activities. In order to have a person-centered approach, it is important to keep the whole person and family in mind; this means that providers should try to avoid an exclusive focus on overcoming symptoms, functional impairments and diagnoses and instead also recognize the individual's strengths, effort, motivation and accomplishments.

Historically, there has been a range of documentation standards for recording the provision of services, commonly referred to as progress notes, service notes, case notes, and so on. These entries should be used to document services and should reference the specific objectives under which the service is provided. Notes can include unstructured narratives, as well as highly structured formats such as:

PIE: **P**roblem identification, **I**ntervention, **E**valuation

SOAP: **S**ubjective, **O**bjective, **A**ssessment, **P**lan

DAP: **D**escription, **A**ssessment, **P**lan

GIRP: **G**oal(s) and Objective(s), **I**ntervention, **R**esponse, **P**lan

These four formats share some important elements in common beyond the fact that they are structured, which is in and of itself important. They all require *assessment* to be part of the note.

The DAP format is effectively the same as the SOAP and collapses subjective and objective into one category or field (i.e., description). *Subjective* was meant to capture the individual's own words while *objective* was to include the provider's data or observations, but often the subjective report was forced and inaccurate, which is why the SOAP format drifted into DAP. The *description* section should include what is also found in the *P* part of the PIE format: a combination of the individual's self-report of his or her status, feelings and symptoms, and the provider's observation of the same. The *I* in PIE should include a description of the service or intervention delivered. In GIRP, the *I* means Intervention and is a specific description of the activities and services provided by staff. *R* is the individual/family response to the specific intervention. Providers are encouraged to include individual/family *self-assessment* of response as well as staff assessment.

Documenting the impact or outcome of services is equally important. What happened? Too often progress or service notes list a host of services and interventions but there is little said about what effect they had. The *assessment* section of DAP and SOAP, equivalent to *evaluation* in the PIE, should include the provider's impressions of the impact of the intervention, the individual's overall progress to date, the apparent effectiveness of the service and plan, and other related thoughts and observations that inform the decision-making process. These could be considered "micro-assessments" as they are generally very specific, narrow in focus, and for the most part tied to the intervention and the objective.

The *plan* section should describe next steps. With the GIRP format, the plan for next steps should be within the context of the intervention/response to the documented service. If progress is being made that is consistent with what had been anticipated in the overall recovery plan, and consistent with the intended impact described in each intervention, then a simple notation referring to the plan is sufficient. However, if progress is significantly lagging, then rethinking the strategy and possible next steps should be included the note.

There are advantages and disadvantages to each format. The GIRP was developed to be more of a recovery-oriented progress note, with an emphasis on starting off documentation related to the goal and short-term goal or objective of the plan. The PIE, SOAP and DAP formats have often been referred to as part of a "problem-oriented record" but can just as well be used in a recovery model to support an *objective-oriented* or *recovery-oriented* record. Regardless of the format, if an objective on the person-centered plan is correctly structured, and a service or intervention is written that specifies the provider, modality, and most importantly the intended purpose or impact as it relates to the objective, then a formatted structured note greatly simplifies the obligation to document services, substantiate the medical necessity and satisfy the expectation that there be a reassessment at the point of service.

Writing a formatted note that includes a mini-assessment is beneficial for a few important reasons. One is that it keeps the provider clear and focused on what the task is for each individual, and the purpose or relevance of the intervention and service is apparent. With this approach, it is difficult to provide ineffective services for an extended period of time; the lack of progress becomes too apparent for all, and the provider and team are compelled to re-evaluate. At the same time, if the service is proving to be an effective intervention and helping to support the change identified in the objective, then this approach to documentation, review and reassessment generates enthusiasm and support for moving forward and maintaining momentum. This is the proverbial win–win approach. Hopefully the efficiencies in service delivery, documentation and accountability that come from using a structured note are focused and compelling. It makes it clear that assessment is both initial and ongoing, both real and valuable.

Writing concurrent or collaborative progress notes is another approach. This strategy grew out of efforts to improve provider efficiency and consistency, but is also person-centered in many ways. Concurrent documentation involves writing the note while the individual/family is actually meeting with the provider/team, and having them check it out for accuracy. This ensures transparency of the process and a good use of time for providers in terms of not having to wait until the person leaves to complete documentation. The practice appears to enjoy high levels of satisfaction with service recipients. In fact, research has demonstrated improved medication adherence for an individual receiving mental health services associated with person-centered planning and concurrent documentation suggesting that this practice does enhance engagement and the individual's experience of care[1].

An example of how a person-centered progress note might read is: "Celia is extremely fearful of going outside of her house and concerned that she will miss her psychiatrist's appointment. She has no nearby relatives and explains that in her culture a woman does not go to the doctor alone. A rehab specialist (RS) supported her in asking a roommate to accompany her to her appointment, and provided coaching to her on stress-reduction skills to reduce her anxiety. RS will follow up with Celia and her roommate after the doctor's appointment to learn about results." In this example, Celia's goal is that she wants to be able to return to work someday. Her main barrier to doing so is her extreme anxiety about leaving her home, which is stress related. One of the objectives of her plan is for her to better manage her anxiety and the resulting limitations by utilizing stress-reduction techniques within the next six weeks. The recovery plan intervention states that every week the RS will provide cognitive behavioral therapy to help Celia improve her stress-reduction skills. The plan also includes an intervention by the psychiatrist who is to provide Celia with monthly medication management.

There are a few "noteworthy" parts to this documentation example that warrant attention. The note speaks to the objective and the two interventions, and helps to explain how Celia's cultural heritage impacts her help-seeking and progress. The overall approach documents a recovery focus in that the RS does not intervene by taking Celia to the doctor himself/herself. Instead, the RS arranges for a natural support in Celia's life, her roommate, to accompany her to the doctor. This note will support a billable service because it is clear that the RS is providing skill building with Celia, as well as coordinating/arranging/supporting her access to medical services.

Timeliness of Review

As stated earlier, the individual plan can be considered a contract between the provider and the individual and family, so that the objectives become the equivalent of the short-term or interim deliverables, the sum of which is the goal. The provider has an obligation to honor the target dates on the objectives and to conduct a review and update of the plan when the target dates on the objectives occur. In some settings, there may be external mandates to review individual plans or conduct plan updates within specified timeframes appropriate to the level of care. This can range from weekly for acute care to monthly for short-term care and between quarterly to semi-annually for more long-term care.

While the target dates on objectives should always be determined by what is most appropriate for the individual and their needs, the provider is often able to satisfy externally imposed requirements by setting objective target dates below those thresholds. It is often better to have more short-term and modest but attainable objectives that are reviewed more frequently than to have "larger" longer-term objectives that default to the mandated timeframes for review. Regardless, these target dates should prompt a team meeting to review the plan and make modifications as necessary.

When the review occurs, there are multiple but essential questions to consider: Have the deliverables been produced? Has the objective been met? If the answers are yes, the process is in many ways relatively simple, but additional questions remain. Have there been significant changes for the individual or family—for better or for worse? Should the overall goal remain the same? With the current objective accomplished, what is next? What lessons were learned in the process? How does this success inform the selection of the next objective? What was learned about what works best in terms of services and interventions that promote and support change? What did not help? What, if anything, seemed to hinder the process? All of these questions are effectively a form of reassessment, but they are rather targeted and specific to the circumstances. The focus is on understanding a recent success and accomplishment, appreciating what there is to learn from it, and deciding how to build upon it to support the individual and family in pursuit of their goal.

Another approach is to reconsider the individual's stage of recovery and any significant changes. For individuals addressing substance abuse problems, the six dimensions of the American Society of Addiction Medicine's (ASAM) *Treatment Criteria for Substance-Related, Addictive, and Co-Occurring Conditions*, the American Association of Community Psychiatry's (AACP) *Level Of Care and Utilization Scale* (LOCUS) tool or Prochaska's stages of motivation can all be useful frameworks. In the mental health field the use of the MORS (Milestones of Recovery Scale) developed by Dave Pilon, PhD, and Mark Ragins, MD, both from Mental Health America of Los Angeles (MHA), has proven to be an effective evaluation tool to measure recovery progress that is growing in acceptance and popularity[2]. Together, this information can help to re-inform the planning process.

On the other hand, if the objective was *not* met, the focus of the review and update needs to be on understanding why. Was it partially met? Would more time make a difference? Was it the right objective? Did other circumstances change? Were the interventions helpful? Were the services provided in the right location with the necessary frequency and intensity? Should the objective be scrapped or modified? What should the objective be? What steps can be taken to assure success in this next interval? Perhaps it is simply a matter of extending the time; perhaps it is a matter of bringing new services and interventions to bear, or providing the services with greater intensity or frequency.

The insights gained in this process often help to further inform both the provider and the individual and family about strengths, as well as challenges and barriers, that need to be overcome. This, in turn, may well cause some discussion about formulations/integrated summaries, priorities and even goals. All of these factors need to be taken into consideration when reviewing the plan at target dates, particularly for objectives that were not met.

In considering this review process, it should become more apparent that setting relevant and attainable objectives with reasonable timeframes—not too short and not too long—is beneficial. The setting of objectives is not a paper exercise to be filed in the record, or buried in the electronic health record (EHR), and forgotten. Rather, the objectives are the documented agreement for change between the provider and the individual and family. They should be reviewed regularly and serve as a point of short-term accountability which is all part of making the process meaningful and effective. It is much more satisfying for everyone to see a pattern of meaningful progress than recurrent failures. Asking the tough questions when an objective is not met can help to assure success in the next interval. And nothing succeeds like success!

Reassessment

It is not unusual to review a record for an individual or family with a long service history in a community mental health center or an addiction recovery program and find that there is one formal assessment completed some 10 years ago without current documentation of any formal reassessment or update. Oftentimes there have been multiple staff transitions and changes over those years and one is left to wonder exactly who knows what about this individual. What are his or her strengths and needs at this point? What information serves as the basis for the development of any meaningful individual recovery plan? All too often there is none.

There is an emerging consensus that a formal annual reassessment, following the domain-based approach for the initial assessment, is a reasonable practice standard to follow for those individuals and families requiring services over extended periods of time. Certainly a full reassessment on a more frequent basis can be done, but this may not yield enough benefit to justify the effort and expense. However, if there are significant unanticipated or unexplained changes in the appearance, presentation, status, health or function of the individual, then reassessment is clearly indicated.

In some cases this expectation of a formal annual reassessment has been written into code, regulation, accreditation standards, licensure requirements and the like. Sometimes it is merely a matter of organizational policy. In some settings, it is more frequent, while in others it is less and yet in others the requirements do not exist at all. Obviously, providers must meet those requirements where they exist. However, the temptation to default to the lowest possible standard should be resisted. While reassessment and review can appear to be burdensome, timeliness is an essential component of quality care. When periodic reassessments become a routine component of care, both the provider and the individual are handsomely repaid for their investment with improved outcomes and satisfaction.

The focus in reassessment should be on building upon the existing clinical database and understanding what, if anything, has changed in each of the domains—accomplishments, improvements and the acquisition of new abilities and strengths as well as losses, setbacks, new challenges and barriers since the last evaluation was completed. It does not need to be a complete recantation of the entire original assessment. Instead, highlighting those significant and relevant details describing changes that are meaningful in support of the individual's and family's recovery goals and journey is sufficient.

In a paper record system, this reassessment can potentially be recorded on a single page that is tacked onto the original assessment. This way, each year another page is added onto the assessment and its evolution can be followed progressively through the years. Many of the systems for electronic clinical records have the ability to update an assessment, by automatically populating fields with data, so that current facts and narrative do not have to be retyped, and only new information has to be entered. Care should be taken to ensure that new information which changes the formulation and fundamental understanding of the individual and family, their strengths and their needs is included in a revised and updated version of the integrated summary. The possibility that out of these processes new goals may emerge or that current goals may have changed also needs to be considered. Attention should also be paid to changes in priorities, barriers and strengths, all of which may need to be reflected in the individual plan.

While some level of reassessment is occurring through the course of the year in the "micro-assessments" that are tied to the service notes, and assessments that are part of reviewing the objectives, neither of those is intended to be comprehensive. In contrast, the annual reassessment is intended to provide a formal, thorough and comprehensive review. In this way there is some assurance that important concerns, which may not have been a particular focus in the recovery process over the preceding year, are not overlooked or neglected. It is an opportunity to ensure that while there is a focus on specific issues and change strategies, the importance of recognizing the whole person is not forgotten. Annual reassessment provides an opportunity to reconsider a holistic approach to understanding the individual and family, their strengths, their needs and the remainder of the journey yet to be traveled.

Along with a formal reassessment, some providers and organizations may want to consider a formal and comprehensive review of the entire individual plan on an annual basis. Other reviews and updates discussed in this section have focused on particular elements of the plan, the objectives and the services. The risk is that over time, drift occurs. There is always the possibility that in the course of events the individual has actually shifted their goal and it is no longer reflected in the plan or in the discharge and transition criteria. As a result, the integrity and coherency of the plan can be lost and objectives may no longer relate to the goal as they once did. One strategy is to consider a thorough and comprehensive review of all of the elements of a plan for those individuals and families whose length of service significantly exceeds that which is typical for the provider or setting.

Transition or Discharge Planning

A true commitment to recovery means fostering the independence of the individual and the family, not fostering dependence on service-delivery systems and professionals. This means that planning for and anticipating transition or discharge must be a part of every individual plan. Where do people who have received services go once their goals have been met? Hopefully they develop coping skills and other resources and learn to rely on themselves, family, friends, church, peer support and civic groups—the natural supports and resources within the community. Providers have an obligation to repeatedly re-evaluate the individual's and family's readiness to discontinue services entirely or to transition to a lower level of care. Sometimes some individuals do need ongoing professional services and supports, but can preserve their gains and/or make continual progress with a mix of community, family and peer-based support, along with limited professional services, as compared to dependence on a full menu of comprehensive care.

Providers will frequently ask how to write an individual plan and demonstrate the medical necessity of "maintenance." Admittedly, this is difficult. Although the idea of maintenance has long been a part of at least the mental health lexicon, it is a concept that is effectively foreign to the notion of recovery. In recovery, individuals and families are always working to the point where they are self-sustaining, living beyond the challenges of mental illness and addictions, and relying on the natural supports of the community. Perhaps they have need for limited and specific professional services, such as medications, but that is a far cry from the idea of being "maintained" in a state of illness.

As much as possible, individual plans should reflect the individual's recovery goals and not foster dependence and promote disability and maintenance. There is little question that many individuals are impacted by the disincentives of disability benefits as well as a legacy of misinformation about mental illness and addictive disorders and their potential for recovery. The obligation of the provider is to educate and encourage; the review, update and reassessment can be seen as yet another opportunity for providing hope and encouragement.

When individuals have reached a point of readiness for transition or discharge, a final review and reassessment is in order. Ideally, all case or episode-of-care closures and transitions are anticipated and consistent with the individual plan. Regrettably, people all too often leave mental health and addiction recovery services by simply never returning, either celebrating their success or expressing their frustration and disappointment with their feet. This is something to be avoided as much as possible. A planned and thoughtful transition is an opportunity for the members of the team to share their experiences in working together for the success of the individual and family. It provides closure and a chance to wish them well as they continue on their recovery journey—perhaps to return at some point in the future, perhaps never to be seen again.

Some of the questions to consider at transition or discharge include: Is their discharge or transition planned or precipitous? Are they ready? Have the goals been achieved to the individual's and family's satisfaction? Have they received the services and help they were hoping for? Do they have the skills they need in order to succeed? Are they ready for the next leg of the journey? Do they have a map? Do they have their provisions? Do they know the way back if they need to return? What barriers exist to their re-entry?

Ensuring that the needs of the individual and family at transition or discharge are met is critical to their success. Much of this should have been anticipated prior to the actual time of transition. However, at the moment of transition, it is important to reassess the individual's and family's readiness and the availability and appropriateness of post-transition arrangements and resources—either professional, community and/or peer based. Ensuring that the individual and family fully understand what they need to do, and how to access the resources that they need, is all part of the process.

Assessment of ongoing service needs is highly individual and somewhat setting specific. Individuals leaving an inpatient or residential setting will likely have fairly immediate needs for some sort of outpatient follow-up; someone completing a brief course of individual psychotherapy may have no anticipated future needs; and many of the persons completing drug rehab counseling will need to be participating in community-based 12-step programs as part of their recovery promotion plan. Involving the individual and family in this planning process is essential, and their preferences and choices must be the guide. The availability of resources will also inevitably play a role in shaping the plan.

Arrangements for follow-up and continuing care need to create a continuum of services for individuals that may include linking individuals and families with relevant supports in the community, follow-up with the person at regular intervals, access to peer or aftercare groups and educating individuals about continuing care options, such as pharmacotherapy. Increasingly community health clinics and Federally Qualified Health Clinics (FQHCs) provide some range of mental health services and are able to manage ongoing treatment needs, including pharmacotherapy, after discharge from specialty mental health services. For many individuals and families, part of the journey of recovery is accepting the risk of relapse or recurrence and the possibility that mental illness and addictive disorders may require additional treatment or supports at some future point in time. Systems must be designed so that individuals do not face barriers to reassessment, re-entry into services and reactivation of service plans should that become necessary.

A person-centered approach, focused on a long-term view of recovery, should consider including a mechanism for providing ongoing monitoring, feedback and encouragement. This should also include linkage to natural supports in the community and, when necessary, re-engagement and early reintervention monitoring, feedback and support. White et al. propose a Behavioral Health Recovery Management model which calls for "sustained monitoring and recovery support services [which] contrasts with models that provide repeated episodes characterized by 'assess, admit, treat, and discharge,' as is traditional in the treatment of substance use disorders[3]. It also contrasts with mental health programs that focus on stabilization and maintenance of symptom suppression rather than on recovery and personal growth."

Another aspect of the review process at transition or discharge involves the preparation of a summary document. Whether this record of services and accomplishments attained by the individual and family is a document maintained in the clinical record, is given to the individual and family, or is transmitted to another provider, it is still very useful to have what is, in essence, a final integration of the plan. This summary should include at minimum:

- a brief description of the reasons that the individual and family initially sought services
- the formulation that guided the development of the plan
- the strengths that were recognized and built upon
- the discharge/transition criteria—the goals
- the major services or interventions provided
- the changes and growth that occurred as a result of the interventions and service
- current and anticipated future service needs

As appropriate, the transition or discharge summary may include additional information such as diagnosis, medications, health concerns, medical treatments, and so on. Accreditation standards all require that a "transition summary," "continuing care plan" and/or "discharge summary" be prepared and include essential elements such as those previously listed. This plan can then be utilized to facilitate continuity of services as individuals and families move from one provider and setting to another. These records are also helpful if an individual or family leaves services and then returns seeking help anew.

Evaluating Provider Performance

Not only is it essential to evaluate the progress of the individual and family in their journey towards wellness and recovery, from time to time it is important to evaluate how well the provider is doing in meeting the needs of those seeking services. Recovery is not only about the destination; it is also about the journey. Understanding the provider's role in helping individuals toward their final destination should be a part of the process of ongoing learning and quality improvement. In a sense, the provider is on a journey as well, to be the best possible coach and facilitator of others' recovery.

Providers have at least two masters to satisfy. In a traditional sense, their supervisor, agency director, and/or payer is their boss. However, in a recovery-oriented approach, the ultimate judges of the performance of the provider (and system) are the individual and family receiving services. A formal evaluation process to assess provider performance should include these three components of feedback, evaluation and accountability. Ideally feedback is gathered from service users and their families, other team members, referring agencies and the like in order to get a balanced picture. The information gathered should be used to support ongoing staff development and quality improvement initiatives.

Evaluating the Experience of Care

Over the past 10 years there has been increasing use of formal participant survey tools to gain feedback from the recipients of services and from their family members about their perception and experience of services. This is different from a mere evaluation of satisfaction and instead attempts an understanding of key or critical points in the service-delivery process.

The Person-Centered Care Questionnaire (PCCQ) developed by Tondora and Miller at the Yale Program for Recovery and Community Health (2009) has four versions for measuring the experience of care and satisfaction with person-centered planning approaches; the Person in Recovery version, the Provider version, the Administrator version and the Stakeholder (families, employers, other agencies, etc.) version[4]. The Person in Recovery version can be found in Table 7.1. The PCCQ includes a list of key indicators (32 items) that inquire about the extent to which treatment planning reflects person-centered values and principles. Items assess the *process* dimension of PCP (i.e., the meeting and dialog that informs the plan) as well as the associated *documentation* aspects (i.e., the resulting written plan itself). Using the scales provided, stakeholders will indicate the extent to which they agree or disagree with each of the items when thinking about their experience of treatment planning. It is recommended that all four versions be administered in order to obtain different perspectives and inform the team as to how to improve practice.

Table 7.1

Person Centered Care Planning Questionnaire — Person in Recovery (PIR) Version

Tondora, J., & Miller, R. (2009). Yale Program for Recovery and Community Health.

Please indicate the degree to which you agree or disagree with the following statements about your experiences of care or treatment planning.

The scale ranges from 1 for strongly disagree to 5 for strongly agree, with the following options inbetween. It also is possible to check DK if you feel you do not know how to rate a specific item.

1	2	3	4	5	DK
Strongly disagree	Somewhat disagree	Neither agree nor disagree	Somewhat agree	Strongly agree	I don't know

		Strongly agree					I don't know
		1	2	3	4	5	DK
1.	My provider reminds me that I can bring my family, friends, or other supportive people to my treatment planning meetings.						
2.	I get a copy of the treatment plan to keep.						
3.	My goals are written in my own words in the plan.						
4.	My treatment plan is written so that I can understand it. Words that I don't understand are explained to me.						
5.	I was able to include healing practices based on my culture in the plan.						
6.	I can invite other providers, like my vocational or housing specialist, to the meeting if I want.						
7.	My strengths and talents are talked about in my plan.						
8.	In my plan, I can see how I'll use my strengths to work on my goals.						
9.	In my plan, there are next steps for me and my provider to work on.						

Continued

Table 7.1 —cont'd

	1 Strongly disagree	2 Somewhat disagree	3 Neither agree nor disagree	4 Somewhat agree	5 Strongly agree	DK I don't know
10.	Those areas of my life that I want to work on (like health, social relationships, getting a job, housing, and spirituality) are talked about and included in my plan if I want them.					
11.	My treatment team really understood how I explained what was going on for me, based on how I see it in my culture.					
12.	The goals in my plan are important to me.					
13.	I feel like when my provider and I work on a treatment plan, we work together as a team.					
14.	I decide how the meeting is run and what we'll talk about during my treatment planning meeting.					
15.	In my plan, my provider refers to me as "a person with" a mental health issue and does not define me by a label, e.g., "a schizophrenic" or "a bipolar."					
16.	Cultural factors (such as my spiritual beliefs and my cultural views) are considered in my plan.					
17.	I know ahead of time about when my treatment planning meeting is going to happen.					
18.	My plan talks about what I want to get back in my life, not just what I'm trying to get rid of.					
19.	I know what amount of time I have to work on each step in my plan.					
20.	As part of my planning meetings, I get education about my rights and about my responsibilities in treatment.					

21.	As part of the plan, I have things that I'm supposed to do to work on my goals.												
22.	Other people, like my friends and family, have things that they are supposed to do to help me work on my plan, and those things are written in the plan.												
23.	I am offered education about personal wellness, advanced directives, and Wellness Recovery Action Planning (WRAP) as part of my planning meeting.												
24.	I feel like my plan helps me get back involved in my community, not just in places that provide services for people with mental illness.												
25.	My provider asked me about parts of my culture that she or he did not understand to make the treatment plan better for me.												
26.	I feel like my provider supports me in working on things like getting a job and managing my money, even if I still have other issues.												
27.	I got information about peer support as part of my planning meeting.												
28.	If needed, I was able to get a bilingual/bicultural translator for my treatment planning meeting.												
29.	I feel like my culture was really taken into consideration when working on my treatment plan.												
30.	I feel involved in the treatment planning process.												
31.	It is clear to me in my plan how certain interventions/treatments will help me achieve my goals.												
32.	I have the chance to review and make changes to my plan.												
The best part of the treatment planning process has been													
If I could change something about treatment planning, it would be													

The Mental Health Statistics Improvement Project (MHSIP) consumer survey was first developed in 1996 and has become a virtual standard in the field; its use is still required by the US Substance Abuse and Mental Health Services Administration (SAMHSA) as a part of federal block grants to the states[5]. The survey is included in Table 7.2. It has been used successfully with a wide range of service recipients in many different settings to obtain feedback from individuals and families. Many of the items pertain immediately to how the individual and family perceive and experience the process of treatment planning and the role that they as consumers play in determining their goals and treatment. These surveys are an excellent tool for providing feedback to providers about their performance at being person-centered.

Building on the PCCQ development in 2009, in 2010, Tondora and Grieder developed the Person Centered Planning Quality Indicators (PCPQI) at the request of the New York Association of Psychosocial Rehabilitation Services (NYAPRS). This evaluation tool includes a total of 17 items for a medical record review that effectively defines the person-centered planning process and helps to better determine the actual performance of community-based programs serving adults. Using information from both persons receiving services (a seven question tool that can be conducted via a survey or a focus group), as well as the chart record, the PCPQI can provide a snapshot of person-centered practices to use as the basis for making program improvements and celebrating successes. The findings can be used as an educational tool to demystify the process and can also help to evaluate the impact of training and process improvement efforts. It can also serve as a tool for clinical supervisors to create clear expectations and to help shape employee performance development plans, as well as to validate/reward excellent performance/efforts. The PCP Quality Indicators and the subscales are included in Table 7.3 on page 212.

Quality Assessment

Providers, either solo practitioners or members of large organized care delivery systems, should have some periodic ongoing and formal quality assessment and review of their work. This should include, at minimum, a review of records that not only considers the quantity and timeliness of record documents but also addresses the "quality" of the documentation. There are multiple purposes to such reviews, including efforts to improve the quality of services provided to each individual, assess appropriateness and patterns of utilization of services, and identify training needs.

Table 7.2 MHSIP Adult Consumer Survey

	Strongly Agree	Agree	I am Neutral	Disagree	Strongly Disagree	Not Applicable
1. I like the services that I received here.						
2. If I had other choices, I would still get services from this agency.						
3. I would recommend this agency to a friend or family member.						
4. The location of services was convenient (parking, public transportation, distance, etc.).						
5. Staff were willing to see me as often as I felt it was necessary.						
6. Staff returned my call in 24 hours.						
7. Services were available at times that were good for me.						
8. I was able to get all the services I thought I needed.						
9. I was able to see a psychiatrist when I wanted to.						
10. Staff here believe that I can grow, change and recover.						
11. I felt comfortable asking questions about my treatment and medication.						

Continued

Table 7.2 MHSIP Adult Consumer Survey—cont'd

	Strongly Agree	Agree	I am Neutral	Disagree	Strongly Disagree	Not Applicable
12. I felt free to complain.						
13. I was given information about my rights.						
14. Staff encouraged me to take responsibility for how I live my life.						
15. Staff told me what side effects to watch out for.						
16. Staff respected my wishes about who is and who is not to be given information about my treatment.						
17. I, not staff, decided my treatment goals.						
18. Staff were sensitive to my cultural background (race, religion, language, etc.).						
19. Staff helped me obtain the information I needed so that I could take charge of managing my illness.						
20. I was encouraged to use consumer-run programs (support groups, drop-in centers, crisis lines, etc.).						

In order to provide the best possible mental health services, we need to know what you think about the services you received during the last [specify time period], the people who provided it, and the results. There is space at the end of the survey to comment on any of your answers.

As a direct result of services I received								
21. I deal more effectively with daily problems.								
22. I am better able to control my life.								
23. I am better able to deal with crisis.								
24. I am getting along better with my family.								
25. I do better in social situations.								
26. I do better in school and/or work.								
27. My housing situation has improved.								
28. My symptoms are not bothering me as much.								

Table 7.3 Person-Centered Planning Quality Indicators—Person in Recovery Subscale

We Want to Know: Tell us about your experience in treatment/recovery planning…				
As part of a broader effort in _____, our agency is working hard to redesign our services so that they are consumer-centered, and driven by the needs and preferences of the people we serve. One important part of this effort is thinking about how we go about the process of treatment planning—sometimes also called service planning or recovery planning. We would like to hear from you about your experiences planning with your team, and would appreciate your feedback on the items listed below.				

Person-Centered Planning Indicators: Person In Recovery Perspective

Item #	RESPONSE	Yes	No	I Don't Know
A1	My provider reminds me that I can bring my family, friends or other supportive people to my treatment planning meetings.			
A2	My plan has goals (hopes and dreams) that are important to me and they are about more than just symptom management. My plan focuses on things like making friends, getting a job and pursuing new interests.			
A3	My provider asked me about parts of my culture (such as my spiritual beliefs and my cultural views) that she or he did not understand to make the treatment/service/recovery plan better for me.			
A4	I am offered education about personal wellness, advanced directives, personalized relapse prevention plans and Wellness Recovery Action Planning (WRAP) as part of my planning meeting.			
A5	I have the opportunity to work with a Peer Specialist/Coach if I want help getting ready for my planning meeting.			
A6	I am offered a copy of my plan to review and keep.			
A7	Staff support me in making my own decisions/choices to take risks/try new things (e.g., work, hobbies, relationships, a new apartment) instead of delaying/waiting until my symptoms are better.			

© Janis Tondora, Psy.D (Janis.tondora@yale.edu) and Diane Grieder, M.Ed (diane@alipar.org) 2011. Please contact primary authors for permission to use.

Table 7.3 Person-Centered Planning Quality Indicators—Person in Recovery Subscale—*cont'd*

Person-Centered Planning Quality Indicators—Chart Review Subscale			
As part of a broader effort in _____, our agency is working/striving to redesign our services so that they are maximally consumer–centered, and driven by the needs and preferences of the people we serve. One important part of this effort is thinking about both the process and documentation of treatment/service/recovery planning. Please use the below quality indicators checklist to evaluate the presence/absence of key PCP documentation indicators.			
	Person-Centered Planning Indicators: Documentation Quality		
	Item #	**Yes**	**No**
B1	The assessment (can include a psychosocial assessment/assessment update/narrative summary/comprehensive psychiatric rehabilitation assessment, etc.) includes the person's strengths. Strengths include, but are not limited to: environmental strengths, positive previous treatment experiences, interests/hobbies, abilities and accomplishments, unique individual attributes, recovery resources/assets.		
B2	The plan/plan update actively incorporates the person's identified strengths into the goals, objectives or interventions.		
B3	The narrative summary includes the following required elements: Strengths, interests, and current and/or desired life roles and priorities Any interfering perpetuating factors, e.g., trauma history, co-occurring medical or substance use disorders, etc. Ideally, a narrative can succinctly capture very relevant as well as more recent factors—these are the barriers that get in the way of the person achieving their goal on their own Individual's stage of change (stage of change readiness for any relevant behavior change that could help them move towards their goal(s)) Available natural supports or community resources Cultural factors and any impact on treatment A clinical hypothesis/understanding/core theme re: what drives the individual's experience of illness and recovery (this incorporates the individual's perception of their problems in how they relate to their goals, as well as the team's/practitioner's observations).		

Continued

Table 7.3 Person-Centered Planning Quality Indicators—Person In Recovery Subscale—*cont'd*

	Person-Centered Planning Indicators: Documentation Quality		
Item #		Yes	No
B4	The goal statements on the plan/plan update are about having a meaningful life in the community, not only symptom reduction or compliance.		
B5	The plan/plan update includes interventions beyond the paid professional clinical/rehab services and notes self-directed action steps/and/or action steps by natural supporters. (Note: These are typically identified within the assessment process and build upon the person's strengths.)		
B6	The plan/plan update uses "person-first" language (i.e., a *person living with schizophrenia* NOT a *schizophrenic*) and/or the individual's name throughout the document.		
B7	The plan/plan update is developed collaboratively and there is evidence of direct input from the person, e.g., includes quotes from the individual and/or statements such as "Jose stated…" It is important that the person's "voice" is heard.		
B8	There is evidence in the record that the person was offered a copy of their plan. (Note: This may be found in a progress note following the planning meeting or directly on the plan itself.)		
B9	The target dates of short-term objectives on the plan/plan update are individualized rather than all objectives defaulting to a standard update cycle, e.g., every 90 days.		
B10	The plan/plan update describes attempts to help the person to connect with chosen activities in the community rather than relying on social supports coming solely from mental health agencies.		

© Janis Tondora, Psy.D (Janis.tondora@yale.edu) and Diane Grieder, M.Ed (diane@alipar.org) 2011.

One way that practitioners can do a quick check of the quality of their work in person-centered planning is to actually review the person-centered plans that are in the records to see if there are logical links between the plan elements. For instance, to make sure that plans are coherent and logical, it can be useful to review the plan from "the bottom up" as well as from the top down. Starting with the descriptions of each intervention, and then looking at the objectives, the goals, the integrated summary and finally the assessment. From this perspective, the interventions should be logical strategies likely to help the individual achieve objectives, and the objectives should be tied to resolving barriers that keep the person from their goals. The rationale for the interventions should be embedded in the understandings that make up the integrated summary. All these elements should support the medical necessity of the interventions and be consistent with the individual's stage of change.

There are a number of tools and resources that can help with quality focused record review. Accreditation programs are increasingly focused on the importance of person-centered approaches to wellness and recovery services. Both CARF International's and the Joint Commission on Accreditation of Healthcare Organizations' (JCAHO) behavioral health accreditation manuals have standards that address the need for person-centered assessments, including an integrated summary, along with person-centered treatment planning and care. Standards typically require that records be reviewed on a periodic and ongoing manner to determine if:

- the psychosocial assessment is comprehensive
- the written plan follows the assessment conclusions
- goals and objectives are based on active input from the individual and are understandable to the individual
- objectives are measurable and appropriate
- services delivered relate to the goals and objectives
- co-occurring disorders are addressed
- progress is documented and relates to the plan
- the plan is regularly reviewed and updated

The Council on Quality (CQL) is a unique accrediting organization that has taken a different approach. Its accreditation standards are virtually entirely driven by the values and principles of person-centered care. Its accreditation key factors and success indicators for behavioral health include Person-Centered Assessment, Discovery and Person-Centered Planning, as detailed in their reference manual *What Really Matters, A Guide to Person-Centered Excellence*[6]. For instance, their criteria for person-centered planning requires that:

- The plan identifies and integrates natural supports and paid services
- Informal community resources are used
- Planning is responsive to changing priorities, opportunities and needs
- Planning and funding are connected to outcomes and supports, not programs

A new evaluation of Assertive Community Treatment (ACT) programs utilizes the TMACT: Tool for Measurement of Assertive Community Treatment, developed by Monroe, Moser and Teague, and is a contemporary update to the Dartmouth Assertive Community Treatment Scale (DACTS)[7]. This evaluation tool uses a variety of measures and approaches, including interviews and chart reviews to determine fidelity to ACT; one of its six subscales is devoted to person-centered planning and practices. This subscale has items including:

- strengths identified in assessment informing the plan
- interventions target a broad range of life domains including physical health, employment, housing, and so on
- consumer self-determination and choice
- items concerning the planning process itself and the revision of plans

The TMACT also evaluates integrated addiction and mental health treatment practices for ACT teams via the Integrated Dual Disorders Treatment (IDDT) model[8]. Those standards require that the entire team uses a strengths-based, stage-wise approach to understanding the individual's needs, motivational interviewing and cognitive behavioral principles[9].

Records may be reviewed for a whole host of other reasons or concerns, including documentation of service provision for billing and the assurance of medical necessity. Rather than being prescriptive or comprehensive, the above list is meant to suggest at least some quality of care concerns that should be reflected and documented in the record. Some organizations have gone so far as to quantify the record review by assigning points to the different elements and then arriving at a total score for that record and the responsible provider. Other organizations have developed automated databases that capture the findings of a record and prepare reports that can be easily given to providers and their supervisors. No matter the methodology, the goal is to give providers feedback about their performance and to continually improve the person-centeredness of assessment, planning and services provided.

Ideally, record reviews should be tied directly into the organization's quality management activities system and should be used to improve the quality of services. Regular reports of overall performance should be made available to key staff responsible for advancing person-centered recovery and wellness-oriented practices. Typically such reports are analyzed for trends and are reported in aggregate form to a larger audience; however, findings should also be shared with individual providers so that they have an opportunity to make necessary corrections and improvements. Examples of organizational changes that can occur as a result of quality records review may include additional training or the allocation of funding for staff training, program design and implementation, personnel assignments, evaluation of staff competencies and improved outcomes.

A record review to assess the quality and person-centeredness of services may also be organized as a peer-review effort and involve direct-care staff. By involving the actual providers in the review, direct learning occurs through the process of understanding and reviewing a set of criteria that reflects appropriate documentation of quality services. If the organization is truly recovery oriented, then it may also include recovery coaches and other persons with lived experience in the peer-review process—with all necessary precautions required to assure the confidentiality of records.

No matter who the peer reviewers are, they all need to receive training on how to evaluate records from a quality perspective and an understanding of quality theory and quality improvement practice. Such reviews should never be seen as an effort at fault-finding but rather as a mechanism for service delivery system improvement. When such training does not occur, the strength and purpose of the peer-review process is at risk of being devalued by the recipients of the review. Initially, staff members may be somewhat resistant to a peer-review process, as they are hesitant to examine and comment upon their colleague's work, and equally reluctant to have their own work evaluated. However, if presented as a learning tool for overall program improvement, the process is usually accepted and becomes a dynamic method for staff to support each other in improving their skills, knowledge and abilities. Additionally, it is important to educate staff that the process provides aggregate information to assist management in making decisions related to the organization's staff education and training.

Another approach is to utilize supervisors in the review process or engage external reviewers such as contract quality improvement (QI) organizations or consultants. If the review process is linked to responsibilities for clinical supervision, then this review and its findings can become part of an employed provider's annual job performance review. Such a review can also serve as a compliance or quality assurance (QA) audit as well as a tool to support a continuous quality improvement focus; even in an organization with a strong commitment to ongoing quality improvement there must also be a mechanism to assure regulatory compliance. QA-type reviews are often conducted to assure that there is adequate documentation to support the medical necessity of all billed services—ranging from assessments and services plans within specified timeframes to notes documenting each service provided.

Clinical supervisors can be the linchpins to the sustainability of person-centered practices in any organization. As such, they should be given time and encouragement to make record reviews a routine part of their work. This does not necessarily require a formal chart review process using established timelines, sample sizes, checklists, and so on; supervisors can conduct more informal reviews of person-centered plans when reviewing individual "cases" and in supervisory sessions with staff, either individually or in groups. This implies that the supervisor has the competencies and skills to complete quality documentation themselves, as well as to provide staff with examples of how they want documentation completed, and provide strengths-based feedback to staff. A supervisor should have the ability to determine the following in a review:

- Does the plan meet all the definitions of person-centered elements?
- Is information from the strengths assessment being reflected in practice?
- Are strengths used to develop the goals, objectives and interventions?
- Are naturally occurring resources identified and used in the plan?
- Are the individual's skills and abilities identified and used, along with any personal medicine strategies, as appropriate?
- Do the progress notes reflect a continuous search for or development of the individual's/family's strengths?
- Does the work reflect purposeful movement toward goals and objectives?
- Does the clinician appear stuck, frustrated or reactive in their work?

Table 7.4 includes a sample review tool that provides an example of how a record review can be organized and the review points highlighted. This particular sample is a combination of both quantitative and qualitative measures that are derived from a range of sources including licensure and certification requirements along with accreditation standards. The required "due dates" for completing the various elements of the record are arbitrary and only meant to be illustrative. An organization should determine the elements of a record review form that best meets its needs in order to support conformance to internal policies and procedures, billing documentation, external accountability and regulatory demands.

Yet another useful tool for review of person-centered treatment plans was developed under the auspices of the Minnesota Department of Human Services Direct Treatment and Care Division: the *Treatment Plan Fidelity Review*[10]. Although adaptable to many settings, this review matrix was specifically developed for the review of hospital records for inpatient care. A sample of this review form is in Table 7.5.

Regardless of exactly how such a review is conducted, the purpose, ranging from quality improvement to compliance assurance, it is essential that the expectations and values implicit in the review be consistent with the principles of a person-centered approach to assessment, formulation,

Table 7.4 Recovery Record Review Form

Indicator	Criteria	Frequency	Critical value	Reviewer's comments
1. Initial intake/screening	Intake form is completed	Same day as admission		
2. Medical exam	History and physical form is completed	Within 5 days of admission		
3. Preliminary recovery plan	Form is completed and filed in the record	Within 5 days of admission		
4. Orientation completed	Orientation checklist is signed and filed in the record	Within 7 days of admission		
5. Complete and thorough psychosocial assessment	Includes all domains and the person's strengths, needs, abilities and preferences	Within 10 days of admission and annual update		
6. Interpretive summary	Includes the person's strengths, needs, abilities and preferences, level of care, duration of treatment, co-occurring diagnoses	Within 10 days of admission		
7. Complete recovery plan	Includes documentation of a planning meeting, the person's signature and filed in record	Within 15 days of admission		
8. Goals on plan follow the assessment summary	Goals relate to the assessment summary information			
9. Goals are understandable to the person and are based on his/her input	Goals are expressed in the words of the person			

Continued

Table 7.4 Recovery Record Review Form—cont'd

Indicator	Criteria	Frequency	Critical value	Reviewer's comments
10. Goals are broad, long term, written positively	They represent the person's needs and are not deficit based			
11. Objectives are on the plan	They relate to goals, are action oriented, steps to achieving the goal(s)			
12. Objectives are measurable and understandable	It can be identified when they are achieved and the person is actually able to do them			
13. Objectives are time framed	Each objective has an anticipated timeframe to be accomplished			
14. Interventions are identified	These can be services provided by the staff, others, natural supports, family members			
15. Interventions are provided by...	Identification of who is providing services, including credential, title or affiliation			
16. Interventions happen when and how often	Frequency of services is identified			
17. The plan is reviewed and updated	Progress notes indicate a planning meeting has occurred, the plan itself is revised, a quarterly report is written	At least quarterly		
		TOTAL		

Critical value = points on a scale of 1–3, with 3 representing full compliance, 2 partial compliance, and 1 no compliance. Highest possible score is 51.

Table 7.5 Treatment Plan Fidelity Review for AMH & MNS

Reviewer:	Patient Record #:	Admission Date:
Date of Review:	Date of Treatment Plan Reviewed:	

Technical Areas:

0 = **Not Met** (Comments Required) 0–90%	1 = Not applicable—cannot be used	2 = **Met** (Comments Optional) 90% or Better

Person-Centered Areas:

0 = **Not Met** (Comments Required) 0–50%	1 = **Partially Met** (Comments Required) 50–90%	2 = **Met** (Comments Optional) 90% or Better

Strengths, Needs, Narrative Summary & Case Formulation

Areas of Focus		Score		Comments
Technical	**Strengths:** The strengths listed under this heading should be the specific "patient strengths that can be utilized in treatment…" CMS 482.61(c)(1)	0	2	
	Needs: These are resources and skills not currently possessed by the patient that will be necessary to achieve the identified goals and overcome identified barriers. These are needs the patient has and should not be mistaken as staff needs.	0	2	
	Narrative Summary: Has the information gained from assessing/evaluating the patient been utilized to create an individualized treatment plan? CMS Probe: 482.61 (C) (1)	0	2	
	Narrative Summary: Does it capture the patient's story?	0	2	
	Case Formulation: One to two sentences that give the reader the "so what" from the narrative summary and then the focus of treatment, for this hospitalization as well as the immediate direction for the next week.	0	2	

Continued

Table 7.5 Treatment Plan Fidelity Review for AMH & MNS—*cont'd*

	0	1	2
Case Formulation: Prioritization of problems is evident. Physical problems are identified with problem statements, goals, and objectives ONLY if they require active treatment or interfere with treatment during the pt's hospitalization.	0		2
Reason for Continued Hospitalization: Beyond being filled in, this field has to clearly support the need for continued hospital level of care.	0		2
Discharge Criteria: Describe what is necessary for this patient to meet the minimum requirements needed for discharge to a lower level of care.	0		2
Person-Centered — **Narrative Summary**: Starts with 2–3 sentences that provide a description of this patient as a person, aside from their illness.	0	1	2
Patient statements about their treatment problems and discharge are incorporated in the plan, beginning with the Narrative Summary (CMS Tag B119 Probe).	0	1	2
Descriptions of the patient's Strengths and Needs and the Narrative Summary and Case Formulation are written in **person-centered language**.	0	1	2
Individual patient's values and priorities are taken into account.	0	1	2

Quality Area	Quality Concern?	Detailed Explanation of Concern(s) & Coaching Recommendations
Strengths/Needs	@ Yes @ No	
Narrative Summary/Case Formulations	@ Yes @ No	
Assessments	@ Yes @ No	

Most Recently Updated Treatment Plan

Areas of Focus			Score		Comments
Technical	**Reason for Continued Hospitalization:** Beyond being filled in, this field has to clearly support the need for continued hospital level of care.		0	2	
	Discharge Criteria: Describe the changes in the patient's current needs and circumstances to meet the minimum requirements for discharge to a lower level of care.		0	2	
	Update Note	Gives a clear picture of how the patient is doing clinically: successes in the past week, medical status/changes in the past week, VRRP changes carried forward. Documents rationale for decisions regarding Goals, Objectives, and Interventions.	0	2	
		Captures active involvement of others by phone, in person, or through correspondence during the past week (family, county, other support providers).	0	2	
		Summarizes discharge planning activities.	0	2	
		Includes the direction of treatment for the upcoming week, based on new or revised information obtained through ongoing assessment.	0	2	
Pers–Cent	Patient statements about their treatment problems and discharge are incorporated in the plan, (CMS Tag B119 Probe).		0	1	2
	All major components of the treatment plan are updated to match the most recent patient Update Note, which includes the direction of treatment.		0	1	2

Continued

Table 7.5 Treatment Plan Fidelity Review for AMH & MNS—cont'd

Quality Area	Quality Concern?	Detailed Explanation of Concern(s) & Coaching Recommendations
Updated Treatment Plan/Updated Note	@ Yes @ No	

Problem Statement

Areas of Focus		Score		Comments
Technical	**Comprehensive Treatment Plan:** Does each Problem Statement follow logically from the Case Formulation? **Updated Treatment Plan:** Does each Problem Statement follow logically from the direction of treatment as indicated in the updated note?	0	2	
	Does each problem statement describe what specific problem will be treated during the hospitalization? (CMS Probes 482.61(C) (1)(i).	0	2	
	Does each problem statement identify and precisely describe a problem behavior (not generic descriptions such as "paranoid", "aggressive", "depressed", "alteration in thought process", or "ineffective coping")? (CMS Probes 482.61(C) (1)(i).	0	2	
	Comprehensive Treatment Plan: Does each problem statement describe the pattern of behavior that brought the patient into the hospital. **Updated Treatment Plan:** Does each problem statement describe what the current problem that is being focused on right now to move this patient forward – should flow from the Update Note.	0	2	
	No more than one problem area is identified in each Problem Statement.	0	2	

Quality Area	Quality Concern?	Detailed Explanation of Concern(s) & Coaching Recommendations
Problem Statement	@ Yes @ No	

Goals

Areas of Focus		Score			Comments
Technical	No more than one change in behavior or status is identified in each Goal statement.	0		2	
	Does each treatment plan goal relate to the problem statement?	0		2	
	Each goal indicates an outcome to be achieved by the patient and not an intervention to be provided or which patients are to comply with? (CMS Probes (C) (1)(ii)	0		2	
	Are the criteria used to measure success for each goal readily apparent? (CMS Probes (C) (1)(ii)	0		2	
	Goals are the addition of positive or desirable behaviors, not the reduction or absence of negative behaviors.	0		2	
	How relevant are the treatment plan goals to the patient's condition? (CMS Probe (C) (1) (ii)	0		2	
Person–Centered	Individualized/personalized goals are used.	0	1	2	
	Goals can be reasonably expected to resolve the patient's problems for treatment success and discharge.	0	1	2	
	Barriers that keep the patient from attaining their goal are identified.	0	1	2	

Continued

Table 7.5 Treatment Plan Fidelity Review for AMH & MNS—cont'd

Quality Area	Quality Concern?	Detailed Explanation of Concern(s) & Coaching Recommendations
Goals	@ Yes @ No	

Objectives

Areas of Focus		Score			Comments
Technical	No more than one behavioral change is identified in each Objective statement.	0		2	
	Each Objective is behaviorally specific.	0		2	
	Each Objective is measurable.	0		2	
	Each Objective is a step toward meeting the Goal.	0		2	
	Each objective addresses an identified Barrier.	0		2	
	Target Date not over 7 days without rationale documented in Weekly Summary; should never be over 14 days. (AMRTC: Target Date not over 14 days without documented rationale.)	0		2	
Person-Centered	Each Objective is described in positive terms (presence of desirable behavior or symptom change).	0	1	2	
	Objectives are specific to the patient and their unique treatment needs.	0	1	2	

Quality Area	Quality Concern?	Detailed Explanation of Concern(s) & Coaching Recommendations
Objectives	@ Yes @ No	

Interventions

Areas of Focus		Score	Comments
Technical	Interventions are written as actions staff will take, that are specific to that patient to address a specific need/issue/objective (i.e. makes an intervention unique for that patient and does not read as a job description for the staff providing the intervention).	0 2	
	The intervention must state the purpose or intended impact as it relates to the patient's objective.	0 2	
	Discipline/classification needs to be identified in the intervention statement.	0 2	
	Frequency is stated in the intervention..	0 2	
	Do the disciplines represented in the treatment plan interventions represent the patient's *current* needs?	0 2	
Person-Centered	Interventions are tailored to the patient's stage of change readiness.	0 1 2	
	Interventions are individualized to accommodate the learning, understanding or communication needs of the patient.	0 1 2	

Quality Area	Quality Concern?	Detailed Explanation of Concern(s) & Coaching Recommendations
Interventions	@ Yes @ No	

Continued

Table 7.5 Treatment Plan Fidelity Review for AMH & MNS—*cont'd*

General Elements

Area of Focus		Score		Comments
Technical	Is the treatment plan individualized, i.e. patient specific, or is there a predictable sameness from plan to plan? (CMS Probes 482.61(C)(1)	0	2	
	Do the pieces of the treatment plan work together to achieve the greatest possible gain for the patient? (CMS Probes 482.61 (C) (1)(iii)	0	2	

Progress Notes (Including Engagement Log Entries)

Areas of Focus		Score			Comments
Technical	Do the progress notes indicate what staff is doing to carry out the treatment plan?	0		2	
	Does the content of the progress notes reflect the impact of the interventions on the objectives?	0		2	
	Do the progress notes indicate what the patient did or said in response to treatment?	0		2	
	Do the progress notes document Active Treatment.	0		2	
	Overall quality of documentation in Progress Notes.	0		2	
Person-Centered Centered	Progress notes include information that captures how staff are modifying approaches to accommodate unique patient characteristics.	0	1	2	
	The progress notes show evidence of staff eliciting patient input in modifications to Interventions.	0	1	2	
	The progress notes reflect the patient perspective of their treatment experience.	0	1	2	

Quality Area	Quality Concern?	Detailed Explanation of Concern(s) & Coaching Recommendations
Progress Notes	@ Yes @ No	

planning and providing services. Few things are more maddening and demoralizing for staff than to be taught one set of values and expectations only to find that in reality they are held to another set of standards. In organizations attempting to shift from earlier practice approaches to a recovery-oriented, person-centered model, inconsistencies between training expectations and performance review findings can seriously undermine staff spirit and ultimately erode quality of care. There must be an alignment of expectations and standards throughout the system; providers (especially those working in organized systems of care) cannot effect the necessary changes on their own, no matter how committed to the principles and values they may be. Real change must occur at all levels of a system in order for the vision and hope of person-centered recovery-oriented care to be a reality for all individuals and families served.

Outcomes

No matter how well written standards are, how well designed the system is or how well trained the reviewers may be, standards and criteria are always open to interpretation. Determining the quality of documentation and the fidelity of a person-centered approach to planning will always be seen through the eyes of the observer. Each evaluator, despite using the same set of standards, will bring their own set of values and experiences and potential bias into the process and might view the same criteria differently. The most important consideration overall is to remember that the ultimate evaluator of quality is the individual receiving services, based on the *outcomes* for each individual.

However, measuring outcomes from services is an enormously complex and in some instances controversial issue. The challenges in measuring outcomes are many and have challenged the mental health and substance abuse fields for many years without a general consensus about best practices and strategies. The topic is worth a book of its own. Many providers and provider organizations do want accurate information about the benefit they provide to individuals and families, while others get concerned that they will be found to be underperforming especially in comparison to other providers. More than that is the ongoing debate about what to measure and what instruments should be used to gather and analyze data about outcomes. And then there is the issue about whether outcomes should be measured by persons served only, providers or both, and what level of aggregation should be used in evaluating the findings.

Table 7.6, *Milestones in Recovery from Mental Illness,* presents an integrated set of outcomes or milestones developed by individuals, families and providers from Stanislaus County, California[11]. This is offered simply as an excellent example of how one could go about identifying outcomes from the perspective of adults with mental illness—there are countless others that could have been selected for discussion. The eight clear milestones described in the recovery process are all components of successful person-centered outcomes. These milestones, similar in thought and process to the Alcoholics Anonymous 12 Steps to Recovery, are also aligned with the stages of change model. In addition, subjective and objective indicators make explicit

Table 7.6 Milestones in Recovery from Mental Illness

There are many paths to recovery. The following key milestones in the recovery process were developed by consensus groups involving individuals, families and providers. They were developed from the individual's point of view and identify those key accomplishments that are commonly part of the progression in the recovery process. There are many other accomplishments in numerous life domains that may be part of the breadth of an individual's recovery that are not included in this table.

	Subjective	Objective
R	I begin to ***Recognize*** my inner distress but may be unable to identify what it is.	Beginning awareness of problem(s) within oneself.
E	I begin to ***Examine*** my distress with the help of others.	Willingness to discuss problems and accept help.
C	I ***Choose*** to believe that hope exists.	Begin to believe that hope and recovery are possible.
O	I start ***Overcoming*** symptoms that keep me from examining what is important to me.	Coping with symptoms and examining life circumstances.
V	I ***Voluntarily*** take some action toward recovery.	Take action step(s) directed towards recovery.
E	I start to ***Enjoy*** the benefits of mutual recovery.	Actively participates in mutual aid, peer support and experiences benefits of recovery.
R	I am ***Responsible*** for my own recovery.	Takes ownership and responsibility for one's own recovery.
Y	***Yes***, I am helping others strengthen my recovery.	Being of service to others strengthens one's own recovery.

what one could expect to experience within the eight milestones. There are successes for each person's milestone, not a finite end to the individual's journey.

One of the challenges and controversies in outcome measurement is that historically outcome measures have tended to focus on predefined social goods, such as employment, housing, school attendance, reduced hospitalization, incarceration, and so on. There is no question that these are, for the most part, desirable benefits from services, but they are neither necessarily universal nor person-centered. For the individual who, for whatever reasons, is *not* interested in working, measures of employment do not match well and are not a meaningful assessment of outcome and the value and benefit derived from services that have been provided. The eight milestones offer an alternative approach to evaluating outcomes that focus on the individual and family and their recovery process, as well as their capacity to make choices and manage their own lives.

Clearly there is a real need for more work and research in the mental health and addictive disorders field in developing meaningful and relevant approaches to outcome measurement. The challenge is to rethink past approaches and to create outcome measurement tools that are consistent with person-centered approaches to services and individual self-defined recovery goals. The Stanislaus milestones are only one example of how this could be accomplished.

Some of this work is under way and ongoing. The Patient-Centered Outcomes Research Institute (PCORI) is an independent, non-profit, United States-based research organization created by the Patient Protection and Affordable Care Act of 2010 (PPACA). The mission of PCORI is to help people make informed health care decisions—and improve health care delivery and outcomes—by producing and promoting high-integrity, evidence-based information derived from research guided by individuals, caregivers and the broader health care community[12]. In the United Kingdom the NHS National Institute for Health Research (NIHR) has funded a five-year (2009–2014) program of research around recovery in adult mental health services, called REFOCUS. This provides an infrastructure to create a new informal and inclusive network to support recovery-focused research relevant to mental health services[13].

At the level of health care systems outcomes, *efficiency* is a growing concern and is likely to become ever more important as efforts are made to lower the cost of health care while preserving quality and improving outcomes. The Institute of Medicine's report *Best Care at Lower Cost: The Path to Continuously Learning Health Care in America* offers findings, conclusions and recommendations for implementation by key stakeholders to achieve a health care system that is consistently reliable and that constantly, systematically and seamlessly improves[14]. Recommendation Number Two from the report is to provide "patient-centered care." The report goes on to say that individuals and their families should be engaged at all levels of care, involved in their health care decisions and have community-based interventions to promote health. So while person-centeredness can be linked to improved outcomes and lower costs, exactly how best to measure and evaluate performance remains problematic.

Since the first edition of this book, much research has occurred around shared decision making, motivational interviewing, stages of change (see Chapter 1) and person-centeredness. Unfortunately, nine years later, person-centered planning itself is still not considered to be an evidenced-based practice; however, it is increasingly recognized as a "best practice" with an emerging evidence base to support its implementation and dissemination. Much is being looked at around the world in terms of research on recovery, including person-centered care. Still, much work remains.

III. MAKING IT HAPPEN

Ultimately all the values, principles, ideas, tactics, approaches, strategies, examples and tools presented in these pages need to be incorporated into daily practice so that integrated whole health approaches to person-centered care based on shared decision making become the new standard of routine care. But like the barriers faced by people embarked on their individual recovery journey, providers of health, mental health and substance abuse services face barriers in changing and improving current practice. Virtually any significant change process does, and in many instances a move to more person-centered care is virtually a paradigm shift rather than a matter of relatively minor modifications of existing practices and processes. This change requires not only new skills for providers but in many instances systems-level change in terms of how series delivery systems are designed and operated. Wagner's model provides some insight into the challenges that we face.

The first impulse when trying to change practice and systems is often to provide training to all who might be impacted with the change. However, our experience is that training is necessary but not sufficient. And not all training is alike or equally effective. The impact of didactic training such as lectures, webinars, seminars or even conferences is short lived beyond the training event itself—rarely does it translate into new skills and practices. Didactic training can be helpful in raising awareness and piquing interest in learning new ways, but more experiential approaches to learning are required to begin to develop some mastery of new skills—and with that practice and feedback and ongoing learning seem to be necessary to really help learners to become competent.

But competency is also necessary but not sufficient. The real issue is capability. Can providers take new knowledge, skills and abilities and apply them in real-world everyday practice? That is where the proverbial rubber meets the road in terms of meaningful and lasting paradigmatic change. Oftentimes the barriers to capability are not the lack of knowledge or ability, but rather systems-level and administrative issues which maintain the status quo. These must be addressed in parallel with the development of new skills if lasting change in practice is to be achieved. We have found working with small groups of providers and providing experiential training, followed by technical assistance that focuses on how to address, work with and work around those barriers, can be a successful change strategy—but it takes time, effort and consistency and a real commitment to make the change happen.

Health care reform, the push towards integration, the emphasis on Person-Centered Healthcare Homes and the implementation of the Affordable Care Act provide us all with an opportunity to make our service delivery systems more person-centered—and it is absolutely the right thing to do. Hopefully this book can be a resource to those who are committed to making our health care systems more humanistic, efficient, effective and recovery oriented.

REFERENCES

1. Stanhope V, Ingoglia C, Schmelter B, Marcus S. Impact of person-centered planning and collaborative documentation on treatment adherenc. *Psychiatr Ser.* 2013;64(1).
2. http://www.milestonesofrecovery.com/what_is_mors/.
3. White W, Boyle M, Loveland D, Corrington P. *The Behavioral Health Recovery Management Project: A Brief Primer.* Peoria, IL: Fayette Companies and Chestnut Health Systems.
4. http://www.ct.gov/dmhas/lib/dmhas/publications/PCCQprovider.pdf.
5. http://www.nri-inc.org/projects/SDICC/TA/Ganju.Smith_1.pdf.
6. The Council on Quality and Leadership. *Guide to Person-centered Excellence.* MD: Towson; 2010. http://www.thecouncil.org/pceguideforminandsubstanceabuse.asp.
7. Monroe-DeVita M, Moser LL, Teague GB. The tool for measurement of assertive community treatment (TMACT). Unpublished measure; 2011.

8. Mueser K. *Integrated Treatment for Dual Disorders: A Guide to Effective Practice.* Guilford Press; 2003.

9. Monroe-DeVita M, Teague GB, Moser LL. The TMACT: a new tool for measuring fidelity to assertive community treatment. *J Am Psychiatr Nurses Assoc.* 2011;17(1):17-29.

10. This tool was developed by Dr. Erwin Concepcion, Steve Dahl Penny Hogberg, Nicole McMahon, Carol Olson, Pamela Peters, Dr. Steven Pratt and Tona Willand.

11. Carroll A. Personal communication. Modesto, CA: Stanislaus County Behavioral Health and Recovery Services.

12. http://www.pcori.org/about-us/mission-and-vision/.

13. www.researchintorecovery.com.

14. Institute of Medicine. *Best Care at Lower Cost: The Path to Continuously Learning Health Care in America. Washington DC;* 2012.

Implementing Person Centered Recovery Planning

contributed by Laurel Blackman, DO, Austin State Hospital

I am thankful to the authors for inviting me to contribute to this important book with a few closing remarks about actually implementing Person Centered Recovery Planning (PCRP) on a State Hospital Inpatient Psychiatric Unit. In my experience, translating recovery values and principles into daily practice can be challenging and must account for organizational culture change as well as other barriers to system transformation. Below are a few notes about some lessons and successes achieved from our efforts at improving care at Austin State Hopsital in Texas

LESSON #1: WHAT PCRP ON A STATE HOSPITAL INPATIENT PSYCHIATRIC UNIT IS *NOT*

Person Centered Recovery Planning (PCRP) is not an idea or outcome on a piece of paper. It is not something patients do when they are better or keep handy for later reference after they discharge from the hospital. It is not something staff might do or try when they have the time or external motivation to do so. It is not some new age philosophy or academic think tank consensus for better delivery of mental health care and services. It is not a band-aid for staffing, environmental, funding, and programmatic challenges mandated by well-meaning administrators who rarely work the floor and regulatory surveyors who stroll through the campus whenever alerted or only when it is time to re-certify. It is not time limited, constrained to particular persons and situations, or narrowly applied to only some areas of life and living and never to others. So if it is not all or intended to be any of that, which is certainly what it can feel like much of the time, then what is it?

LESSON #2: WHAT PCRP ON A STATE HOSPITAL INPATIENT PSYCHIATRIC UNIT *IS*

PCRP is action and activity and connection and consideration at every possible exchange or juncture involving staff and patients occurring at any time of day on any day of the week. It is what we try, do, or help make happen with individuals who come to us either by external mandates or choice. It is a far and wide reaching priority for the preferences and things of importance to those with whom we partner–whatever that might be whenever and however voiced–as we go about our workdays to offer the best care we can to the wide variety of people who are our patients. Each detail and interaction, large or small, counts. Resoundingly, perhaps counter-intuitively, it is more often the littlest of things routinely overlooked that make the biggest difference in how far along we get how quickly as well as what we think and feel about what was needed to achieve and sustain any desired outcome. It includes all disciplines, functional groups, and identified supports. It is all encompassing, and everyone plays a part.

LESSON #3: PCRP IS MUCH HARDER TO PRESCRIBE AND PRACTICE THAN IT IS TO ENVISION ON A STATE HOSPITAL INPATIENT PSYCHIATRIC UNIT

PCRP on a state hospital inpatient psychiatric hospital unit is challenging for a whole host of reasons, but two particularly stand out. First, what person, employee, team, group, unit, hospital, agency, or system can be so super aware and accommodating every second, every day, for so many people? And how many of us really see how our part connects to the big picture and appreciate their inputs and actions as so essential? Right from the start with just the mention or introduction of PCRP, it already seems almost impossible and unclear to whom the responsibility and accountability falls. The short answer is that each and every person working on, or with the unit is responsible for promoting person–centeredness; for assuring that patients are treated as people first can–succeed even on an under-resourced state hospital inpatient psychiatric unit.

To make the idea of PCRP more readily understood and applicable to any and all of the unit's business, I think of PCRP as a verb. It is anything a person or group of people does or carries out in cooperation with a particular person who in this context we identify as a patient. It can be a huge thing or small thing. It can be an action, e.g. looking for an extra snack for someone who says they are hungry, or an occurrence, e.g. working out a time for out of town family to visit outside of regular visiting hours, or a state of being, e.g. taking time to listen or problem solve with someone who's angry, frightened, or upset.

There is a very subtle quality to PCRP that is tough to capture and point out, or artificially generate for teaching and training purposes. That quintessential quality is one of attentiveness. Attentiveness is an overarching value that guides PCRP. You just simply cannot have PCRP without attentiveness. While attentiveness is paramount to doing PCRP successfully, on the flip side, inattentiveness, or lack of attentiveness, absolutely cripples PCRP while also impacting lots of other important facility provisions–like quality of life, safety and risk mitigation, comfort and clarity in treatment relationships, patient and employee satisfaction, along with unit order and work flow.

Attentiveness is very hard to inspire, instill, and infuse. Solidifying in people charged with carrying out PCRP the value and practice of attentiveness is a tall order. Unfortunately it is easier to point out what inattentiveness is or looks like and what attentiveness is not than the opposite. However, developing a bank of actions that demonstrate, recognize, reinforce, and reward attentiveness is well worthwhile.

LESSON #4: PCRP WORKS FANTASTICALLY ON A STATE HOSPITAL INPATIENT PSYCHIATRIC UNIT AND CAN ENDURE THE STRUGGLES THAT PREDICTABLY ACCOMPANY ANY FULL-SCALE SHIFT OR CHANGE

Some of the successes we have seen using PCRP are nothing short of miraculous. We have had the honor and experienced the awe that comes with helping people who have been mired for years to decades in despair and strict limits, surpass all expectations and reintegrate into peer groups and less restrictive settings. Many have blossomed into futures that thankfully no longer include us here at the hospital because they have discharged to the community where only imagination and what the person wants to do next is the limit.

Name: Diana.

Age: 12.

Identifying Info: Latina girl who speaks Spanish and English. She lives with her mother Teresa, father Jorge, grandmother, two older brothers and one younger brother (ages 14, 10 and 3). She is in the 7th grade.

Presenting Problems: Diana has been referred for assessment and possible treatment by the school counselor because of changes in behavior and school performance since the beginning of the school year. Diana acknowledges that she is having school problems and states "I just want my teachers to be nice to me."

Teresa says that she has some idea about what the teachers are concerned about because at home Diana is often "hyper," seems very distractible and moody and has trouble completing homework. Mostly she has done well at school, but teachers have complained recently about her being more disruptive in class with refusing to follow directions, some back talk and talking with other students during assignments over the past six months. She gets intensely (over)involved with other girls, and seems to get very preoccupied with gossip and concerns about boys, her appearance and her popularity. She has frequent tantrums and is very demanding and argumentative with parents and siblings. She fights with her brothers but also seeks support and protection from the oldest brother, Jose.

She had a traumatic incident two years ago when she was stuck in a locked room with other children at school until nearly midnight when a lock broke and emergency personnel were required to open to door. She now feels anxious in rooms with closed doors. She has continued to have occasional bedwetting incidents since early childhood—possibly related to a tendency to recurrent urinary tract infections—but these incidents have increased in the last year.

Theresa is at a loss to explain her daughter's problems. Diana says she is upset because her mother is mean, expects her to be a "good little Mexican girl" and doesn't understand her "gringo" ways.

Family History: Parents immigrated to the USA from Michoacán, Mexico, 13 years ago. One of her brothers is in Special Ed due to developmental delays. Mother works full time, sometimes graveyard shifts at a fast food restaurant and father is not fully employed.

Teresa struggles to feel connected to her daughter and finds her hard to please (though Diana is attached to her grandmother and has less conflict with her father). Due to Teresa having experienced trauma in the past, she has difficulty expressing physical affection especially to a daughter. Teresa does not feel they had an easy time bonding when Diana was an infant, as she had to go back to work quite soon after the birth and had a hard time soothing her baby when she was upset. Teresa and Diana hoped the youngest child would be a sister for Diana and were both disappointed when another boy was born.

Grandmother has a strong leadership role in the family and influences rules. Jorge grew up without a father and believes a father is very important to his children. Mother, however, feels resentful that he seems to spend a lot of time watching TV and drinking beer. Mother has a lot of resentment about how much she has to be the one working to support the family. This takes away her quality time with husband and children or to supervise homework and adds stress getting out of the house in the mornings.

Historically—and even now—Diana is generally well liked by teachers and peers. Recently she has emerged as a star in her local church folklorico group. However, the family has difficulty transporting her to and from the dance group on a regular basis. She is verbal, expressive and artistic.

During the assessment interview there was significant family conflict observed. Diana made multiple efforts to engage her mother in argument, and the mother seemed not to know how to respond. Teresa stated that she often feels emotionally and physically intruded on by her daughter and she is aware that Diana does become more intrusive and demanding as her frustration increases. Teresa is very worried about her daughter's bedwetting, but Diana would not allow further discussion of this and became angry and tearful.

Teresa feels Diana is old enough to understand that she cannot always or instantly have everything she wants. Diana for her part states that her wish is for her mother to love her and accept her for who she is. Father and mother argue a lot and father thinks mother creates unnecessary conflicts with daughter. Father admits that he worries mother will leave him as a result of this and other conflicts. The family used to attend church together on a weekly basis and found the priest's sermons to be helpful—but for reasons that are unclear, they have not been attending in recent months.

Mother has a "comadre" who she calls for support when her frustration is high. This person will sometimes have Diana stay for a weekend as Diana and her daughter enjoy each other's company. There, Diana seems to have few behavioral problems and has not had any bedwetting.

As derived from the CANS assessment, Diana's strengths and needs can be summarized as follows:

Strengths: Some good relationships between siblings, good interpersonal skills, ability to develop healthy friendships, connected to others who share cultural identity, folklorico dance skills source of pleasure and self-esteem, does well academically, likes to read and learn.

Needs: Frequent arguing, mild to moderate problems with social development, mild behavior problems in school, clear evidence of impulsive, distractible or hyperactive behavior that interferes with functioning, suspicion of depression due to moodiness and irritability, recent history of defiance in family, bedwetting.

DIANA'S INTEGRATED SUMMARY

Diana is a bright and friendly 12-year-old girl who has grown up in the USA, and at the same time enjoys her Mexican heritage. She has until recently been a good student. She is proud of her abilities as a folklorico dancer. Diana makes friends easily and is verbally expressive.

Diana is aware that she and her mother have a strained relationship and expresses that she wants her mother to love her and to be a leader with her friends. She would like once more to be seen by her teachers as a positive student in her class. She is at a stage where peers are becoming more important and where she is capable of observing and questioning the situations in her life. As a pre-teen she is beginning to deal with her understanding of the role of being a girl in a Latino family, and what it looks like to become an adult woman.

At this time Diana appears to be struggling to manage intense feelings and often feels anxious, disappointed and frustrated. It is likely that some of her tantrums and arguments are a result of her early relationship and problems in bonding with her mother. PTSD secondary to a recent traumatic event at school may also play some role. Diana is also likely to be affected by conflicts between her parents and other members of her family. Recently she has had increasing unexplained problems with nocturnal enuresis along with difficulties with attention and impulsivity at both home and school which are suggestive of Attention Deficit and Hyperactivity Disorder (ADHD).

It is not clear the extent to which Diana's problems are psychological, biological or social; regardless she has multiple strengths to draw upon to help with current challenges. Further evaluation for urinary tract problems is warranted along with formal testing for ADHD. Regardless, Diana would likely benefit from an opportunity in group and individual therapy to sort through her feelings about her relationship with her mother, her trauma and ways of dealing with family conflict. Family therapy might also be helpful in reducing the level of conflict in the home that is a source of distress for everyone. Diana is in need of help in developing a sense of mastery, confidence building and personal connection as she transitions from childhood to adolescence and struggles with her own cultural identity as a Latina.

DIANA'S RECOVERY PLAN

GOAL(S)	Goals should be stated in the **individual's or family's own words,** and include statements of dreams, hopes, role functions and vision of life.

I want to be happy (stop fighting with my mother).

BARRIERS	Describe the **challenges, including challenges as a result of the mental illness or addictive disorder,** that stand in the way of the individual and family meeting their goals and/or achieving the discharge/transition criteria. Identifying these barriers is key to specifying the objectives as well as services and interventions in the following section of the plan.

- Frequent arguing with mother
- Mild to moderate problems with social development
- Mild behavior problems in school
- Impulsive, distractible or hyperactive behavior that interferes with functioning
- Possible underlying depression
- Recent history of defiance in family
- Bedwetting
- Anxiety due to past traumatic experience

INDIVIDUAL/FAMILY STRENGTHS	Identify the **individual's and family's strengths, past accomplishments,** current aspirations, motivations, personal attitudes, attributes, etc. which can be used to help accomplish goals.

- Some good relationships between siblings
- Good interpersonal skills
- Ability to develop healthy friendships
- Connected to others who share cultural identity
- Folkloric dance skills are a source of pleasure and self esteem
- Bright—does well academically, likes to read and learn
- Good relationship with grandmother
- Comrade who is a natural support to mom and Diana
- Used to attend church and have a good relationship with the priest
- Family committed to working together

OBJECTIVE WORK SHEET

Which barrier is this objective intended to overcome?
family conflict, irritability, arguing

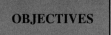

*Objectives = **Incremental step toward goal/measure of progress.** HOW will person know they are making progress? Using action words, describe the near-term specific changes expected in measurable and behavioral terms. Include the target date for completion, e.g., "Within 90 days, Mr. S will..."*

Diana will have improved academic performance within two months as measured by having at least one week with 100% completion of homework with a grade of C or better as reported by her classroom teacher and parents.

INTERVENTIONS *Describe the specific activity, service or treatment, the provider or other responsible person (including the individual and family), and the **intended purpose or impact as it relates to this objective.** The frequency, duration and span of time service should also be specified.*

Children's Specialist, Janis Hudson MSW, to provide Incredible Years Parenting class to teach behavior management skills and facilitate emotional support to Diana's parents once per week for three months.

Therapist, Nancy Martinez, to provide cognitive behavioral therapy for Diana and her mother two to four times a month for three months to help mother and daughter to become more aware of and responsive to each other's cues.

Care Coordinator to arrange for Pediatric Consult to evaluate enuresis and psychological testing to evaluate intentional problems through Diana's health plan and report findings to treatment team within three weeks.

Family Action Step

Once a month for six months Teresa will attend a support group for women who have experienced abuse as children so she can learn ways to protect and show kindness to herself which will also help her express affection to her daughter.

Individual/Family Action Steps

Diana and Teresa will practice breathing and relaxation exercises twice a week outside of sessions.

Family Support

Parents will also use resources in their church community to help them transport Diana to dance class on a weekly basis.

Family Action Step

Parents will implement "special time," child-directed play for 10 minutes each day and will apply new parenting strategies such as praise and rewards from Incredible Years Parenting class each week.

JR'S ASSESSMENT

History and Demographics: JR is a 21-year-old, Caucasian male. For the past two years, since his freshman year in culinary school, JR has been struggling with symptoms of schizophrenia. Since coming onto the ACT team in November 2011 after he withdrew from school, JR has experienced delusional thinking, visual hallucinations and problems with self-care most evident in his poor hygiene. In addition, he has gained a lot of weight and cannot keep track of when or what he has eaten.

Currently JR is experiencing a number of symptoms/problems including a lack of energy, anxiety about being around other people and difficulty with thinking clearly. As a result he takes a long time to respond to questions and can't seem to get himself organized to get out of the house. He believes that his symptoms are a result of spirits moving in and out of his body, which are ultimately controlled by God and the church. When he does leave the house he seems unable or unwilling to use public transportation.

JR has had a lot of concerns about his medications and side effects and he has in the past stopped taking them before he and his doctor could reasonably evaluate its effectiveness. He complains that his shots insert spirits into his body, causing him to feel "numb, like I don't care about anything and like I have no energy."

Currently, JR is fixated on his own death and "the spirits." He believes that he will die around Christmas and has seen a variety of signs, including the cover of a CD case with a suitcase on it and a title of "Go Home." He believes when he goes to church, the good spirits replace these bad spirits. However, of late he has been unable to go to church because of his withdrawal and anxiety.

JR has had some recent periods where he has been able to identify some of his goals, including his desire to work or go back to school. He at times talks about wanting to have his own apartment and a car, as well as participate in groups and trainings. However, JR is unable to identify the things that get in the way of his pursuing these goals or how his team might help him to succeed.

Strengths and Assets: JR has a strong faith in God and feels very connected to his church and Pentecostal faith. He has a gentleness and warmth about him that make him approachable and easy to talk to. In high school,

245

JR reports that he was popular, athletic and did well in school. JR was on the chess team and was nationally ranked. He graduated high school with honors. In addition to chess as a hobby, he states that he likes to cook.

Family Background: He lives in Smallville with his parents, brothers and sister. His family, specifically his mother, seems to have lost patience with him and he says that his family "hates him." During the family interview it did in fact appear that the family has become worn out with JR's problems and at this point are not very supportive.

Education/Employment Accomplishments: During high school JR was a good student, popular with classmates and was on the varsity football and volleyball teams. Following high school graduation JR enrolled at the Culinary Institute, but left school during the second semester of his freshman year because of his problems with extreme anxiety around other people, and beliefs that spirits were taking over his body and telling him what to do. He was active in working in restaurants in high school and college. After leaving school he worked at a local coffee shop part-time for nearly a year. Now, he is too anxious and having problems with concentrating and organizing this thoughts to be able to work.

Health Status: JR overall has good health, other than being overweight.

Alcohol/Drug Use: JR acknowledges drinking alcohol and smoking marijuana from time to time since the 11th grade. He states that smoking pot "calms him down" a bit and improves his mood—over the past several months he reports smoking a joint at least three times per week. He also reports drinking beer daily but he is vague about the amount when questioned.

Medications and Treatment: For the past four months he has been receiving Invega-Systena injections every four weeks. His doctor has recommended increasing the dosage but JR refuses; however, he has recently agreed to a trial of adding Abilify to his medication regimen.

Diagnostic Considerations/Differential Diagnosis: Schizophrenia, paranoid type; major depression; cannabis abuse; consideration should also be given to a diagnosis of religious or spiritual problem.

JR'S INTEGRATED SUMMARY/FORMULATION

JR is a 21-year-old man, with many strengths, who is now facing significant challenges. His past accomplishments include academic and athletic success and a reputation for being passionate about cooking. He is generally seen as intelligent, possessed of a kind amicable nature and a strong faith-based approach to life. For the greater portion of his life, JR has been socially engaging, warm, open and comfortable with friendships.

For the past two years, since his freshman year in culinary school, JR has struggled and claims that he hears voices, has visions as well as some beliefs about God that his family tell him can't be true. He also has had feelings of depression, frustration and hopelessness about his circumstances. The impact of these experiences, thoughts and feelings is significant—they have interfered with his ability to function on a daily basis. He believes that his problems and suffering will be relieved through faith and prayer and he is sometimes ambivalent about "mental health" treatments.

The ACT team is trying to balance respect for his spiritual beliefs with providing services to alleviate symptoms of his illness and support his recovery. For the past three months JR has been receiving once-monthly Invega-Systena injections because of his past difficulties taking oral medications as prescribed. Despite this intervention, his hallucinations and preoccupation with death have persisted and because of his continued distress he has agreed also to take Abilify.

JR and the team have agreed that his primary recovery goal is to get a job—but his symptoms interfere with his motivation and ability to concentrate and pursue employment. JR appears to be getting ready to make some changes in his life (contemplative stage of change) since he at times accepts that he has an illness and he is willing to accept some help. He does not see his use of alcohol and marijuana as a problem that he needs help with despite the possibility that this may play a role in his difficulties with motivation and concentration (pre-contemplative).

JR'S RECOVERY PLAN

GOAL(S)	Goals should be stated in the **individual's or family's own words,** and include statements of dreams, hopes, role functions and vision of life.

Get a job as a cook in a restaurant.

BARRIERS	Describe the **challenges, including challenges as a result of the mental illness or addictive disorder,** that stand in the way of the individual and family meeting their goals and/or achieving the discharge/transition criteria. Identifying these barriers is key to specifying the objectives as well as services and interventions in the following section of the plan.

- Anxiety around people
- Low mood, problems concentrating, low motivation, poor self confidence
- Family no longer supportive of him
- Religious conflicts—confusion between religious beliefs and delusions
- Auditory and visual hallucinations
- Alcohol and marijuana use to self-medicate

INDIVIDUAL/FAMILY STRENGTHS	Identify the **individual's and family's strengths, past accomplishments,** current aspirations, motivations, personal attitudes, attributes, etc. which can be used to help accomplish goals.

- Likeable—kind and easy to get along with
- Likes to cook
- Strong faith-based approach to life
- Previous work history
- Intelligent: some college/culinary school
- Athletic in high school

OBJECTIVE WORK SHEET

Which barrier is this objective intended to overcome?
lack of energy, depressed mood, anxiety around people

OBJECTIVES	*Objectives = **Incremental step toward goal/measure of progress.** HOW will person know they are making progress? Using action words, describe the near-term specific changes expected in measurable and behavioral terms. Include the target date for completion, e.g., "Within 90 days, Sam will…"*

JR will be able to manage his symptoms so that they do not interfere with his ability to look for work as evidenced by his completion of at least two job applications for two consecutive weeks within three months.

INTERVENTIONS	*Describe the specific activity, service or treatment, the provider or other responsible person (including the individual and family), and the **intended purpose or impact as it relates to this objective.** The frequency, duration and span of time service should also be specified.*

Nurse Practitioner, Sally Strong, to meet with JR weekly to monthly as needed for medication management in order to up-titrate Abilify to maximum tolerated dose and monitor for benefit/side-effects and tx adherence.

Therapist, Allison Jones, will work with JR one hour weekly in individual sessions utilizing CBT for depression for the next three months to help him gain skills to better manage his depression and anxiety and hallucinations.

Peer Support Specialist, Noah Samuels, will coordinate JR attending two hours of Cognitive Enhancement Therapy skills training group one time per week for three months to provide JR with social skills and social cognition training to reduce his anxiety and to improve his problem solving and reasoning capability.

Joe Jobster, employment specialist, will provide twice weekly counseling, rehab skills training and field-based support to help JR overcome his anxiety and problems concentrating so that he will have developed the ability and confidence to learn how to make job applications.

RN Claire Egeberg will provide one hour of PSR training related to symptoms of schizophrenia and the role of medication in order to help reduce JR's reluctance about taking medication, one time per week, for three months.

CM, Dean Brown, will arrange a meeting with JR's pastor to address medication issues, examine possible ways that the team, pastor and JR can collaborate concerning JR's treatment, and to provide some counseling on his religious/existential questions within one month.

Sally Hughes, SA Specialist, will provide education to JR once weekly for two months on the pros and cons of using substances while taking psychotropic medications.

Self-directed intervention(s)

1. JR will try to volunteer at his church to cook meals during the monthly after-service breakfast, and picnic lunches.
2. JR will attend the local peer-operated wellness center to play chess and/or volunteer to teach chess to others one time per week.
3. JR will allow a minimum of 20 minutes per day for exercise.

Family involvement

Mom and dad will be encouraged to attend the family support group at monthly NAMI meetings one time per month.

History and Demographics: Keisha is a 38-year-old African American female who has been challenged by the symptoms and stigma of mental illness since she had her first breakdown at the age of 21 while living at home and working. At that time she began to experience confusion, auditory hallucinations and thoughts of suicide and admitted that she had been silently struggling with these problems "for years." She was hospitalized on multiple occasions after that first episode, but by the age of 25 she became more stable and free of symptoms and was able to get a part-time job and, over time, establish an independent life for herself. She has not been hospitalized for over five years.

For the past five years Keisha has been receiving outpatient services at the ABC Mental Health Center. She has been treated at the Center and her current diagnosis is major depression with psychotic features. Her ongoing mental health problems have made it difficult for her to develop and maintain relationships or to participate in activities outside of her home. An exception to this experience is her connection to her local Baptist congregation. Keisha's faith and involvement in church activities, especially singing in the church choir, have historically been a cornerstone of her identity, regular routine and life satisfaction.

However, two months ago, during a period of particularly intense symptoms, Keisha attended a church service and began displaying behavior that was alarming to her pastor and fellow parishioners. She was standing in the church aisle, shouting loudly "take me Lord…I am a worthless sinner." When the pastor attempted to calm Keisha down, she became very agitated and started spinning around wildly, flailing her arms and throwing herself against the pews and floor. After several minutes of this behavior, the pastor contacted the local emergency services for assistance. Both police and ambulance personnel arrived at the church. After an unsuccessful attempt to diffuse the situation, she was forcibly restrained in the presence of the church community and taken to the nearest emergency psychiatric center for evaluation. She was subsequently hospitalized for a period of two weeks during which time her medications were adjusted and her mood, thinking and behavior gradually improved.

She has since been able to return to her part-time job as a museum security guard, and is continuing to benefit from receiving pharmacotherapy and counseling at the ABC Center. However, she has not resumed any church activities—something which she told her therapist "has left a gaping, dark hole inside me…" She was deeply hurt by the incident and feels betrayed by her pastor, but she has been unable to speak to him since this event despite several efforts on his part to connect with her. She feels he will never understand the "illness that torments me," and she fears that something like this will happen in the future. Her sister has encouraged Keisha once again to attend services and church events, but every time Keisha has attempted this, she has been overcome by anxiety and distress, stating: "My heart pounds, and my head spins…all their eyes are on me. I can never go back." She is extremely fearful of having another episode in church.

Family Background: Keisha is the youngest of three siblings, one of whom resides locally and is very supportive of Keisha and her recovery. This sister is a nurse's aide and is a respected leader in their shared Baptist faith community. Keisha still lives in the community she was raised by her mother and father. Her father, who was diagnosed with schizophrenia, was verbally and physically abusive to her mother and her siblings during childhood; Keisha reports that he treated her like the "golden child" because she was "the baby." She has always felt tremendous guilt for having "been spared" her father's wrath, and was deeply ambivalent about his leaving the family home when he was "committed to a mental institution" when Keisha was age 13. While her siblings were much relieved at this change in the family's life, Keisha felt a great loss and regrets that she never saw her father again as he died several years later while institutionalized. When Keisha herself began to experience mental health problems, she believed that it was her "curse to go crazy and die like my father." She continues to believe she is meant to suffer and to live/die alone. The only important connection she has in her life, other than her sister, is to her cat which she rescued from a shelter and has nurtured for the past five years.

Education/Employment Accomplishments: Keisha is a high-school graduate who was always an above-average student. But she describes herself as extremely shy and reclusive—openly admitting that she feared her peers would know she was "going crazy" so she rarely spent time with people outside her family home. After graduating from high school, Keisha began working in a series of different full-time jobs in different roles at the local university—including as a file clerk, a library assistant and a dining hall server—until her breakdown at age 21. After that she went several years where she was unable to work; now she has been employed part-time for the last eight years as an evening security guard. She has cordial relationships with her co-workers and supervisors but does not describe being "close" to any of them. She returned to her job after her most recent hospitalization, and states that she continues to enjoy this position because it is slow in the evening and she enjoys the quiet.

Health Status: Keisha reports that she has suffered from asthma since she was 10 years old; the condition is now stable with oral medications and inhalers and she has not had a crisis for three or four years. After she was started on antipsychotic medications, she noticed a persistent weight gain that has now leveled off. Her doctor tells her she is 55 pounds overweight and as a result she feels very self-conscious and uncomfortable with her appearance.

Alcohol/Drug Use: Keisha does admit that she drinks alcohol by herself while she is alone in her apartment to "calm my nerves." She says that she drinks "a few glasses" nearly every day.

Medications and Treatment: Keisha uses a twice-daily dosage of Risperidone, 1 mg, to control her symptoms. She and her team believe this to be an effective tool for her in managing intermittent symptoms of psychosis and her mood also seems to be stable with this regimen. It was discovered during her most recent episode of acute symptoms that she had run out of medications several weeks before the church incident that led to her hospitalization. While things are stable, Keisha continues to complain of persistent periods of deep depression for a few days a week accompanied by a continued general lack of interest in activities, and social isolation. Although encouraged by staff and family, Keisha is unwilling to attend activities at the ABC Center's Helping Hand peer-operated support center, as she does not want to be reminded that she is "crazy."

Diagnostic Considerations: Keisha is currently being treated for symptoms associated with a diagnosis of major depression with psychotic features. There is also some concern that her use of alcohol is more significant than she reports and that alcohol abuse/dependence may complicate her problems of mood and psychosis. Consideration should also be given to a diagnosis of a religious or spiritual problem in that she feels she cannot return to her church, which has been a major source of support for her.

KEISHA'S INTEGRATED SUMMARY/FORMULATION

Keisha is a hard working and independent woman who has successfully maintained part-time competitive employment for most of her adult life despite periods of significant difficulty managing symptoms of psychosis and depression. Beyond work, she describes a life of social isolation and a general lack of involvement in activities outside her home, which she attributes to feelings of stigma and shame. However, she has been an active member of her local Baptist church community, including singing in the choir for many years, which has been perhaps the most important aspect of her life. She has a sister who lives locally who is also a member of the church and is very understanding and supportive of Keisha and her mental health issues.

Three months ago Keisha had a sudden breakdown during a Sunday morning service and this resulted in her forcible removal by psychiatric emergency personnel from the church service. Following this she was hospitalized for two weeks for the first time in five years. In the past Keisha actively pursued and benefited from therapy and peer supports as part of her recovery, although she had been reducing her visits to only once a month for the four months prior to her recent crisis. It is not clear why she began to cut back and how if at all this may be associated with her setback as it now appears she had run out of her routine medications (Risperidone 1 mg twice a day) several weeks prior to the episode in church. Although Keisha seems to have returned to "baseline" and is now back at work, she has not experienced much improvement with her problems of depression and social isolation.

Keisha continues to drink alcohol daily while at home alone. She also has a history of asthma, and since starting on her medicines she has become overweight. There is a real possibility that her drinking and self-consciousness about her obesity may be contributing to her continuing to isolate and feel depressed.

After her hospitalization, Keisha is highly motivated to re-engage in regular weekly treatment and wants to continue moving forward in her recovery. Along with suffering a setback and loss of her sense of well-being associated with her hospitalization, she is experiencing her separation from her church as a tremendous loss, and both may be contributing to her current experience of depression.

Her self-identified priority goal at this time is to rebuild her connection to her faith community—she recognizes how important that connection has been for her overall well-being. However, feelings of intense anxiety and fear and worries about having another breakdown—whenever she attempts to go to church—have kept her from achieving this goal. She also recognizes that she is angry with her pastor and cannot reconcile this with her previous experience of respect and admiration; the possibility that ambivalence toward her pastor is somehow tied to her past experiences with her own father, who she perceives as having betrayed and abandoned her at her time of need, may warrant further exploration in therapy. She may also benefit from re-evaluation of her diagnosis and current pharmacotherapy.

She is between the preparation and action stage of change, and is seeking help to decrease her depression and social isolation and to reconnect with her Baptist church. However, she is pre-contemplative about considering that her alcohol use is playing a role in her current difficulties.

KIESHA'S RECOVERY PLAN

GOAL(S)	Goals should be stated in the **individual's or family's own words,** and include statements of dreams, hopes, role functions and vision of life.

I want to get back to my Baptist Church.

BARRIERS	Describe the **challenges, including challenges as a result of the mental illness or addictive disorder,** that stand in the way of the individual and family meeting their goals and/or achieving the discharge/transition criteria. Identifying these barriers is key to specifying the objectives as well as services and interventions in the following section of the plan.

- Anxiety fear and distress which increase during attempts to speak with her pastor or return to church —"I am so embarrassed and angry about the way I was treated. I don't want to go back"
- Social isolation and avoidance
- Vulnerability to and fear of relapse
- Lack of illness self-management strategies
- Physical health concerns and some possible limitations from being overweight
- Lacks understanding of how alcohol use can contribute to depressive mood

INDIVIDUAL/FAMILY STRENGTHS	Identify the **individual's and family's strengths, past accomplishments,** current aspirations, motivations, personal attitudes, attributes, etc. which can be used to help accomplish goals.

- Motivation for change and recovery success
- Supportive sister who is caring and compassionate
- Strong faith/belief system
- History of active involvement in volunteer activities at the church
- Support of therapist and peers at ABC program
- Regular employment

OBJECTIVE WORK SHEET

Which barrier is this objective intended to overcome? *Anxiety, fear and distress*	

OBJECTIVES	*Objectives = **Incremental step toward goal/measure of progress.** HOW will person know they are making progress? Using action words, describe the near-term specific changes expected in measurable and behavioral terms. Include the target date for completion, e.g., "Within 90 days, Mr. S will…"*

Keisha will be able to better manage her anxiety and avoidance of social interactions as evidenced by her participation in at least part of one service at her church within 90 days.

INTERVENTIONS	*Describe the specific activity, service or treatment, the provider or other responsible person (including the individual and family), and the **intended purpose or impact as it relates to this objective.** The intensity, frequency and duration should also be specified.*

Psychiatrist to meet with Keisha for 30 minutes every other week for the next three months to continue to evaluate medications and other strategies for minimizing the experience and impact of anxiety/depression.

Primary clinician, LCSW, to provide weekly CBT for 45 minutes for three months to help develop coping skills/strategies for self-soothing/calming when she is challenged or stressed.

Case Manager/Care Coordinator will meet with Keisha for 30–45 minutes weekly for six weeks to help her identify and attend alternative social activities/church functions in the community.

Rehab specialist will provide Coping Skills Training by walking with Keisha weekly for 30 minutes while reinforcing practice of CBT-based coping skills.

Rehab specialist will provide education on the interactions of alcohol use and depression, as well as tools available for support as alternatives to drinking every other week for three months.

Care Coordinator will discuss with Keisha's primary care physician how to better coordinate/address impact of physical health issues on her mental health and well-being within two weeks.

Self-directed Intervention(s) Keisha will:
- Practice singing each day for ½ hour while at home, to help bring some joy into her life.
- Participate in bi-weekly Wellness Recovery Action Planning group (facilitated by her peer recovery mentor) for the purpose of developing and implementing a relapse prevention plan which will increase her sense of control in her life.

Family Involvement Keisha's sister will:
- Meet with pastor at least once within next month in an effort to help him better understand Keisha and what she needs in order to reconnect and attempt to heal the rift.
- Role-play to help Keisha practice forgiving her pastor 15 minutes three times per week.

Current Circumstances: Roberto, a recent veteran who has just returned from the Iraq war, was brought to the emergency department of his local hospital three days ago by his parents because they said their son had "lost his mind." For the preceding two days Roberto had locked himself in a closet to hide from the military police who he was convinced were searching for him to send him to Guantanamo Bay prison for interrogation as a terrorist and war criminal. When they tried to get him out, he asked them for a gun so that he could "take care of his business." Roberto had been increasingly preoccupied and withdrawn over the preceding week and typically spent time alone in his room and could be heard repeatedly talking to himself and occasionally shouting "run...run." When he came out for meals, he ate little and often left the table in tears. Twice in the past week he had come home very late after spending time with his veteran friends, and his parents reported that he seemed both drunk and jumpy. When Roberto was evaluated in the emergency room he acknowledged that he had been feeling a little low and worried but denied any further problems. He denies hearing voices, but was observed by nursing staff to be responding to internal stimuli and giving them hostile and threatening looks when they passed by. His urine tox screen was positive for amphetamines and opioids. Inpatient admission to "give Roberto a rest" was suggested by the emergency room physician. Although Roberto was initially reluctant, his parents were able to convince him it was best for him and his family to seek some help and he gave his consent for further evaluation and treatment.

History: Two months ago Roberto returned from his second tour of duty in Iraq. He had a mission where he was conducting a helicopter evacuation of an Iraqi family (husband, wife and two children). The direct and specific order was to evacuate the family in which the father had been an informant for the US. Roberto landed in the backyard of the home as the insurgents (on a mission to assassinate the family) were rapidly approaching the village. He quickly learned that the family had taken in six orphans. He did not have any time to call his commanding officer to determine if the "family" also included the orphans. As the insurgents approached, he made the decision to follow orders and just take the original family members with him. As they are taking off in the helicopter the insurgents arrive and the last thing that Roberto sees are the six orphans being killed.

Roberto received an honorable discharge from the military with commendation for his heroism in rescuing civilians in Iraq. He returned home to his wife and children without a job. After a month of being at home, his wife sought legal separation because of repeated angry and threatening outbursts toward towards her and their children exacerbated by his hypervigilance toward his sons. For example, he was unable to tolerate his children being out of his immediate sight and wouldn't allow his four-year-old to have friends over.

Since leaving his wife, Roberto has been living with his parents. While his parents are supportive and understanding, Roberto is ashamed to be living with them. He says he is not sleeping well at all and is having nightmares that awaken him. He typically sleeps for an hour or two and then gets up and paces the house until the early morning hours and then is unable to get himself out of bed until mid-afternoon.

Family Background: Roberto is a 26-year-old Latino who was married at age 20 and has two sons, ages four and two. Roberto is the oldest of four siblings who have previously looked up to him as a role model. His parents came to the USA from Mexico and Roberto was born in the USA. His parents are monolingual Spanish speaking and Roberto is bilingual. They are an observant Catholic family.

There is no acknowledged history of mental illness in the family but his grandfather died of alcoholism and a maternal uncle committed suicide.

Education/Employment Accomplishments: Since age 15, Roberto has always had some sort of job; however, he has had periods in high school when he had a hard time getting out of bed and going to school and work which has always concerned him. While in high school, he participated in several athletic teams. He is a high school graduate who has also had some college courses. He had hoped to become a chemical engineer one day. He is currently unemployed and had considerable difficulty in looking for work since returning home.

Health Status: Upon his return from Iraq, Roberto was diagnosed with an orthopedic injury that resulted in compressed discs in his back with a moderate amount of pain that continues to bother him.

Alcohol/Drug Use: He admits to some drug use, stating he typically uses amphetamines five time per week with his veteran friends and he drinks alcohol at least three times per week, typically five beers per night.

Medications and Treatment: Roberto has been prescribed 20 mg a day of fluoextine for his "depression" and back pain problems by his primary care physician which he takes only three or four days a week. He has also been prescribed oxycotin for his back pain which he does not use routinely as prescribed and instead often takes twice as many pills as directed at a time when the pain becomes severe. Roberto's wife and parents have suggested he go to the local clinic for counseling but Roberto had previously refused to do this, seeing it as a sign of weakness and saying that "real men" don't need counseling.

ROBERTO'S FORMULATION/NARRATIVE SUMMARY

Roberto is an intelligent young man with strong family ties and support. Until his experience in Iraq, he served as a successful role model for his younger siblings. Roberto has had high expectations for himself and his future as evidenced by his success in high school, his desire to become a chemical engineer, his hopes for a successful marriage, and all family members looking up to him as someone to emulate.

Now, however, Roberto finds his life spinning out of control and his future seriously in doubt. He is having difficulty adjusting to civilian life as evidenced by fighting with/separation from his wife, being overvigilant with his children, an inability to sleep due to nightmares, and difficulties in gaining employment. He misses being with his wife and children. He is used to being independent and "in charge"; instead of being able to benefit from his family's supports, he finds that he is embarrassed to be around them and is ashamed of his perceived failures.

Over the past week Roberto has become increasingly withdrawn, exhibiting bizarre behaviors and engaging in significant substance abuse according to his parents. He recognizes that he needs to take some action to get his life back on track, but is fearful to admit the extent of his difficulties and the effort it will take to turn things around.

Roberto appears to be experiencing numerous symptoms of a psychiatric disorder including anxiety, dysphoria, withdrawal, irritability, fearfulness and psychotic symptoms including delusions and possible hallucinations. Several diagnoses warrant consideration including post-traumatic stress, major depression with psychotic features, psychosis not otherwise specified, (NOS), mixed substance use/abuse and possible psychosis secondary to amphetamines. His condition is complicated by back problems which require narcotic analgesics for pain control.

Roberto is in the contemplative stage of change. He is distressed but cannot seem to understand what has happened to him and is uncertain about his need for treatment. As a Latino man from a traditional background, his family and their advice are very important to him and his sense of worth and self-esteem is very much tied to his ability to be a capable provider for them. It appears that feelings of survivor guilt and the trauma he experienced/witnessed during his military service have exacerbated an underlying vulnerability to depression. His ideas about pride and self-sufficiency and providing for a family are impacting his ability to seek help and aggravating his feelings of guilt and failure. He may be using alcohol and drugs in an effort to maintain social connection with peers as well as gaining some relief of his anxiety and sadness.

ROBERTO'S RECOVERY PLAN

GOALS	Goals should be stated in the **individual's or family's own words,** and include statements of dreams, hopes, role functions and vision of life.

Recovery/Life Goals

I want to be back with my family…Eventually go back to school so I can be a good provider for my wife and kids.

Inpatient Treatment Goals

I want to be less anxious so I can cope at home.

ANTICIPATED DISCHARGE/TRANSITION SETTING AND CRITERIA	Describe the setting in terms of location, level of care, length of stay and service needs. Describe changes in the individual's and family's current needs and circumstances that will need to occur in order to succeed in discharge or transition.

1. Roberto will be able to manage his feelings of anxiety, depression and fearfulness without inappropriate anger withdrawal or suicidal feelings.
2. Roberto will have a harm reduction plan to minimize his drug and alcohol use at home following discharge.

BARRIERS	Describe the **challenges as a result of the mental illness or addictive disorder** that stand in the way of the individual and family meeting their goals and/or achieving the discharge/transition criteria. Identifying these barriers is key to specifying the objectives as well as services and interventions in the following section of the plan.

- Unresolved feelings about trauma experienced in Iraq
- Probable psychotic symptoms interfering with ability to adapt/cope
- Amphetamine and alcohol abuse possibly causing/exacerbating distress and psychotic sx
- Feelings of inadequacy and low self-esteem
- Lack of structured/purposeful activity upon discharge
- Difficulty in getting adequate restorative sleep
- Difficulty reintegrating into civilian life
- Physical pain

OBJECTIVE WORK SHEET

This objective is related to which goal(s) or transition/discharge criteria (i.e., treatment goal) or barrier?
I want to be less anxious so I can cope at home—sleep disturbance.

OBJECTIVES	Using action words, describe the **specific changes expected** in measurable and behavioral terms. Include the target date for completion.
Roberto will sleep seven hours a night without interruption for five consecutive nights as evidenced by nursing staff report.	
TARGET DATE	March 15, 2014.

INDIVIDUAL/FAMILY STRENGTHS	Identify the individual's and family's past accomplishments, current aspirations, motivations, personal attitudes, attributes, etc. which can be used to **help accomplish this objective.**
Strong family connection, religious/spiritual connections, aware of his distress, intelligent, supportive family, history of past accomplishments/success.	

INTERVENTIONS	Describe the specific activity, service or treatment, the provider or other responsible person (including the individual and family), and the **intended purpose or impact as it relates to this objective.** The intensity, frequency and duration should also be specified.

Dr. Pfizer, Psychiatrist, to provide daily pharmacotherapy during hospital stay to help alleviate symptoms of anxiety, depression, psychosis and insomnia.
Sally Goodheart, Psychologist, will provide one hour 1:1 trauma-resolution therapy three times per week while inpatient to educate Roberto on symptoms and treatment of PTSD to better understand his nightmares.
Florence Nightingale, RN, to train Roberto in a program of sleep hygiene skills on a daily basis for 30 minutes daily until discharged to give him self-management tools/strategies to improve sleep habits/patterns.
Father Deldios, Hospital Chaplain, to provide spiritual counseling two hours/week in hospital help Roberto find ways to use his faith as a support for healing and self-forgiveness.

Objective Work Sheet

This objective is related to which goal(s) or transition/discharge criteria (i.e. treatment goal) or barrier?
I want to be less anxious so I can cope at home—use of substances.

OBJECTIVES	*Using action words, describe the **specific changes expected** in measurable and behavioral terms. Include the target date for completion.*
Roberto will complete a written harm reduction plan that is appropriate to support his controlling his drug and alcohol use upon discharge as evidenced by sharing his plan with the treatment team.	

TARGET DATE	March 15, 2012.

INDIVIDUAL/FAMILY STRENGTHS	*Identify the individual's and family's past accomplishments, current aspirations, motivations, personal attitudes, attributes, etc. which can be used to **help accomplish this objective.***
Strong family connection, religious/spiritual connections, aware of his distress, intelligent, supportive family, concern about his drug/alcohol use, hx of past self-control.	

INTERVENTIONS	*Describe the specific activity, service or treatment, the provider or other responsible person (including the individual and family), and the **intended purpose or impact as it relates to this objective.** The intensity, frequency and duration should also be specified.*
Joe Sixpack, Rehab Therapist, to provide daily substance abuse treatment group for one hour during hospital stay to help Roberto understand the role of substance misuse in his current problems.	
Will Helpyou Dual Dx Peer Counselor, to provide supportive counseling 3 times a week while inpatient to assist in identif ying triggers and developing a relapse prevention plan.	
Hope Forall, Psychologist, to provide one hour of family therapy twice per week for until dischareged to help Roberto and family find ways of working together to support his recovery following d/c.	
Roberto to attend hospital AA/NA meetings for one hour twice a week while inpatient to begin 12 step work and gain support for recovery.	

INDEX

Note: Page numbers with "f" denote figures; "t" tables; "b" boxes.